FROM
HITLER
TO
ULBRICHT

FROM HITLER TO ULBRICHT

The Communist Reconstruction of East Germany 1945-46

GREGORY W. SANDFORD

PRINCETON UNIVERSITY PRESS

To
M. Gale Hoffman
and
Jacques E. Legrand
in acknowledgment of an old debt

Contents

Contents

Preface

The Soviet Union, alone among the Big Three victors of World War II, saw the problem of Germany's democratization as one of social and economic restructuring. While the British and Americans advocated some decartelization and reform of land tenure, their efforts focused on punishment and reeducation of the German people. In the Communist view, however, fascism was but another expression, albeit a virulent one, of the moribund economic system, of monopoly capitalism. Destroying it meant destroying the dominance of reactionary classes and transferring their property and power to the control of progressive social forces, led by the Communists themselves. The purpose of this study is to trace the theoretical development of this socio-economic approach to democratization, its practical implementation by Soviet and German Communists during the decisive first year of occupation, and its effect on the shaping of postwar Germany.

There has been a dearth of reliable information in the West about the German Democratic Republic and its origins. During the Cold War period, the GDR was written off as a mere extension of the Soviet Union, and analysis of developments there was left largely to the propagandists of the Bonn government. This attitude has changed dramatically in recent years with the advent of *Ostpolitik* and the international recognition of the GDR, now a major industrial power. However, remaining political sensitivities and the inaccessibility to scholars of important archives have continued to hamper historical research. I undertook the present study in the conviction that such difficulties will probably persist for some time to come, and that a beginning not only can but, in view of the growing importance of the GDR, should be made now on the basis of available materials.

Although the resources of the GDR state and party archives for the postwar period remained closed to me as to all but approved East European scholars, I did have a unique opportunity to use the archives of the Confederation of Free German Trade Unions (FDGB) and the Peasants' Mutual Aid Association (VdgB), both of which also have hitherto been unavailable to Western researchers. Some recently declassified documents from the OMGUS records in the National Archives in Washington and from Foreign Office archives in London were also helpful. Otherwise, my research has relied heavily on published documents (large collections of which have been released by the GDR itself); memoirs; contemporary newspapers, pamphlets and official gazettes; and a number of East German dissertations and other monographs based on research in archives I was unable to use. A few recent West German works were quite valuable, too, and were all the more welcome since a dispassionate study of East German history is still something of a novelty in the Federal Republic.

If historical research on the GDR has been scarce in West Germany, it has been all but nonexistent in English-speaking countries. I owe an especial debt of gratitude to my mentor, Professor Theodore Hamerow, for his encouragement in pursuing an unusual and at first rather intimidating topic, and for several years of continuing help and guidance in overcoming the many hurdles along the way. I would also like to convey my warm thanks to Professor Melvin Croan and Dr. Erwin Welsch, both of whom have been more than generous with their valuable time and expertise.

My research in Germany was made possible by the financial support of the Council for European Studies, the Deutscher Akademischer Austauschdienst (DAAD), and the University of Wisconsin Graduate School; as well as by the joint efforts of the International Research and Exchanges Board (IREX), the U.S. Information Agency, and various agencies of the German Democratic Republic in arranging a three-month academic exchange program for me in the GDR. I am also indebted to a number of libraries and archives whose collections I was permitted to use and whose staff were unfailingly patient and considerate in helping me to locate the materials I needed. These include the University of Wisconsin Memorial Library, the Hoover Institution for War, Revolution and Peace, and the National Archives and Records Service in this country; the Public Record Office in London; and in West Berlin the Otto Suhr Institut and the Institut für sozialwissenschaftliche Forschungen of the Free University, and the Deutsches Institut für Wirtschaftsforschung (DIW). A special word of thanks is due to Agnes Peterson of the Hoover Institution, Dietrich Staritz of the Otto Suhr Institut, and Hartmut Zimmermann of the Institut für sozialwissenschaftliche Forschungen. Nor can I fail to mention the great generosity of veteran SPD leader Karl Germer in sharing with me his private documents and unique firsthand knowledge of the creation of new parties and trade unions in Berlin.

I am particularly grateful for the cordial reception given me by a number of individuals and institutions in the GDR whose assistance was invaluable to this work. First and foremost, my deep appreciation goes to Rainer Hagen of the Institut für Internationale Beziehungen, who has been a tireless friend in helping me to track down materials and make contacts for my research, and who with his charming wife Renate made my visits to Berlin enjoyable as well as useful. I also want to extend sincere thanks to Professor Walter Bartel and Dr. Siegfried Prokop of Humboldt University, Dr. Claus Montag of the GDR Foreign Ministry, Dr. Siegfried Thomas of the Akademie der Wissenschaften, and KPD/SED veterans Kurt Smettan and Hein Peglow; and to the staff of the FDGB and VdgB libraries and archives, the Deutsche Staatsbibliothek, the Deutsche Bücherei, and the Institut für Agrargeschichte. The ability of all these people to rise above the mutual animosities of an unfortunate past and to share their knowledge and resources so graciously with an American historian is a credit to them, and a testimony to the progress our two societies have made in learning to understand and deal with one another. Political differences will undoubtedly remain; nevertheless it is my earnest hope that this progress will continue, and that the present work may repay the efforts of all who have contributed to it by serving, however modestly, to promote that end.

Last, but most of all, I want to thank my wife Nancy for her years of loving support. Surely she never guessed she was capable of such patience.

All opinions and analysis of events presented in this book are strictly those of the author, and do not in any way represent the official views of the U.S. Department of State or any other agency of the United States government.

Fresno, California
October 1981

Abbreviations

ADGB	Allgemeiner Deutscher Gewerkschaftsbund (General Confederation of German Trade Unions)
BdS	Bund demokratischer Sozialisten (League of Democratic Socialists)
BzG	*Beiträge zur Geschichte der (deutschen) Arbeiterbewegung*
CDU	Christian Democratic Union
DFB	*Der Freie Bauer*
DIW	Deutsches Institut für Wirtschaftsforschung (German Institute for Economic Research)
DVZ	*Deutsche Volkszeitung*
FDGB	Freier Deutscher Gewerkschaftsbund (Confederation of Free German Trade Unions)
FDJ	Freie Deutsche Jugend (Free German Youth)
GDR	German Democratic Republic
IHK	Industrie- und Handelskammer (Chamber of Industry and Commerce)
IML	Institute for Marxism-Leninism (of SED)
KPD	Kommunistische Partei Deutschlands (Communist Party of Germany)
LDP	Liberal Democratic Party
NARS	National Archives and Records Service (Washington, D.C.)
NKFD	Nationalkomitee "Freies Deutschland" (National Committee "Free Germany")
OMGUS	Office of Military Government, U.S.
OSS	Office of Strategic Services
PRO	Public Record Office (London)
RGO	Revolutionäre Gewerkschaftsopposition (Revolutionary Trade Union Opposition)

Abbreviations

SED	Sozialistische Einheitspartei Deutschlands (Socialist Unity Party of Germany)
SMA	Soviet Military Administration
SPD	Sozialdemokratische Partei Deutschlands (Social Democratic Party of Germany)
TVZ	*Thüringer Volkszeitung*
VdgB	Vereinigung der gegenseitigen Bauernhilfe (Peasants' Mutual Aid Association)
VEB	Volkseigener Betrieb (People's Enterprise)
ZfG	*Zeitschrift für Geschichtswissenschaft*

FROM
HITLER
TO
ULBRICHT

ONE

The Communist Strategy for Germany, 1935-1945

On 30 April 1945—the day of Hitler's suicide—two Soviet transport planes touched down on a makeshift runway a few miles from the flaming ruins of Berlin. Aboard, under the leadership of Walter Ulbricht, member of the Politburo of the Communist Party of Germany (KPD), was the first advance group of German Communists to arrive from Moscow. The returning exiles brought with them the KPD's plans for a new German state and society.

The greatest surprise these plans held for the German people was that they did *not* call for creation of a Communist, or even socialist, state. Rather, the KPD's goal, as stated repeatedly in speeches and printed propaganda over the following months, was the establishment of a bourgeois democratic republic. This new republic, however, was not to be a revival of the weak and reactionary Weimar Republic that preceded Hitler. Its "progressive" character was to be guaranteed by the "leading role of the working class," both within a ruling political alliance of anti-fascist parties and in the institutions controlling the levers of economic and social power—what Communists called the "commanding heights" of society. In practice, this meant the hegemony of the KPD.

THE POPULAR FRONT OF THE 1930S AND THE
"DEMOCRATIC PEOPLE'S REPUBLIC"

The idea for such a new order had its origin in the Communist "Popular Front" strategy of the 1930s. Convinced

by mid-1934 that the Nazi regime was relatively stable
and not, as had been thought, just a brief episode in the
progress toward socialist revolution, the emigré leaders
of the KPD and the leadership of the Communist International (Comintern) began reassessing the policies that
had led to their failure to defeat fascism. Their conclusions, and the revised strategy that resulted, were promulgated during 1935 as the new Comintern line.[1]

At the Seventh Congress of the International that year,
Wilhelm Pieck of the KPD declared that his party had
made a serious error in attacking all bourgeois regimes as
fascist, including those which in fact represented a more
moderate form of bourgeois rule. So long as proletarian
democracy remained beyond reach, Communists must re-
alize their stake in preserving "every scrap of bourgeois
democracy." Speeches by Comintern chief Georgi Dimitrov and others reinforced the conclusion that Communist parties had overestimated the level of consciousness
of the masses, isolating themselves from the people by an
excess of Marxist rhetoric and undue preoccupation with
ideological purity. In the future, the emphasis must be
not on wordy statements about revolutionary goals, but
on winning respect and influence for the Party through
political action to attain immediate and tangible advantages for the workers. Alliances must be forged with other
political groups opposed to fascism, as had been done successfully by French Communists, and an attempt made
to guide these alliances toward realization of Communist
goals. To this end, each individual party would have greater
latitude to adapt the Comintern line to its own national
circumstances.[2]

The implications for the KPD were already being spelled
out as early as January 1935. According to Comintern
instructions, German Communists were to work for "a
broad anti-fascist Popular Front, which should include not
only Communist and Social Democratic but also Catholic
workers, and discontented elements of the peasantry, the

middle class, and the intellectuals; thus, all those who are prepared to fight against the fascist dictatorship." Proletarian leadership of these forces was to be assured in turn by a "United Front" of Communists and Socialists.

Pieck further clarified the new strategy at the KPD "Brussels" Conference in October 1935. The Comintern, he explained, had now recognized the possibility of a situation in which the masses were not yet ready for the rule of workers' soviets, but could nonetheless be united against fascism. The KPD must therefore approach them as the champion of their respective goals and grievances. The disaffected bourgeoisie should be appealed to in terms of the traditions of 1848, with a call for a "struggle for the democratic freedoms"—for freedom of speech, press, assembly and election—that were being suppressed by Hitler. The peasants would be won over by exposing to them the fraudulence of Hitler's promises of land reform, and reminding them of the KPD's commitment to a radical land redistribution. Similarly, other classes and economic groups would be united by the common denominator of their resentment at Nazi betrayal of their particular interests.[3]

Central to KPD strategy for the Popular Front was that it be based on a more intimate alliance between the KPD and the Social Democratic Party of Germany (SPD): a United Front guaranteeing unified working class leadership of the anti-fascist movement. Abandoning its longstanding campaign of vilification against the SPD as the "social-fascist" betrayer of the proletariat, in January 1935 the KPD Central Committee made an open offer of cooperation to the SPD's exile leadership in Prague. In contrast to offers of this sort in past years, intended to embarrass the SPD with blatantly unacceptable terms, this one seems to have been seriously intended. The Comintern was urging the KPD to make real gestures of conciliation, such as support for SPD candidates in some factory-council elections inside Germany. In the resolution of the

"Brussels" Conference, special emphasis was placed on action to promote pet SPD goals such as improvements in pay and working conditions for workers.[4]

Unfortunately, the KPD's timing was off. Two years earlier, in the first shock of Hitler's seizure of power, sentiment among Social Democrats had been for rejection of the discredited policies of the party's moderate Weimar leadership and a sharp swing to the left. Under pressure from its own left wing, from radical young resistance leaders in Germany, and from socialist parties of other countries, the Prague party leadership had issued a manifesto in June 1933 calling for a revolutionary class struggle against the Nazi dictatorship, and another in January 1934 containing its own proposal for an anti-fascist coalition led by a united working class party. The latter provided for a proletarian-dominated dictatorship, eradication of all "counterrevolutionary agitation," and elimination of the power of the "ruling class" by immediate expropriation of all large estates, key industries, and major banks.[5]

The 1934 manifesto represented the high point of this development within the SPD, though, and soon a reaction set in which, for various reasons, strengthened the hand of more moderate leaders in Prague during the remainder of 1934 and 1935. For the sake of appearances and to mollify their left-wing colleagues, these leaders agreed to a meeting with KPD representatives on 23 November 1935. At the meeting, however, the SPD delegates informed the Communists that no cooperation was possible so long as the SPD had no concrete proof of the sincerity of KPD claims to support democracy or of its honest intention to stick by a "nonaggression pact" with the SPD. They further explained that it would be very difficult for the SPD to cooperate under any circumstances with a party that did not represent primarily German interests, but rather those of a foreign power.[6]

In protest against this decision, one group of left Social Democrats split with the Prague majority and attempted to work with the KPD toward a unified party. Their experience soon proved the soundness of the Prague leaders' skepticism. The Communists' terms of cooperation amounted essentially to assimilation into the KPD. Even at the "Brussels" Conference no bones had been made about the ultimate goals of KPD strategy: "soviet power" (i.e., all power to the workers' soviets) and a united socialist party based on the Leninist principle of "democratic centralism." While it was making its offers of cooperation to the SPD and other groups, the KPD was simultaneously tightening its own internal party discipline and intensifying ideological indoctrination of its members. Its unconcealed intention was to use United Front and Popular Front organs to wean the masses, including Social Democrats, away from reformism toward revolution, isolating moderate SPD leaders and achieving KPD leadership of the anti-fascist movement.

The KPD succeeded instead in isolating itself. The breakaway SPD group began disintegrating in 1936, with most of its disillusioned members returning to the Prague fold. The main SPD leadership continued its drift to the right throughout the remainder of the decade, with the growing conviction that its role was to coordinate the activities of all liberal-democratic opponents to Hitler. It repeatedly rejected renewed Communist offers of cooperation right up to the outbreak of war.[7]

After the defeat of its first United Front initiative, the KPD turned its attention to developing a more detailed program for a post-Hitler regime in Germany, hoping that its program might have enough universal appeal to serve as a basis for alliance with other anti-fascist forces. In view of the SPD's rebuff, Communist strategists made a particular effort after late 1936 to present an attractive package to potential non-socialist allies. The result was a plan for a "democratic people's republic," similar to the contemporary Spanish Republic, providing for a broad-based anti-fascist government with KPD participation. For the first time, there was no suggestion that this would be merely a transitional phase on the way to socialism (an omission that many rank-and-file Communists had difficulty accepting). On the other hand, the KPD summarized in the resolution of its 1939 "Bern" Conference the measures it considered necessary to guard against the resurgence of pro-fascist elites: "Expropriation of the fascist trust-capitalists. Implementation of an economic policy that serves the purposes of peace and a higher standard of living for the people. . . . Democratic land reform to benefit peasants and agricultural workers." The strength of democratic institutions was to be founded on the assurance that key positions of power in industry, bureaucracy, army, and police would be controlled by the working class and its allies and not, as in Weimar times, by the upper bourgeoisie.[8]

Such plans were to remain for the time being the KPD's private pipe dream, in the absence of any important allies with whom to collaborate. By 1939 the KPD was in fact, despite its continued Popular Front rhetoric, withdrawing into something like its pre-1935 political isolation. The Hitler-Stalin Pact and the coming of war in the West completed this isolation by removing the major impetus that had inspired the Popular Front strategy in the first place: the Soviet campaign for a similar coalition with Western powers against Hitler. Only with the German invasion of the USSR in 1941 and the renewed importance of Soviet-Western relations did the KPD's relations with other antifascist German groups regain its significance for the Kremlin in a unique new way.[9]

THE KPD AND THE "FREE GERMANY" MOVEMENT

The passing of the military initiative to the Soviets at Stalingrad in February 1943 opened new possibilities for political initiatives. From the Soviet point of view, no moral bond existed between them and the Western Allies that outweighed what had long been the primary goal of Soviet diplomacy: to keep the USSR out of any inter-capitalist war. It is not surprising that by December 1942 Stalin was already extending peace feelers to Germany.[10] Stalin was playing a double game. If his efforts toward Hitler failed to produce a separate Soviet-German peace, the mere possibility might nonetheless frighten the Western powers into making concessions to the Soviets—such as the quick opening of a second front in the West or agreement to Stalin's territorial claims in Eastern Europe—to keep them in the Alliance. The turn of the tide on the Eastern Front gave the Soviets a chance for new leverage in both directions. If Hitler's military losses could be used to undermine support for the war and for his regime within Germany, the result might be either a quicker and more advantageous Soviet-German agreement or a cheaper Allied victory, either way bringing maximum advantage to the USSR.

With these possibilities in mind, the Soviet Union engineered the foundation, in summer 1943, of the National Committee "Free Germany" (Nationalkomitee "Freies Deutschland," or NKFD), a new anti-Hitler organization designed to appeal to German nationalist sentiment. Its first members were recruited from Soviet prisoner-of-war camps, into which the captives taken at Stalingrad had introduced a new and gloomier outlook on the war and the Nazis. The Soviets were particularly interested in the captive officers; especially several generals who, if properly approached, might have an influence on powerful military circles in Germany, as well as greater weight with the German public at large.[11] It fell to the KPD, aided by Red Army officers, to enlist these POWs for a "Free Germany" organization and a program strong enough to have serious political influence, yet amenable to Communist control. The experience was to prove an invaluable opportunity to develop techniques that were later used to control the development of the political system in East Germany.

Up to this time, KPD work in the POW camps had consisted of debriefings of German soldiers for intelligence purposes and ham-handed attempts at political indoctrination through various combinations of propaganda and pressure. Despite the dismal results, the KPD was at first reluctant to make the kind of sharp break with its ideological traditions demanded by the Soviets as an overture to the POWs: abandonment of all class-warfare rhetoric in favor of an appeal to common national loyalties. At the NKFD's founding conference on 12-13 July 1943, the Communists and a group of German officers presented mutually unacceptable platform drafts: one purely nationalist in tenor, the other a stereotype of Marxist dogma. The Soviets, however, were in no mood for lengthy negotiations. Realizing from their own experience the force of nationalism, and fearing that Western powers would soon make a similar move to coopt conservative sentiment against Hitler for their own aims, they extracted a quick agreement on a compromise draft of their own.[12]

The Soviet solution was to force the KPD to abandon temporarily any ideological baggage impeding an agreement and to maintain a façade of equal cooperation, while assuring that real power rested in Communist hands. The NKFD manifesto emphasized the desire for national self-preservation and the danger of Hitler's "catastrophic" policies. "Stein, Clausewitz and Yorck were invoked; and an emphatic demand was made to preserve the army, shun Weimar, and drop all of the slogans of class war that are not connected with the punishment and disowning of war criminals." The KPD goal of radical land reform was ignored (out of deference to the Junker officers), and repentant followers of Hitler were promised amnesty. On the other hand, Nazis, war criminals, and their accomplices—terms not carefully defined—were to be subject to trial and punishment, including expropriation. While bourgeois freedoms and property rights were to be guaranteed under a "strong democratic state power," nothing precise was said about the form of government or the structure of power. The door was thus left open for a social transformation.[13]

Despite their concessions and their efforts, especially in the first months of the NKFD's existence, to create a spirit of good will in their dealings with the soldiers, the KPD emigrés always regarded the Free Germany organization as having its "motor mounted on the left," in the words of one NKFD veteran. The accuracy of this assessment was not really altered by some further changes in the organization's professed aims in order to win the cooperation of the highest-ranking POW officers later in 1943. Speculating on the chance that the influence of these officers might help bring about a military coup against Hitler, the Communists were willing to agree to cooperate with an intact Wehrmacht in a postwar regime. Captive generals were given generous opportunities to appeal to their colleagues for such a plan on radio and in print, with minimal censorship. NKFD information media remained under KPD control, however, and the work of NKFD propaganda agents at the front and in the POW camps was controlled from KPD headquarters in Moscow. Recruitment, too, was handled by the left wing of the organization, and demanded of new members a rigid adherence to Marxist dogma.[14]

As it became clear that the POWs' efforts were neither turning the German army against Hitler nor weakening it through massive desertions in the field—that is, that they could have no influence either in ending the war or in shaping the peace thereafter—the NKFD became ever more forthrightly a Communist tool. After early 1944, its propaganda broadcasts ceased commenting on the future German government or advertising the NKFD itself as the force that would lead the nation out of catastrophe, and began concentrating primarily on calling for resistance within Germany. "Free Germany" popular committees were now to be formed, comprised of all anti-fascists of whatever political stripe. These were to undermine Nazism from below and help the Allies in the democratization of Germany. Meanwhile, through indoctrination of its more cooperative members and isolation of the rest, the Communists progressively prepared the NKFD for its final role, as a source of cadre to help the KPD establish its political hegemony in postwar Germany.[15]

In all other respects, the NKFD had exhausted its usefulness as of the Teheran Conference in November 1943. Here, the Western Allies—suitably responsive to the threat of a Soviet-German accommodation implicit in the NKFD—offered Stalin major concessions on the Polish question and the promise of a second front in the West shortly. With Germany's eventual defeat now inevitable, Stalin's interests were no longer served by an ambiguous posture toward the Allies, and he assured them that the NKFD was merely a propaganda tool against Hitler.[16]

Hereafter, Soviet strategy was based on the assumption of a military defeat and joint occupation of Germany, whose resurgence as a threat to the USSR was to be prevented at all costs. This could be accomplished by several external measures which Stalin urged on his American and British counterparts, including execution of political and military leaders, territorial amputations and divisions, and destruction of industrial capacity. Simultaneously, however, the Soviets intended to attack what they considered to be the root of all political evil in Germany: the economic and political power of the reactionary landowners and capitalists. The instrument for this internal solution was to be the KPD.

The KPD Work Commission and its "Action Program" for Germany

Detailed Soviet planning for postwar Germany began in January 1944. In London that month, Soviet and Western representatives of the European Advisory Commission began negotiations on an Allied policy toward the Reich. Almost simultaneously, Wilhelm Pieck and Georgi Dimitrov met for a preliminary discussion of the "main political tasks" of future KPD work inside occupied Germany.[17]

The KPD program that emerged was based on the ideas of a Popular Front developed during the 1930s, and in fact amounted to a renewed call for the "democratic people's republic" conceived at that time. The circumstances now confronting the KPD were vastly more complicated than before, though; both the challenges and the opportunities were far greater. On the one hand, KPD leaders realized that the psychological and political climate in Germany after twelve years of fascism, and the anticipated occupation of large areas of the country by capitalist powers, rendered any open commitment to socialism unrealistic and unwise for the present. Having failed so miserably to resist Nazism before and during the war, the German working class would be in no position to make a successful socialist revolution soon thereafter. Should the Western powers suspect the Communists of such a plan, moreover, they would be less inclined to cooperate in destroying the old order in Germany. They might even, as after World War I, collaborate with the old elites to combat the revolutionary threat.

On the other hand, if the Communists could overcome their radical stigma and gain broad popular support for their own program of anti-fascism and national reconstruction, their chances for political leadership were better than ever before. Backed by the Soviets, they could use their organizational head start to seize and keep the initiative among the splintered and disoriented political factions in Germany. The economic and social reforms sought by all the Allies could then be carried out in a way that favored Soviet and KPD interests.[18]

Such considerations of *Realpolitik* led the KPD lead-

ership to ground its postwar program on a profound theoretical reassessment of the revolutionary situation in
Germany. According to the new line, the German
bourgeoisie had, like that of Russia before 1905, failed in
its historic task of overthrowing the feudal power structure. The first goal of the working class was therefore not
the proletarian revolution, but the completion of the bourgeois democratic revolution. In an address to fellow party
members in November 1944, Pieck chose the following
citation from Lenin's 1905 tract *Two Tactics of Social
Democracy in the Democratic Revolution* as a sort of
leitmotiv for KPD policy:

> While absolutely recognizing the bourgeois character of
> the revolution, which cannot *immediately* go beyond
> the bounds of a merely democratic revolution, our slo-
> gan ["the revolutionary-democratic dictatorship of the
> proletariat and the peasantry"] *pushes forward* this par-
> ticular revolution and strives to mould it into forms
> most advantageous to the proletariat; consequently, it
> strives for the utmost utilisation of the democratic rev-
> olution for a most successful further struggle of the
> proletariat for socialism.[19]

According to Lenin, the working class must seek to ally
itself at this stage with the relatively progressive petty
bourgeoisie against the more reactionary bourgeois elements, and thus to become the dominant and guiding
force even within the capitalist state. By using their political power to push through land reform and other measures to eliminate repressive features of rural and factory
life, the workers could create "a consistent and full democracy."[20]

On February 6, 1944, the KPD Politburo resolved to
convene a "Work Commission" of twenty influential party
figures to map out a detailed program based on the above
principles. In its eighteen regular sessions from 6 March
to 21 August, this commission heard presentations on a

variety of major issues, including future German political leadership, the German economy and KPD economic policy, agricultural policy, and the role of the trade unions. These presentations, and the "Action Program of the Bloc of Militant Democracy" into which they were incorporated in late 1944, reflected the central role that economic transformation played in KPD planning.[21]

In conformity with express Allied intentions, the Action Program called for arrest and punishment of Nazis and war criminals, including confiscation of their property. War profiteers, too, were subject to expropriation to offset the costs of reparations and reconstruction. In addition all war industries, public utilities and transport facilities, mining, pharmaceutical manufacturing, and energy production were to be nationalized, along with major banks and those public corporations "which are under the control of the 80 best-known major monopolists." Corporation laws were to be rewritten to limit the power of large shareholders. The stated purpose of these measures was to destroy the private economic power of anti-democratic elites and to enable reconstruction to begin. Another consideration emerged in the deliberations of the Work Commission, however, as observed by a modern East German historian: "The object behind this orientation was to create a sector with socialized ownership of the means of production, and thereby to guarantee a stable socio-economic basis for the anti-fascist, democratic order."[22]

A second such guarantee was to be central direction of the economy by the organs of the new state. Here the trade unions had a critical part to play. Hermann Matern, in his report to the Work Commission, noted that the unions would retain their traditional function as representatives of the workers' economic interests. At the same time, though, being the most comprehensive working class organization, they must also become the party's main link to the masses. In this capacity they would have important functions to perform, not only of educating the workers to class-consciousness, but of mobilizing them behind the economic and social policies of the KPD.

The creation of such a trade union movement, Matern added, would entail considerable difficulties. Not least of these would be a tendency for old Weimar leaders to form separate organizations in an effort, probably supported by Western powers in areas under their control, to revive the pre-1933 unions. For this reason, the KPD should immediately begin taking steps to secure the initiative in trade union reorganization. It should open negotiations with union leaders in exile and in Germany itself, aimed at an agreement on basic principles; it should recruit and train new trade union cadre in the Soviet POW camps; and it should prepare its own experienced trade union functionaries for future responsibilities under the new regime. These efforts should be aimed at creation of a single, unified organization with voluntary membership and a maximum of internal democracy (to neutralize the influence of the Weimar leaders). Effective political and economic power should be guaranteed by a clear division of authority among its component trade unions, based on the principle of one-union shops.[23]

Outside the industrial sector, KPD economic policy was closely related to its Leninist strategy of class alliances. Thus, the petty bourgeoisie was courted not only with the prospect of parliamentary democracy, but also with promises of economic freedom and state credits to restore small private artisan and commercial enterprises. In calling for state support of cooperatives and professional organizations serving the interests of small business, the Action Program hinted that these organizations, too, would have their role to play in the planned economy.[24]

The Party's main enticement to the peasants was the promise of land reform. The KPD plan, based on recommendations by its veteran agricultural expert Edwin Hoernle, was to create a "land fund" of at least 10,000 hectares to be redistributed to the land-hungry peasantry. Sources for this fund would include the expropriated holdings of fascists, war criminals, land speculators, "saboteurs of the people's food supply," and all proprietors of estates exceeding 150 hectares. The fund and the distribution process were to be administered by special land commissions composed of representatives of both the peasants and the state.[25]

The economic aims of this plan were similar to those behind the intended industrial expropriations: to eliminate fascist and reactionary elite groups—including, in this case, the class of large landowners—and to secure a sound economic basis for the new regime, meaning control over the food supply. Another important political dimension was also involved, however, which explains why this plank, the only one in the Action Program with no basis in Allied agreements, had such a high priority for the KPD and its sister parties throughout Eastern Europe. In the Communist view, no revolution was secure without the support of the peasantry. In this light must be seen the fact, too, that the Action Program contained no call for collectivization that might alienate "individualistic" German peasants. Rather, a period was foreseen during which these peasant proprietors would be educated to the advantages of cooperative farming methods. Within KPD circles, discussion was already underway about the use, for this purpose, of the "free farmers' cooperatives" promised in the Action Program.[26]

The political framework within which the KPD would seek to implement its program of economic transformation was still unclear by the end of 1944. The "Bloc of Militant Democracy" was envisioned as a sort of successor to the Popular Front, uniting all the anti-fascist political groups and "mass organizations" expected to spring up in Germany after Hitler's fall. Well into 1945, however, two possible forms for the Bloc were considered: a loose alliance of organizations and individuals led by the KPD, and a more formal coalition of recognized parties. Also unresolved was the exact part to be played by the "People's Committees," the local resistance groups being called for in KPD/NKFD propaganda broadcasts. The Work Commission foresaw an important role for these, particularly early in the occupation and in rural areas, as agents of denazification and initiators of economic reconstruction. The actual extent of their political influence, though, would certainly depend on their contribution to Hitler's defeat. Indeed, the Work Commission took pains to persuade the German people that Germany's continued national existence itself would be decided by their own "successful struggle against German imperialism" as well as by "the internal restructuring of Germany in an anti-fascist, anti-imperialist spirit."[27]

FINAL ADJUSTMENTS: FROM YALTA TO THE OCCUPATION

Ultimately, of course, Germany's future as a nation was in the hands of the Big Three. Up to the Yalta Conference in February 1945, Soviet policy on the German question was no clearer than that of the other Allied powers, nor did it need to be. On the issues of greatest immediate concern, such as Poland, reparations, the Oder-Neisse line, and the dismantling of Germany's military and economic power, Stalin was able to reach agreements to his satisfaction, at least in principle. The Allies' public commitment to "eliminate or control all German industry that could be used for military production" and to "remove all Nazi and militarist influences from public office and from the cultural and economic life of the German people" also gave the KPD an adequate basis for pursuing its transformation program throughout all of Germany. At the same time, the decision to assume Allied sovereignty over Germany, and acceptance of the Soviet position that the individual powers would have supreme authority within their own zones, assured that in any event a sizable portion of Germany would remain under Soviet control.[28]

It was thus in the interest of the USSR to support the Yalta agreement in practice, as it did, and not to insist on immediate resolution of more abstract issues at the cost of straining Allied relations. While Stalin called at the conference for a decision on partition of Germany, reminding Roosevelt and Churchill of their earlier support for this idea and expressing his own, he did not press the point when his allies' misgivings became clear. The formal agreement that finally resulted left dismemberment open as a future option.[29]

Stalin's flexibility on this issue was further dramatically demonstrated shortly after the Yalta Conference when, in an apparent reversal of policy, he began supporting German unity himself and disclaiming any intention to partition or destroy Germany. Again, the key to Soviet motives seems to lie in short-term tactical considerations. As the Allied armies now began their advance into Germany, relations with the German people assumed a new importance. Already their rabid Russophobia, fanned by Nazi propaganda, was manifested in a stiffer resistance in the East than in the West, and rumors were current of a last-minute Anglo-American-German alliance against Bolshevism. That Stalin seriously feared some such secret arrangement was evident in his extravagantly suspicious reaction when informed by the Americans of German attempts to negotiate a separate surrender. Moreover, some thought had to be given to the KPD's need for popular support in order to achieve its aims throughout the country.

The Soviets had shown before, when they founded the NKFD, their appreciation for the power of national feeling and their wariness of being outflanked on the right by their allies in dealing with the Germans. Now, having failed to extract a public commitment to partition from Britain and the U.S., they were not about to hand these powers a propaganda advantage by holding to such a policy unilaterally; rather, they would be the first to appear as magnanimous victors and preservers of the German nation. Similar motives led the Soviets, roughly simultaneously, to abandon their violent anti-German propaganda at home and to republicize a remark Stalin had once made that "Hitlers come and go, but the German nation and the German state remains." Such postures looked good and cost nothing.[30]

The impending problems of occupation loomed larger after Yalta, and their exact nature became clearer. By early 1945, with the Allied invasion of Germany itself imminent, it was plain that no anti-Hitler rebellion was likely to occur or, if it did, to have any real effect on the outcome of the war. On 17 February, in conformity with the Allied agreement to assume sovereign powers, Communist propaganda ceased calling for Hitler's overthrow from within. The following day, the KPD leadership produced a policy document that provided for KPD cadre to be sent into Germany in the wake of the Red Army, to direct the first denazification and reconstruction measures. The Action Program of 1944, as Pieck commented a short time later, was "obsolete."[31]

The necessary reassessment of KPD strategy was accomplished in the Work Commission, which resumed its sessions on 4 January 1945. While it could not revise the Action Program entirely, its deliberations did culminate, on 5 April, in a set of "Guidelines for the Work of German Anti-Fascists in the Area of Germany Occupied by the Red Army," for the realization of that program's primary objectives "under even more unfavorable circumstances." The new planning emphasized a quick restoration of order. Nazis and war criminals had to be apprehended and a functioning economy reestablished, especially rational food production, collection, and distribution. To this latter end—and also in anticipation of the land reform—

abandoned farms and all fallow lands would be made available to peasants willing to work them (although nothing as yet was said about formal expropriation). Barter and "mutual aid" relationships were to be established between city and rural populations.[32]

As late as February 1945, KPD policy had still called for the local "People's Committees" to lay the basis for the new order in the towns. These were to have responsibility for restoring and running all municipal services and utilities, securing vital raw materials, and coordinating and impelling efforts to restore industrial production. The "Guidelines" of 5 April, however, replaced these committees with appointed administrative organs whose first duty would be to enlist public support for the policies of the occupation authorities. They were to be staffed, in order of priority, with 1) pre-1933 members of "anti-fascist organizations" who had remained loyal; 2) workers who had resisted Hitler and the war; and 3) "responsible" members of the intelligentsia not affiliated with the Nazi party or Hitler Youth. Selection of all staff members was assigned to a personnel office to be controlled, if possible, by "a comrade who has spent the last few years working as an anti-fascist functionary outside Germany"; that is, in the Soviet Union.[33]

The KPD did not easily abandon its original Popular Front model. Even as late as May 1945 it briefly considered sponsoring a "People's League for Democratic Renewal" to coordinate the activities of all anti-fascist forces. This idea was quickly discarded, though, in the realization, reflected in the April "Guidelines," that these "anti-fascist forces" were too weak and disorganized to serve as a power base for the KPD and its democratization plans. Such a power base would have to be created from the ground up; cooperation with other anti-fascists would be possible only within a framework of political, economic, and social institutions carefully structured so as to extend, rather than dilute, Communist control. Through these institutions, the KPD could then channel all efforts for national regeneration into what has often and aptly been called a "revolution from above": a directed program of social and economic transformation.[34]

TWO

A New Foundation, Spring and Summer 1945

RESTORING ORDER OUT OF CHAOS

When Walter Ulbricht and his party began their task of reconstruction on 1 May 1945, they found a society in total collapse. Virtually all cities were in ruins and depopulated (Berlin, for example, had been reduced from 4,325,000 to about 2,560,000 residents), and vast areas of Brandenburg and Mecklenburg had been devastated by battle. Refugees from these provinces and the lands beyond the Oder and Neisse, prisoners from Nazi camps, evacuees, and soldiers thronged cities, villages, and roads; heading homeward, or westward, or nowhere. Most surviving leaders of government and the economy at all levels had fled west before the advancing Red Army, taking with them vital documents, equipment, and supplies. In the ensuing chaos, what had not been destroyed in the fighting was subject to plunder by the desperate populace.[1]

The First Measures of the Red Army and the "Initiative Groups"

For the first few weeks of occupation, such order as existed was the result of measures taken by nearly-autonomous local Red Army commanders. Soviet commandants of large cities acted to avert starvation and epidemic by feeding as many as they could directly from Red Army supplies and remaining German stockpiles, and by organizing civilian work battalions to clean up debris and restore power and water. By mid-May, a reasonably adequate food distribution system was functioning in Berlin. Soviet political officers and KPD agents advised commanders in the appointment of new German civil authorities.[2]

The "Ulbricht Group," which concentrated its efforts in Berlin and the surrounding region of Brandenburg, was the first and most important of three "Initiative Groups" dispatched from Moscow to each of the major Red Army operations areas in Germany. The second group under Anton Ackermann landed in Saxony on 1 May, and the last, under Gustav Sobottka, in Mecklenburg-Pomerania on 6 May. Each group was composed of ten selected KPD members, including the Central Committee member in charge, augmented by "up to twenty anti-fascist prisoners of war" from the NKFD who had been trained since fall of 1944 in special "Antifa" (anti-fascist) schools in the USSR.[3]

The Initiative Groups immediately began searching out Communists, Social Democrats, and other anti-fascists to cooperate with them in the new administrative organs. Those Group members who did not assume key posts in the cities were dispatched to towns and villages in the surrounding countryside, where the KPD and SPD were traditionally weak and conservative social and political influences were deeply entrenched. Here, Soviet commanders had been appointing to local and county offices any self-styled democrats willing to assume the responsibility, including some actual fascists or other undesirables. With the commanders' consent, "instructors" from the Initiative Groups purged local government of these elements, installed the most reliable anti-fascists they could find, developed programs for collection of the harvest, and, as everywhere, held mass meetings to rally support behind the KPD and its reconstruction program.[4]

The KPD's aim, as Ulbricht later admitted, was to set its own stamp on the basic institutions of government while the situation was still fluid, before the Communists' adversaries could regroup and reassert their influence. These institutions would then define the limits of acceptable political activity according to KPD standards. At the same time, the Initiative Groups had an educational mission: to arouse the masses to an awareness that the Nazis, Junker militarists, and monopoly capitalists (*not* the Allies) were the cause of Germany's misfortune; and to persuade them that the only way to a better future was through a united popular effort to destroy these groups and rebuild on a democratic basis.[5]

That the KPD was to be the "motor" driving the regeneration effort was implied in deeds as well as words. In the first days of occupation, Communists organized teams of "activists" to begin the herculean tasks of restoring vital public services and distributing food and other necessities. Communists promoted the institution of elected house and block captains as the lowest officials of the city administrations, charged with directing communal efforts to repair housing and utilities, aid needy victims of war and fascism, and so forth. KPD newspapers regularly printed articles suggesting practical measures for the improvement of living conditions, and reporting on exemplary reconstruction activities. Of course, such initiatives reinforced the endeavors of the Soviet authorities to restore order. They also had the advantage, though, of identifying KPD programs with the common interest. The Communists hoped, by presenting their program of economic and social restructuring in the same light, to mobilize support for it as well.[6]

The masses remained frustratingly apathetic, however. At this point most Germans, East and West, proved indifferent to politics, or indeed to anything but their own immediate self-interest. A contemporary SPD organizer recalled,

> In the inferno of the last months of war, our life was reduced to instinctive actions aimed at saving that life. . . . Since all of us stood so close to destruction, even our hatred for those who were to blame for the whole

disaster was blunted and dulled; there remained only the vengeful hope that the truly guilty ones would not survive the end of the war.[7]

The KPD expressed particular disappointment with the lack of class consciousness shown by the proletariat in failing to support its Communist liberators. "Unfortunately," one spokesman declared, "we are now forced to recognize that the fascist ideology has created vast confusion among the workers."[8]

Worse yet, such anti-fascist political activity as did appear was independent of the Initiative Groups, and even competed with them. Responding to earlier KPD and NKFD propaganda, "People's Committees"—also called "Free Germany," "Anti-Fascist," or simply "Antifa" Committees—sprang up spontaneously in cities and towns all over Germany to fill the power vacuum left by the collapse of Nazi authority. Frequently they arose out of resistance groups and, as in Leipzig, even helped overthrow the crumbling fascist regime. Dominated by local Communists and Social Democrats, but often including a few liberal bourgeois as well, the Antifa Committees began fulfilling the role originally foreseen for them in KPD planning. The record of one committee in Dresden is typical:

> Weapons of all sorts were confiscated and secured; suspected Nazis closely watched. . . . Supplies still on hand in grocery stores were controlled. Confiscated hoards were immediately and equitably distributed. Squads of workers tore down anti-tank barriers and distributed the salvaged wood to the citizenry. . . .
>
> Almost by themselves a labor exchange and a sort of housing office arose. Hundreds of homeless people and refugees were provided with food and shelter. . . .[9]

Harried Red Army commandants, grateful for this desperately needed help, granted the Antifas power as pro-

visional city administrations and appointed their nominees to top municipal and county posts.[10]

The Antifa Committees were not without value to the
KPD in remote rural villages and in regions of the Soviet
Zone temporarily under Western occupation. Beyond the
reach of the KPD organization, such loose committees
were for a time the only available instruments of Communist political power, and were still being supported as
late as August 1945. Elsewhere, though, they were a threat
to KPD plans, and Ulbricht and his colleagues eliminated
them while establishing their own system of control.[11]

For one thing, the Antifas were too various in their
political composition and ideological leanings. Some were
dominated by Communists, some by Social Democrats;
some, in predominantly middle-class areas, even had a
strong bourgeois element which diluted their socialist
character and made them "collection points for a variety
of uncontrollable elements."[12] There was, moreover, little
hope of coordinating their efforts beyond the local level.
Whatever chance for political or organizational unity the
Antifa movement may have had, died when the Gestapo
destroyed the last centers of German underground resistance after the attempt on Hitler's life on 20 July 1944.
The individual committees arose as isolated ad hoc groups
of activists. As such they made a great contribution to
relieving the most immediate local needs, but they became counterproductive when the KPD set about constructing a coherent, centralized political and economic
system.[13]

The real problem went still deeper though. Having failed
in their mission to bring about a revolution from below,
the Antifa Committees now threatened to interfere with
KPD plans for a revolution from above by competing with
the institutions required to implement it. To guide Germany through a difficult process of reorganization, reeducation, and class struggle, the KPD leadership wanted
instruments it could control and use to mobilize society

with almost military precision. The spontaneous Antifas could not be controlled this way, nor did they have a broad basis of mass support. By their existence, however, they absorbed the personnel needed to create new German administrations, political parties, and "mass organs" such as trade unions, which could meet the Communists' requirements.

Most important, the Antifas hindered the reconstitution of the Communist Party itself—the pivot on which the entire new system must turn. Veteran Communist cadre reemerging from hiding or imprisonment were sorely needed to rebuild the Party and help implement its program. By devoting their energies to Antifa work instead, they weakened the KPD numerically and (Ulbricht feared) gave rival political forces a better chance to insinuate themselves into positions of power. Further, they endangered party unity by independently forming alliances with other political groups and bandying about slogans of proletarian revolution in contradiction to official KPD policy. It was essential that these cadres be reincorporated into the party organization, carefully schooled in the current party line, and placed in positions where their work would benefit the party.[14]

The suppression of the Antifa Committees was the decisive move by which the KPD emigré leadership asserted both its control over the Communist Party and the Party's leading role in society. Ulbricht set an early example in the capital. On 9 May 1945, a day after Germany's final surrender and a week after Berlin's capitulation, he was able to report to Dimitrov in Moscow that he had disbanded all such committees and "made it clear to the comrades that all energies must now be concentrated on our work in the city administrations."[15]

The administrations were reconstructed along a pattern that was already becoming familiar throughout Eastern Europe. At first glance, the appearance was one of nonpartisan anti-fascist reform and democratization. Despite a rigorous purge of fascists, the traditional structure of municipal government—the breakdown of departments, bureaus, etc.—was retained, and the participation of bourgeois representatives actively sought. Ulbricht instructed his task force to secure the appointment of district mayors, and of deputy mayors for such departments as transportation and economic affairs, who represented the predominant social group in their respective areas. Former members of the Center or Democratic parties were to be recommended for middle-class areas, while working-class districts would have mostly SPD officials and a light sprinkling of Communists. Departments of public health, the post office, and similar technical responsibilities were to be entrusted to any non-Nazis with sufficient expertise to run them.

A few key posts, however, were to be reserved exclusively for Communists, and through these posts the dominance of the KPD was to be secured. One was that of first deputy mayor, responsible for personnel matters and hence, according to the 5 April policy "Guidelines," always to be held by one of the Moscow-trained inner circle. Others included the director of public education (in charge of ideological reorientation), and police chief. Additionally, every effort was made to assure support for the KPD among the many administration personnel not formally affiliated with any party. Wolfgang Leonhard, a former member of the Ulbricht Group who later defected to the West, has recorded the following summation by Ulbricht himself: "It's really quite simple: it must look democratic, but everything must be in our hands."[16]

On 17 May 1945, the new Berlin Magistrat (City Council) was formally installed by the Soviet commandant with a politically unaffiliated and inexperienced engineer, Dr. Arthur Werner, as Lord Mayor. KPD Initiative Group members Karl Maron, Otto Winzer, and Arthur Pieck (son of Wilhelm) assumed office as, respectively, First Deputy Mayor and heads of the departments of Public Education and Internal Affairs. A Colonel Markgraf of the NKFD became Chief of Police. Similar councils were installed roughly simultaneously in other cities of the Soviet Zone. From the first, middle-class representatives were limited to a few representational or technical functions, with Communists or Social Democrats filling almost all positions of real power. In the Berlin district of Lichtenberg, for example, KPD members held five of the top jobs, Social Democrats four, representatives of bourgeois parties three, and one went to a non-party member. In Dresden, forty-three out of fifty-eight "leading staff members" belonged to either KPD or SPD.[17]

The next step was a thorough denazification of the municipal bureaucracy. Beginning in late May in Berlin and continuing into the fall of 1945 throughout the Soviet Zone, Communist personnel directors supervised the systematic purge of tens of thousands of fascists from city administrations. This move was particularly significant in view of the expanded role of local governments in the first weeks of occupation when, as the only German authorities yet permitted by the Soviets, they temporarily assumed control over the local agencies of central and regional government as well. The wholesale dismissal of experienced personnel, coming as it did at a time of chaotic social conditions, greatly complicated the already monumental tasks of the administrations. In general, however, despite the reluctant retention of some indispensable technicians, political considerations won out.[18]

Above all, the Communists were determined to avoid what they saw as a fatal mistake of the 1918 revolution: the failure to democratize the civil service, which the first issue of the KPD organ *Deutsche Volkszeitung* characterized as one of the "three pillars" of reactionary power in Germany, along with large landowners and the military. The grip of this trinity had, the KPD noted, never really been broken by democratic movements of the past; always it had reemerged to block social progress. This time, even at the cost of some additional confusion and inefficiency in the short run, the Communists insisted on appointing bureaucrats upon whom they could rely in the long run, and on letting them develop by trial and error the skills to manage a new kind of state.[19]

For the Communists, denazification was part of the class struggle. Their purpose was not, like that of the Western powers, to eliminate a specific obnoxious political phenomenon, but rather to transform the entire reactionary power structure, replacing bourgeois-aristocratic hegemony with their own. They therefore chose means appropriate to their revolutionary goals. Avoiding the painstakingly legalistic Anglo-American approach of trying to identify and punish all Nazi party members, the KPD worked instead to focus popular resentment on the socioeconomic elites it considered the true authors and beneficiaries of fascism. A steady barrage of KPD propaganda pointed to the interpenetration of economic and political power in the Third Reich, enormous business profits, state aid to large landowners, and the economic motives of Hitler's war. The people were exhorted to remove and punish on their own initiative all those who had actively participated in or supported this fascist system or who opposed the democratic goals of the new regime, regardless of whether those implicated had formally joined the Nazi party. In Ulbricht's words,

> The important thing is to find out who are the war criminals and active Nazis. All others are citizens who must be given the chance, through honest work and by overcoming their Nazi ideology, to participate in the construction of the new democratic order.[20]

Thus, "nominal" Nazis were to have an opportunity to redeem themselves by demonstrating their loyalty to the new system. The ultimate test would be their support for the KPD's attack on the "real criminals." Over succeeding months it would become increasingly clear that the main "criminals" the KPD had in mind included the leaders of the German economy, and that "denazification" in the Communist sense involved expropriation of the principle means of production. For the time being, however, the Communists contented themselves with extending the anti-fascist political purge to business and industry—a move not only popular with the mass of workers, but actually begun spontaneously by them.

Revival of the Economy

Like the Antifas at the municipal level, spontaneous workers' committees led by Communist and Socialist activists arose to seize control of factories throughout Germany at the moment of occupation. An anti-Nazi purge was usually high on their list of priorities. Where this took the form of driving reactionary managers from positions of power, particularly in major industries, the KPD eagerly supported committee actions. All too frequently, though, the workers' vengeance turned also (or instead) against the petty fascists in their own midst, thus weakening the working class rather than the bourgeoisie—and incidentally removing vital skilled manpower from the economy. Communist propaganda strongly condemned this symptom of "ideological confusion" as an objective danger to the anti-fascist cause, and campaigned for general acceptance of the KPD's economic standard of guilt. It urged the workers to overlook the deluded pawns of the fascist system and concentrate on its capitalist mainstays. But only the development of a centralized trade union organization finally enabled the KPD to harness for its own priorities the spontaneous anti-fascism of the workers.[21]

A similar ambiguity in KPD-worker relations arose over the economic role of the workers' committees. The conflict here, although ultimately of deeper significance, was at first overshadowed by the fact that the committees' activities greatly helped to achieve the KPD's number-one objective: to get the economy moving again. Lacking as yet any machinery of economic control, the Communists relied largely on private entrepreneurs to restart production on their own initiative, and in fact urgently entreated them to do so, whether for patriotism or for profit. Where owners and managers had either fled or been purged, though, the task fell to the workers themselves. Led by their elected committees, half-starved men dragged machines from the rubble, repaired them with their bare hands and whatever tools they could assemble, and began amid the ruins of their factories to manufacture anything they could trade for food. Groups of them made excursions into the countryside to barter with peasants, then returned to divide up the proceeds or to add them to the noon meal in their factory canteens. On this hand-to-mouth economic basis, the workers' committees made an important contribution to the revival of Soviet Zone industry, as well as to the sort of worker-peasant relationship the KPD hoped to promote.[22]

Beyond this, the committees helped neutralize the power of the managers. Where entrepreneurs remained in place and participated in reconstruction efforts, they were generally forced by their workers to share power in some degree with the committees. Such "codetermination" arrangements had several advantages for the Communists. For one, it reduced their dependence on a large portion of the old economic elite whose expertise was for the time being indispensable, but whose loyalty was questionable at best. The workers, with their livelihood at stake, tended to inhibit the sort of "sabotage" in which anti-regime managers often engaged, including smuggling of documents, plans, and equipment to the West; and to see to it that the factory produced at capacity. Secondly, the spontaneity of the workers' actions lent an aura of revolutionary legitimacy to the KPD's own efforts to undercut the bourgeoisie. Finally, the power gained by the workers' committees opened an avenue for the KPD to increase its own power in the economy—as soon as new trade unions gave it an instrument with which to gain control of the workers' initiative.[23]

What the spontaneous committees could not achieve, however, was a centrally directed economy. The need for central direction was practical as well as political, and became increasingly evident during summer 1945 as diverse initiatives began setting some factories in motion again. The first to recover were small consumer-goods and food-processing plants serving mostly local needs. Larger and more complex industries followed, having suffered more from bomb damage and from subsequent shortages of fuel and power, due largely to the shattered rail system's inability to transport coal to the cities. With their stocks depleted and all bank accounts blocked by Soviet order, the big factories' immediate need was for working capital. To get it, they too turned to the local economy, and set about producing whatever gewgaws and gadgets would turn a quick groschen in a marketplace flooded with inflated money and hungry for consumer goods:

> One saw ashtrays, painted glass vases and tiles, fireplace pokers, cigarette lighters without flints, eyeglasses without lenses, lamps without bulbs, radios without tubes, razors without blades, etc. In the "food chemistry" field, food spreads, aromatic flavorings and hot beverages were offered.[24]

This sort of production, while it kept the workers employed, obviously did not meet the needs of a people faced with starvation. Still worse, it further depleted remaining reserves of vital raw materials. Even when real necessities were produced, they were often attainable only on the black market, which thrived on a barter economy and tended to perpetuate it. Workers who were paid in kind traded with peasants, and factories traded with other factories, while those with no tangible goods to exchange in this so-called "compensation" system did without. While such conditions prevailed, it made little sense for a factory to produce anything but immediate consumables.[25]

The economic departments of the German administrations had the job of imposing order on this anarchy and restoring a rational economic system. In the Communist view this meant developing plans for assigning production, allocating resources, and distributing finished goods according to the needs of society as a whole. In the process, of course, the administrations would also increase the KPD's social leverage by tightening its hold on the means of production. As a first step, they had taken over from the Antifas in the first weeks the responsibility for organizing efforts to clear debris. Labor exchanges set up by the local authorities registered all able-bodied men and women and assigned those not otherwise employed (especially purged Nazis) to hauling rubble from factories and streets. Subsequently, as industry began to recover, these exchanges helped allocate manpower according to economic priorities. The administrations underwrote loans to local industries, and in fact virtually forced entrepreneurs to accept credits from the new Soviet-licensed banks, so that the entrepreneurs would have the capital to start producing useful goods.[26]

Meanwhile the means of actual economic control were being developed. The new civil servants, many of them recruited from private industry to replace experienced fascist bureaucrats, labored intensively to accumulate the necessary documentation and administrative expertise to coordinate production in an entire city or district. At the same time the administrations worked to bring a significant segment of the economy directly under their authority, by appointing trustees to take over running those enterprises whose owners and managers had fled or been purged. The public sector thus acquired was to be a prime source of economic leverage for the regime. Acquiring it was not always a simple matter, however, since it often involved elbowing aside a syndicalist workers' committee whose members had seized "their" factory and restored it to production on their own. The struggle of the committees to preserve their autonomy (covered in detail in a later chapter) was long and stubborn. Occasionally they even prevailed for a while and were allowed to run their factories as workers' cooperatives. Normally, though, the economic authorities struck a compromise: they appointed a trustee selected by the workers, but made him answerable henceforth to themselves.[27]

The speed of industrial recovery varied throughout the Soviet Zone. Highly industrialized areas like Saxony and Saxony-Anhalt, which had suffered severely from bombing and general economic disruption, were slower to revive; while the relatively simple handicraft industries of Thuringia recuperated more quickly. On the whole, however, by late summer of 1945 some degree of order was returning to economic life, with a number of factories once more engaged in socially useful production. The level of industrial production for the entire zone, which had fallen to an estimated 5 percent of 1936 levels in April-May 1945, was back up to about 25 percent by the end of the year. This was a monumental achievement in view of the enormous difficulties that confronted the East German economy in the postwar period.[28]

Unlike western Germany, the area of the Soviet Zone had practically no mineral wealth or coal (apart from brown coal) and little basic industry. The light industry which had predominated before the war had depended on raw materials from Germany's western and extreme eastern provinces. While the war effort had brought a greater increase in productive capacity here than elsewhere in the Reich, this increase served to make the economy even more disproportionate. Established consumer industries and such little basic industry as existed were neglected in favor of large and highly specialized new metalworking, automotive, electronics, and chemicals plants whose main markets and sources of supply lay elsewhere. Many of the new facilities were suitable only for arms production. Since machine manufacturing concentrated on supplying the needs of such war industries, the region's light industries were left by 1945 with mostly worn-out and obsolescent equipment for peacetime production.[29]

Finally, bombardment and the actual combat that raged through much of the eastern part of the zone destroyed about 45 percent of industrial capacity and 60 percent of transport facilities, and wasted vast agricultural areas. Even the skilled work force which was doubtless East Germany's most important remaining asset was badly depleted, being left with about 13 percent fewer working males than before the war (as opposed to 7½ percent fewer in West Germany). Old men, women, and half-trained youths filled the places of the many workers now dead, disabled, or imprisoned abroad. In general, the population structure was heavily weighted toward women, children, and the very old, and became ever more so as it absorbed a mounting flood of destitute refugees from the East. On the other hand, those fleeing westward out of the Soviet Zone included, as noted above, a number of highly skilled technicians and managers, who often took important material assets with them. That the worst effects of economic collapse were overcome so quickly under these conditions reflected credit not only on the Germans, but on the Soviets as well.[30]

Soviet Occupation Policy: A Paradox

By mid-July 1945 American intelligence, puzzled by the "energetic policy followed by the Russians" toward cleanup and reconstruction in their zone, and by its unclear political implications, could only speculate that these efforts were either deemed necessary for reasons of public health or were "designed to facilitate future Russian exploitation of the human and material resources of Germany." Aside from overseeing German efforts to rebuild cities and factories, the Soviets began even before Germany's surrender to restore vital transportation facilities, especially rail-roads. By June they had reopened a number of critical rail lines, and were also setting up local motor pools of all available commercial vehicles to deliver food to the pop-ulation and coal to the factories. To maximize the food supply, the Soviets and their German allies organized and dispatched into the countryside tens of thousands of city dwellers, factory workers, and uprooted refugees to help with the harvest. In some cases the Red Army itself even pitched in, or lent tractors and horses to German farm-ers.[31]

The occupation authorities encouraged production by instituting a food rationing system that favored workers engaged in hard manual labor and by making special de-liveries of food and manufactured goods to bolster morale in the most critical factories. At the same time, they took steps to create a stable financial basis for recovery. Im-mediately upon entering Berlin, the Red Army command had ordered the temporary closing of all banks and the blockage of their funds. An order of 23 July confirmed this measure and also froze wages and prices at 1944 levels. The stated aim of these actions was to choke off a vast excess money supply which, at a time of scarce consumer goods, was fueling the black market and threatening run-away inflation. Since January 1933, total currency in cir-culation had risen from 5.7 billion to about 65 billion marks, while the backing for this paper money had been siphoned off to finance the war effort.[32]

By closing the banks, the Soviets eliminated the eco-nomic dead weight of private wealth accumulated before 1945 and cut the taproot to power derived from the old order. Henceforth, every able-bodied person would have to work to earn his way in the new economy on the terms of the new regime. Except for some later compensatory payments to holders of small savings accounts, especially in hardship cases, no disbursements could hereafter be made by any financial institution without the granting of fresh credits by the Soviets. These credits were funneled through a new state-controlled banking system, set up after August 1945, into developing industries and agriculture.[33]

One motive behind the Soviets' exertions at restoring their zone's economy was doubtless to strengthen their own hand in Germany as a whole. An economically vigorous Soviet Zone was both a more valuable political asset to the USSR and a good advertisement to the German people for communism. It would be more influential in shaping a reunified German state or, alternatively, more viable as a separate German state. Moreover, in actively leading reconstruction efforts, Soviet and German Communists reinforced the KPD's claim to political leadership and its entrenchment in positions of economic power.

Nevertheless, American observers were accurate in perceiving that economic exploitation was also a motive. Some appropriation of German resources was of course inevitable to enable an exhausted country like the Soviet Union to maintain a distant army of occupation. Thus, in Germany as in Eastern Europe, the Red Army was expected to live off the land, despite the disastrous consequences to the already seriously impaired local food supply.[34] There is likewise good reason to believe that the main immediate purpose for closing the banks was to give Soviet military authorities control over remaining German financial reserves, badly needed to help offset occupation costs.[35]

But the Soviets' intentions went beyond merely covering expenses. A prime occupation aim was to extract from Germany the means to rebuild their own war-ravaged homeland. To the extent that reparations were to be drawn from current production, the Soviets thus had a direct stake in a functioning German economy. A number of factories such as the great Zeiss optics and precision instruments works were restored quickly and under direct Soviet supervision to maximum production for reparations. Textile mills cut off from pre-1945 sources of raw materials received shipments of flax and cotton from the USSR, to be returned in the form of finished goods. The Soviet Zone was deprived of the products of these industries and bore the burden of further depreciation of its productive capital. Nevertheless, it did derive some benefits as well. Important plants were kept intact and their skilled workers remained on the payroll. Moreover, the large reparations contracts had a stimulating effect on the whole economy, promoting manufacture of useful peacetime goods.[36]

Where Soviet and German interests most clearly conflicted was over the second major form of reparations: dismantling. Practically as soon as the guns fell silent, Soviet reparations brigades arrived on the scene to begin stripping factories of their intact machinery for shipment to the USSR. The devastating effect of this action was due not only to the vast amounts of plant and equipment seized (estimated by various West German analysts at about 40 to 45 percent of total productive capacity), but also to the fact that many of the condemned factories were vital to the economy. In a situation of critical energy shortages, fuel and energy production were among the industries hit earliest and hardest. Despite the threat of famine, the key Leuna chemical works lost facilities needed to produce much of the nitrate fertilizer on which the zone's agriculture heavily depended. Tractors and equipment were also removed from farms.[37]

The consequences to morale were equally disastrous. Workers were often forced to dismantle factories which they themselves had just painfully restored to operation, and thus to eliminate their own jobs. Entrepreneurs hesitated to rebuild their plants for fear they would become the next victims. To compound German frustrations, the haste, carelessness, and poor coordination that characterized the work of the reparations brigades resulted frequently in damage to the confiscated machinery, and even more frequently in its being left to rust away on factory yards and railway sidings for lack of transportation.[38]

The dismantling progam could be and was justified by the Communists on a number of grounds. Many of the affected factories (although far from all) were war industries, whose removal had been agreed upon as part of Allied policy to disarm Germany. The occupation authorities also claimed to have seized some machinery bearing Russian and other East European markings, indicating that it had originally been carried off by the Nazis. Finally, the Soviets could certainly be expected to demand restitution for some of the immense ruin wrought in their own country by German invaders, in light of which a certain callousness regarding the well-being of the Germans in their turn is perhaps understandable. Even now, the Berliners were eating no worse than the Muscovites.[39]

Still, the political damage to Soviet interests in Germany was incalculable. Fritz Selbmann, then a leading KPD functionary in Saxony, later recalled: "The dismantling of factories undoubtedly strained for many years the relationship between the Soviet Union and segments of the population of the Soviet Occupation Zone, and later of the German Democratic Republic. . . ."[40] The public image of the KPD also suffered tremendously, although the German Communists could do nothing about dismantling. Even the political officers of the otherwise omnipotent Soviet Military Administration (SMA) were helpless to stop what they saw as a criminally short-sighted policy. The reparations brigades were not under their control, but took orders directly from economic authorities in Moscow. Only in 1946 did these authorities begin to redirect the entire reparations program into levies on current production, having concluded that this method was ultimately more profitable (and having solidified their hold over East Germany's principal industries). Meanwhile, the SMA and its German collaborators could only intercede occasionally to prevent total dismantling of particularly vital plants, and encourage speedy reconstruction of the rest with whatever materials remained.[41]

The conflict between the SMA and the reparations brigades was but one manifestation of an inherent inconsistency in Soviet policy toward Germany and Eastern Europe; a policy showing no single coherent strategy, but expressing instead different and often contradictory interests. The basic contradiction arose out of the very nature of the Moscow leadership, as both a national government and the center of an international revolutionary movement. Thus, the USSR was capable simultaneously of supporting the struggle of East European Communist parties to establish themselves as the leading force for national revival in their respective countries, and of pressing demands for reparations or vast territorial concessions on these same countries.[42] It could likewise contemplate at one time both the despoilment of the German state by the Russian state, and the revolutionary regeneration of German society under Soviet guidance.

Characteristically, Stalin subordinated the interests of ideology to those of national security wherever the two collided, especially so long as the future constellation of power in Europe and the world remained unclear. And it was, as Isaac Deutscher has pointed out, "in Stalin's approach to Germany that the conflict between his nationalism and his revolutionism was sharpest, and that the nationalist element predominated longest."[43] Convinced that the Germans would be "back on their feet again" in a few years[44] (perhaps as one state, for all he yet knew), Stalin first and foremost sought tangible guarantees that they could not once again threaten the Soviet Union. Such guarantees—amputation of German territory and exploitation of the German economy to rebuild the USSR— could only be had at the expense of his own zone.[45]

Yet even had he been so inclined, Stalin could not ignore the revolutionary impulse, least of all in Germany. Indeed, he expressed his own commitment to the "anti-fascist, democratic transformation," albeit in a perverse way, in his notorious remark in 1944 that each victor in this war would impose his own social system "as far as his army can reach."[46] If he thereby betrayed his cynicism about the ability of the intended transformation to succeed without the support of Red Army bayonets, he also revealed a perception that bayonets alone were not enough. Only a restructuring of the societies of occupied countries in the Soviet image could guarantee their permanent incorporation into the Soviet-Communist orbit. To achieve this goal, the USSR depended heavily on the native Communist parties it controlled—its unique asset as an occupying power. Nowhere was this asset potentially more decisive than in Germany, where the military might of all four powers was limited by their joint sovereignty, and the future of the whole nation thus might well hang in the balance of domestic political power.[47]

Raising a Framework of Political and Economic Power

The KPD faced the challenge not only of creating a revolution, but of controlling it: directing it toward calculated political objectives. This involved holding in check those anti-fascists who greeted the Soviet victory as the prelude to Germany's socialist revolution—educating them, if possible, to the subtleties of the KPD policy of class alliances and measured social transformation, or else isolating them. The first and most critical step was to establish the correct party line in the KPD itself.

The Moscow emigrés had had only sporadic contact with Communists in Germany during the war, and virtually none in the final months before occupation. Consequently, although some Communists in Germany were aware of their party's post-1935 "Popular Front" line, they did not know of its commitment to an ostensibly bourgeois democratic regime. The majority apparently assumed that any collaboration with bourgeois forces would be at most a temporary tactical expedient; a brief interlude to be followed by the proletarian dictatorship. Their blatancy in expressing this view threatened to hurt the KPD politically. Thus, shortly after arriving in Berlin Ulbricht complained in a letter to Pieck:

> Some comrades carry out our policy with a wink; some mean well, but then the slogan "Red Front" appears among them nonetheless; and some, above all in the complicated districts of Charlottenburg and Wilmersdorf, speak of soviet power and the like. We have waged an energetic struggle against the misconceptions in the ranks of our comrades, but again and again new comrades appear who start all over with the old mistakes. These short intimations will indicate to you what significance the ideological reschooling of our comrades has.[48]

In addition to reschooling, Ulbricht advocated a speedy change in the composition of the party itself to dilute the influence of these "sectarian" veterans. "Active anti-fascists proving themselves in current work" were to be recruited. The primacy of the emigrés, already affirmed in the elimination of the Antifa Committees, was to be reinforced by importation of more trained KPD cadre from Moscow as quickly as possible. Implementation of these measures was accompanied by serious tensions within the party, fueled by the resentment of the old guard in Germany at being elbowed out of influential positions by the new Soviet-trained elite. Frequent changes in KPD provincial leaderships over succeeding months document the convulsion caused by Ulbricht's determination to remove all who did not adequately support current party policy. The price was high, especially considering the KPD's desperate shortage of experienced functionaries. But, true to their Leninist precepts, The Central Committee leaders placed unity and discipline above all other considerations, particularly at this critical juncture.[49]

The New Political Parties and the "Anti-Fascist Bloc"

In retrospect, 1945-46 appears as a transitional phase for the KPD between its old status as an opposition party of the radical fringe, and its subsequent role (albeit under a different name) as the state party. Earlier the Communists had had no interest in appearing moderate, and later they would have no need to do so. During this anomalous interlude, though, the KPD was forced to behave something like a conventional political party; that is, to compete for the support of the average citizen. It was this that the old "sectarians" could not fully grasp. The KPD needed a new public image. Ulbricht encouraged local party leaders to prepare mass meetings carefully, making sure that the meeting hall was well-decorated and respectable-looking, "so that the people who come get the impression that we are the most important party in that locality." Regarding the use of traditional Communist slogans and emblems, Ulbricht advised: "Certain forms and methods used in our work at a time when our party was still in opposition . . . are no longer applicable."[50]

Likewise, indoctrination of KPD members eschewed the negative, critical political stance of Weimar days in favor of a posture more suited to a party claiming to be the "motor" of reconstruction. "Schooling" sessions, organized at once wherever the KPD established itself, called for concentration on work for the public good rather than on partisan disputes: "a pragmatic, responsible policy, with a view to the general interest of the laboring people and the entire country." The prewar KPD had isolated itself from potential allies among the peasantry, the intelligentsia, the middle class, youth, women, and even the workers themselves. The new KPD, by contrast, must be the party of all "consistent" anti-fascists.[51]

This goal was reflected as well in an eclectic recruitment policy. Virtually any non-fascist was welcomed—provided he or she would submit unreservedly to party discipline. And thus the all-important element of control appeared again. The object of KPD policy was after all to give the Communist Party control of the masses, not the other way around. The lesson the party leaders had learned from the 1930s was that the Communists could not make a revolution alone and on their own terms, but must appeal to the masses in terms appropriate to their present level of consciousness so as to lead them to revolution. Precisely this necessity of cooperating with less enlightened political forces, however, led the KPD's inner circle to tighten its hold on the reins. Only a strict Leninist policy of "democratic centralism" would enable the class-conscious proletariat to hold the party on course despite an influx of unschooled new members. Only iron discipline guaranteed that, whatever the numerical odds against the party itself, it could maneuver its political allies of the moment toward its own objectives, rather than becoming an instrument of theirs.[52]

Ulbricht saw to it that the KPD got a good head start rebuilding its organization. As early as February 1945 he had submitted a plan for "temporary commissions" to be set up in every district of Germany, to supervise establishment of local party organizations and of party "groups" in factories, apartment blocks, and "in the newly-created administrative and economic organs." During May the Ulbricht group installed a network of agents throughout Berlin to register KPD members and act as points of contact with the emigré nucleus. The Initiative Groups in Mecklenburg and Saxony were equally busy enrolling members.[53]

With the fall of the fascist regime, however, survivors of the other Weimar political factions also began emerging from hiding and making contact with one another. Liberal and Catholic leaders like Ernst Lemmer, Andreas Hermes, and Jakob Kaiser met for discussions in Berlin in mid-

May. Almost simultaneously, three separate SPD circles formed in different districts of Berlin. Despite the variety of political conceptions, nurtured in isolation over long years, which appeared in these groups, one idea was common to all of them. This was a perceived need for some sort of united democratic party, particularly a working-class party, to overcome the political fragmentation that had helped Hitler to power. Some Social Democrats saw the KPD as a natural partner in this undertaking, but not all. Thus, on 18 May Karl Germer of the Charlottenburg SPD circle discussed with Jakob Kaiser, a former leader of the Catholic trade unions, the creation of a "comprehensive workers' party" modeled on the British Labour Party, and specifically excluding the KPD. Negotiations also went on between representatives of the old Catholic Center and of former moderate democratic factions toward the founding of a single party of the liberal bourgeoisie.[54]

The organization of other political parties was not unwelcome to the KPD; on the contrary, it played an important part in Communist strategy. Through this vehicle, potential opposition to Communist measures—which might otherwise gain Anglo-American support—could be channeled into a system that would appear democratic, yet be relatively easy to monitor and influence. Parties licensed in the Soviet Zone would obviously have to adopt platforms and policies acceptable to the Soviets, and hence compatible with the Communist idea of democratization. As a test of good faith, they would be expected to cooperate in an anti-fascist alliance (the Popular Front by another name) through which the KPD hoped, as ever, to establish its political hegemony. Nor was this pattern to apply to East Germany alone. Rather, the Communists intended "their" party organizations, headquartered in the capital city of Berlin, to claim national leadership, and thereby to extend the political system of the Soviet Zone throughout all Germany.[55]

A New Foundation

To this end it was important that the parties be founded as soon as possible, and in a configuration that facilitated KPD control. Specifically, the number of parties should be small enough to be manageable, but should include no new political combinations capable of challenging KPD leadership. All the above considerations no doubt figured in strategy talks held in Moscow on 4-5 June 1945 and attended by Pieck, Dimitrov, and the three Initiative Group leaders. Here, the KPD Action Program was once more revised in the light of the situation in Germany and the experiences of other Communist parties in Eastern Europe, and was incorporated into a declaration to announce the formal refoundation of the KPD.[56]

The Allies also completed two important documents on 5 June: one confirming the four zones of occupation as finally agreed upon; and the other asserting Allied authority to "impose on Germany additional political, administrative, economic, financial, military, and other requirements arising from the complete defeat of Germany." On 9 June, the Soviet Military Administration, headed by Marshal Georgi Zhukov, assumed the functions of military government hitherto exercised by the three Red Army commands in Germany. The SMA immediately issued, on 10 June, its Order No. 2 permitting the establishment of "anti-fascist parties and free trade unions." The following day the new Communist Party of Germany was proclaimed, and the Berlin Magistrat let it be known that registration of parties would be limited to the large and familiar anti-fascist parties of the Weimar era—that is, the KPD, the SPD, the old Catholic Center, and a liberal party. Thus within a week the basic preconditions for the new regime were in place.[57]

All this came on the other political groups like a bolt from the blue. None had expected full-fledged political institutions to be permitted again so soon, least of all by the Soviets. The three Berlin SPD groups, already in the process of consolidation, hastily constituted their joint leadership as a Central Committee and rushed their own founding declaration into print on 15 June. A functionaries' conference formally reestablished the SPD two days later. Middle-class forces were less well-organized, but with active Communist encouragement a Christian Democratic Union (CDU) appeared as a successor to the Center Party on 26 June, and on 5 July a small Liberal Democratic Party (LDP) announced itself.[58]

Not surprisingly, the new platforms of all these parties revealed their fundamental acceptance of the Communist viewpoint that the judgment of history had gone not just against Nazism, but against the German society which had produced it. Each recognized both the political and the practical necessity of some important social and economic changes. The CDU leadership reaffirmed its belief in private property "that insures personal development of the individual," but went on to declare, "We are convinced, however, that under present conditions all private property is burdened with a mortgage to the people as a whole, and that its continued existence can only be guaranteed by exercise of the utmost social responsibility in its use." To guard against abuse of governmental authority by the "illegitimate influences of economic power-concentrations," the CDU's founding declaration called for nationalization of all mineral resources and for state control of "mining and other key industries of a monopolistic nature." This document also foresaw a large-scale confiscation of latifundia to provide land for settlement by the greatest possible number of independent farmers.[59]

The LDP was more cautious in its economic formulations, insisting that the retention of private property and a "free economy" was a prerequisite for economic recovery. Even the Liberal Democrats, however, were willing to accept nationalization of such industries and large estates as were "appropriate and ripe" for it, providing such action could be justified by the "preponderant interest of the public welfare." In practice, the LDP proved willing to cooperate with the KPD by interpreting liberally this vague phraseology. The real issue for both bourgeois parties was respect for the *principle* of private property. Property was to be alienated only for a specific reason and, unless the owner was being punished for a crime, due compensation was to be given.[60]

The SPD refrained from an attack on private property per se, but otherwise was committed to a program of sweeping social and economic reform which its founding declaration listed in part as follows:

> Nationalization of banks, insurance companies and mineral resources, of mines and the energy industry. Seizure of large land holdings, of viable large-scale industry and of all war profits, for the purposes of reconstruction. Elimination of unearned income from land and rented housing. Sharp limitation of interest paid on liquid capital. Obligation of entrepreneurs to fiduciary management of the enterprises entrusted to them by the national economy of the German people.[61]

This relatively radical stance reflected the prevailing sentiment among socialists in Germany (both Communist and Social Democratic), whereas that of the KPD was more pragmatically attuned to the exigencies of four-power control in Germany, and of Soviet-Western relations in general.

In other respects, though, the SPD platform was deliberately close to the KPD's, most notably in its adoption of the "anti-fascist, democratic republic" slogan and in its call for working-class unity. The SPD Central Committee in Berlin was in fact dominated by a pro-Soviet faction, led by Otto Grotewohl, which favored immediate union with the KPD. On 25 June, it delegated a member of this faction, Gustav Dahrendorf, to sound out Communist attitudes to the idea of such a merger at a KPD functionaries' conference to which the SPD had been invited to send a representative. Ulbricht demurred: the time was not yet ripe; a period of "ideological clarification" was needed.[62]

By this Ulbricht meant that the necessary control machinery was not yet in place to provide the sort of unified party the KPD leaders wanted. They needed time to assert their absolute authority within the Communist Party and to recruit and train new cadre, so as to be able to out-maneuver the more loosely-organized Social Democrats and dominate a united party. The SPD Central Committee, for its part, had to be given a chance to establish its own authority over the Social Democratic movement throughout Germany. A too-precipitous union might split the SPD, leaving an unassimilated remnant in the hands of its right wing. In the meantime, "working-class unity" was to be secured through a KPD-SPD United Front such as the Communists had sought in the 1930s. (Significantly, SPD leaders were approached about this idea immediately after SMA Order No. 2, but *before* the SPD was formally reestablished.) The United Front, in turn, would dominate a KPD-sponsored bloc of all recognized parties.[63]

The KPD's own founding declaration was intended primarily as a program for this "Bloc of Anti-Fascist, Democratic Parties," rather than as a party platform in the usual sense. Its aims were expressed in terms designed to be acceptable to all anti-fascists. The words "socialism" and "communism" appeared nowhere in the text, and a policy of "forcing the Soviet system on Germany" was specifically rejected. Instead, the KPD called for a cooperative effort to stamp out fascism, restore decent living conditions, and complete the bourgeois revolution of 1848 by establishing a parliamentary democracy "with all democratic rights and freedoms for the people." Its economic program was incorporated into a list of top priorities for that effort. Included were expropriation of "Nazi bosses and war criminals" and transfer of their property, all public utilities and all abandoned enterprises to the control of the "municipal or provincial organs of self-government"; and total liquidation of large land holdings, "the great estates of the Junkers, counts, and princes," for redistribution to peasants ruined in the war. "It goes without saying," the declaration continued, "that these measures will in no way affect the landed property and the economy of the upper peasantry."[64]

This program was calculated to assuage potential resistance to the KPD's leading political role and to seize for the Communists the pivotal issue in German politics. Henceforth, all Communist policies from land reform to the expropriation of key industries would be justified primarily not as positive economic or socio-political measures, but as aspects of the struggle against fascism. To oppose them was by implication to oppose anti-fascism itself—an interpretation that the SMA stood ever ready to reinforce with its own weight if need be.[65]

Likewise, the Communists made it clear quite early that cooperation in the Anti-Fascist Bloc was a condition of legal political activity. At a meeting convened on 12 June to secure acceptance of the bloc idea by the yet-to-be-founded parties, Pieck assured about two hundred veteran Weimar political leaders that the Communists were "making no demands that could infringe upon the independent organization of these parties." Rather, a prerequisite for the Bloc would be a relationship "in which the individual parties encounter each other as equals." Lest this promised independence be misconstrued as a license to debate the merits of the KPD program, however, Pieck also warned that the German people would show no understanding for those "to whom party bickering is more important than the most burning interests of the people."[66]

Like Popular Front coalitions elsewhere in Eastern Europe, the Bloc was intended to give the appearance of a sort of provisional parliament. This appearance was deliberately deceptive, however. The Bloc lacked a popular mandate, clear powers, or (most significantly) any provision for a loyal opposition. Its true purpose was neither to give expression to non-Communist political interests nor to share power with them, but rather to share *responsiblity* for the KPD transformation program: to legitimize each measure with the formal endorsement of all anti-fascist representatives. A KPD-SPD cooperation agreement (the United Front) concluded on 19 June gave the Communists the leverage they needed for effective control. Within the Bloc the two socialist parties had the moral authority of a far greater constituency and of an ideology generally recognized as the antithesis of fascism. In KPD-SPD councils the Communists could insist, with Soviet backing, that theirs was the true interpretation of the faith upon which working-class strategy should be based.[67]

A unanimity rule assured that, in any case, no resolution could be passed by the Bloc without KPD support. A party (or elements thereof) refusing its assent to a KPD-sponsored resolution, on the other hand, could be accused of obstructing the entire process of democratic reconstruction. Although Bloc resolutions technically had no legal force, their representation as the will of the people, plus the fact that the new administrations were staffed with Bloc party members, led to their being interpreted as binding directives by those administrations. Bloc committees were established at all levels of government to coordinate the activities of the administrations with one another and with the policies made in Berlin. Thus, an embryonic legislative mechanism began to function which the Communists regarded hopefully as having "great political import for all Germany." With a central German government yet to be established, the Soviets appraised the Bloc as "an organ whose resolutions were significant not only for the Soviet Occupation Zone, but for all zones."[68]

The New Trade Unions

The creation of new trade unions paralleled that of the political parties, and was in fact the work of essentially the same organizing groups. Their common impulse for anti-fascist unity was reflected perhaps most intensely in their commitment to a unified trade union movement. The argument was generally accepted among them that a single great workers' organization could have barred Hitler's way to power, and would be an indispensable buttress for any future democracy.[69]

This was not a new perception; indeed, a last-ditch effort had been made to forge such an organization even as the Weimar Republic was being liquidated. The SPD trade union league (Allgemeiner Deutscher Gewerkschaftsbund, or ADGB) made overtures in late 1931 to the Christian unions and the liberal-democratic Hirsch-Duncker unions which led to top-level negotiations on the eve of the Nazi takeover. These negotiations produced an agreement in principle on unification. Only after Hitler was in power, however, and had made clear his intention of destroying the unions, did they put aside their political differences and act. On 28 April 1933, after ten days of secret conferences, representatives of the three organizations reached agreement on a common program and formed a joint executive board: a "Leadership Circle of the United Trade Unions." But by then it was too late. Four days afterward, on 2 May, Hitler smashed the unions altogether.[70]

The 1933 unification agreement was nevertheless kept alive by members of the Leadership Circle as a basis for their cooperation in anti-fascist resistance activities. After the war, its principles guided reorganization efforts initiated in part by the same men who had helped frame the agreement, such as Jakob Kaiser of the Christian unions and Ernst Lemmer of the Hirsch-Duncker group. Significantly, these men retained their earlier policy that the KPD unions were to be excluded from any united trade union organization, at least at first. While not completely ruling out any future cooperation with the KPD, non-Communist leaders concurred in wanting to secure their own influence over such an organization before the KPD could move in and impose a Communist scheme.[71]

What was possible in the early 1930s was no longer so in 1945. The Communists had every means of seizing the initiative, and meant to do so. Within a few days of its arrival in Berlin, the Ulbricht Group began rounding up its own trade union veterans. Roman Chwalek and Paul Walter, both former leaders in the KPD's small Revolutionäre Gewerkschaftsopposition (RGO) of the 1930s, were relieved of responsibilities in the new Berlin administrations and put to work recruiting supporters for a KPD-sponsored trade union league. They immediately drew up a list of former functionaries from all the Weimar trade union organizations whom they felt might be willing to work with the Communists, and began visiting them. Concentrating particularly on Social Democrats, by late May they were able to secure the cooperation of several with good connections to ADGB circles, notably Hermann Schlimme, a member of the ADGB Executive Council before 1933; and Bernhard Göring of the clerical workers' associations. With these allies, Ulbricht could make his move.[72]

On 2 June, the Soviets invited representatives of the three non-Communist trade union groups, including Schlimme, Göring, Kaiser, and Lemmer, to a meeting with KPD leaders in the temporary Berlin city hall. There they were greeted by Ulbricht with the information: "Colleagues, Marshal Zhukov has charged me with the task of stimulating the foundation of trade unions." Discussions were set to begin the following day. Ulbricht opened, as chairman, by outlining what he indicated was the Soviet plan for constructing a united trade union: a "preparatory committee" was to be set up as a sort of provisional board of directors, composed of three Communists, three Social Democrats, and two representatives of the "bourgeois unions" (Kaiser and Lemmer).[73]

According to Karl Germer, soon to become the secretary

of this board, the Social Democrats present questioned the fairness of this arrangement, since the ADGB had been by far the largest of the Weimar trade union leagues while the RGO had been insignificant.

> This was received with a smirk and a wink that solicited understanding. But for our consolation we were advised to consider that, should grave differences of opinion arise in the proposed united trade union, there would always be a Social Democratic-bourgeois majority of 5 to 3.[74]

Even this majority was to prove illusory. When Hermann Schlimme hesitated too long in choosing a third SPD representative besides himself and Göring, the Communists suggested Otto Brass, a former left-SPD member whom they themselves had recruited for the new trade unions. Schlimme accepted. About two weeks later, some of Brass's pronouncements prompted Göring to question him more closely, and it emerged that he was in fact working with the KPD, which he subsequently joined.[75]

The Communists' strategy for dominating the trade unions was similar to that used in the political arena: they appeared with a unity program already prepared, and relied on the help of their SPD allies in persuading bourgeois representatives to accept it, at least in substance. As it happened, though, the draft for a founding declaration which the KPD submitted on 12 June (two days after SMA Order No. 2 legalized trade unions) contained some language that even Social Democrats could not swallow. Göring in particular joined Kaiser in rejecting a section aimed at discrediting the leaders of the Weimar trade unions by accusing them, in essence, of selling out the workers to the Nazis. Maintaining that all parties must assume some blame for the failure to stop Hitler, and that nothing could be gained by a public attempt to apportion guilt, the non-Communists at last exacted a compromise. The final document merely characterized 1 May 1933 (when the trade unions had voluntarily taken part in fascist demonstrations) as "the blackest day in the history of the workers' movement."[76]

On another key issue Kaiser and Lemmer stood alone, however: the KPD position that the trade unions would be responsible for "educating the workers to class-consciousness." Kaiser adamantly resisted this terminology, which not only implied a Marxist ideological bent but violated the principle, enunciated in the 1933 unification pact, that the unions should maintain strict political neutrality. Having experienced the divisive political quarrels of the Weimar era (and no doubt also mistrusting the KPD's intentions), Kaiser represented the widely-held view that trade unions should concern themselves exclusively with improving the social condition of the workers. Involvement in politics would tend to pervert them from this purpose and sow dissention. The KPD countered that, as the greatest working-class organization, the unions must be active participants in the highly political process of democratization, including ideological reeducation. The eventual compromise formula entrusted the unions with educating the workers "to a recognition of their social situation."[77]

Any satisfaction Kaiser derived from this change of wording must have been short-lived, since it quickly became clear that no change in policy was intended. The final text of the founding declaration was completed and the Preparatory Committee officially established on 13 June. The same evening General Bersarin, the Soviet commandant of Berlin, received the committee members. As Chwalek later recalled, "He conveyed to us the greetings of the Soviet trade unionists and said, among other things, that the trade unions in Germany must act first and foremost as a class organization of the workers." Bersarin added, paraphrasing the new founding declaration, that the unions must not only struggle for maximum rights of codetermination in the factories, but must cooperate in the anti-fascist purge of these factories, and actively work for the restoration of production. They must (in Bersarin's words) "lead the way as pioneers of the democratic transformation." In short, the unions were to be an instrument of Communist social and economic policy.[78]

As with political parties, the Communists were eager to establish their new trade union system as quickly as possible, particularly since some organizational activity was already being permitted in the U.S. Zone. Bersarin immediately granted the necessary equipment, paper, and other supplies for the Preparatory Committee to begin its work. Buildings and other assets of the Weimar trade unions had, it turned out, already been put at the disposal of the KPD some time earlier, to hold in trust for the planned new organization. The Confederation of Free German Trade Unions (Freier Deutscher Gewerkschaftsbund, or FDGB) and its platform were introduced to the public at a convention of about five hundred veteran trade union functionaries in Berlin on 17 June. With this gathering, the work of organizing new unions began in earnest in the capital city.[79]

In discussions about the structure of the FDGB, the KPD consistently supported "strong" and "unified" unions, meaning maximum uniformity and centralized control. This policy generally won SPD support. Consequently, it was quickly resolved that the FDGB would be organized into a limited number of powerful industry-wide unions on the basis of one-union shops, rather than having the workers in each factory divided among several craft unions as before.[80] Also, the organizational process was to be strictly from the top down: executives of each industrial union and of district-level FDGB committees would be appointed centrally. Independent organizational initiatives were forbidden.[81]

This sort of centralization facilitated KPD efforts to secure at all levels the same numerical "parity" it enjoyed in the Preparatory Committee. The "parity principle" encountered sometimes bitter opposition from veteran trade union leaders, particularly of the SPD, who insisted on resuming the positions of power they had held up to 1933. Recognition of several district committees and industrial-union executive boards was withheld by the Preparatory Committee until an acceptable KPD-SPD balance could be established in them. The KPD's Paul Walter was also active appointing, in the name of the Preparatory Committee, new industrial union leaders who could be relied on to help strengthen the KPD position in key unions, such as the Communist Fritz Rettmann to head the heavily-SPD Metalworkers' Union.[82]

From a broader perspective, centralized control made possible the mobilization of the entire trade union movement for the new social role the Communists intended it to fill. As soon as it was organized, the FDGB started functioning as an agent of the regime's economic policies. Mostly at the KPD's initiative, the FDGB and its member unions began establishing their own production plans and coordinating efforts to restore vital industries. Ulbricht has recorded some examples:

> A Metalworkers' Emergency Program of the Berlin metalworkers provided for the fastest possible repair of rolling stock and locomotives, and designated the plants for this. In Berlin, the trade unions organized a cooperative effort of bridge-building firms which . . . immediately began repairing bridges.[83]

Since all parties agreed on the most urgent priorities of reconstruction, this social involvement of the trade unions enjoyed universal support at the outset. Before long, though, a conflict of interests began to become evident.

A June 1945 KPD Central Committee resolution on trade union policy instructed regional party leaders to introduce piecework wages wherever necessary to maintain worker productivity. It also announced that under present conditions, while upholding the principle of an eight-hour day, "the trade unions feel obliged to attempt to get resolutions for a longer work period passed by the workers in individual factories and branches of industry."[84] In FDGB Preparatory Committee meetings in Berlin, the SPD opposed this position. Göring argued strongly for a return to the traditional trade union standard of a forty-eight-hour week; first because union members were demanding it, and secondly for reasons of health and safety. Temporary exceptions must be made only in cases of real social emergency, as in agriculture and construction. But the Communists saw the FDGB's responsibility differently:

> Colleague Chwalek pointed out that the trade unions had been created only as a means to an end, and that the present task is to rebuild the country and secure the people's food supply. It follows from this that the representation of workers' and salaried employees' interests will take on new forms, and will be directed to a significant degree toward increasing production.[85]

In accepting the new role of the unions as a "partner" in shaping and executing economic policy, the SPD had unwittingly given the Communists the key to transforming them from institutions representing the workers into an instrument of the regime. In the Communist view there was of course no contradiction here, since the regime itself would express the interests of the "working class." Indeed, the FDGB's proper function under present circumstances was not, the Communists reasoned, to pursue the narrow self-interest of Germany's demoralized workers as currently misconstrued by them, but rather to mobilize support for the larger revolutionary goals of the proletariat as interpreted by its class-conscious vanguard, the KPD. One of the unions' main tasks, announced at the outset, would in fact be to raise the class consciousness of the workers themselves: to awaken them to their leading role in the new order, and to the sacrifices required of them in order to secure this new order.[86]

EXTENDING THE SYSTEM TO THE PROVINCES

The efforts of the new political parties and trade unions to extend their organizations beyond Berlin were hampered by the enormous difficulty of communications with other parts of the Reich. Such facilities as did exist were of course under Soviet control. Local bourgeois and Social Democratic political groups often did not receive word of the foundation and subsequent activities of the Berlin party leaderships for weeks, and then only from Communist sources.

Nevertheless, despite their isolation these groups generally organized according to the pattern laid down in Berlin—an outcome reflecting not only the natural lines of political cleavage throughout Germany, but also the deliberate intervention of the SMA and KPD. Where provincial party organizations attempted novel political combinations or resisted the authority of the Berlin party leaders (as occurred particularly in Thuringia), Communist pressure eventually forced them to conform. In this way the Communists solidified the mechanisms of central control and reinforced the national standing of their zone's political leaders, while at the same time demonstrating to these leaders the extent of their dependence on Communist good will.[87]

The Political and Administrative System

The two bourgeois parties, especially the LDP, were at the greatest organizational disadvantage. Unlike the KPD and SPD, they had no organizational remnants in exile or in the underground on which to build, and no coherent ideology. They suffered above all from an almost total demoralization of the middle classes brought about by the collapse of the old order. There remained few liberal democrats with enough intact idealism to take time out from the daily struggle for survival to engage in politics, particularly under a Communist regime. Those who did get involved were variously motivated. Some saw their party as a partner in the anti-fascist democratization process, some as a bulwark against total "Bolshevization," and some as a means of personal advancement or economic protection. The CDU and LDP thus existed mainly as organizational shells until well into 1946, riven with factional differences and unable to exert more than a tenuous central control over their few and feeble outposts in the provinces.[88]

The SPD, by contrast, retained for the most part its large Weimar following and reappeared quickly throughout Germany. Its attraction for many of the left was its forthright call for socialization—a stance which the Communists, hampered by considerations of inter-Allied harmony and their own "Popular Front" strategy, could answer only with petulant charges of "opportunism." The SPD Central Committee in Berlin devoted much effort during spring and summer 1945 to developing a party platform upon which to base its own claim to political leadership. Briefly, the Social Democrats presented their party as the only one capable of bridging the political gulf between East and West, and hence of maintaining Germany's unity. On the one hand they cultivated good relations with the SMA, committing themselves as fellow Marxists not only to a radical social and economic transformation, but to an expressly pro-Soviet policy for Germany. On the other hand, the SPD's traditional adherence to liberal-democratic forms won it the confidence of the Western powers (as opposed to their deep suspicion of the KPD), and even the active support of the British.[89]

Once its organization was unified in all zones, the SPD thus promised to be the most influential party in Germany and the dominant partner in any future merger with the KPD. But unity was precisely the SPD's weak point. The party organization in the West, led by the staunch anti-Communist Kurt Schumacher, rejected the leadership of the Berlin Central Committee. Even within the Soviet

Zone, the Central Committee's lack of trained, full-time cadre and its early preoccupation with drafting a platform prevented it from devoting the necessary energies to rebuilding its provincial apparatus. When it finally began to do so systematically in August 1945, it encountered entrenched opposition from regional leaderships which, like the anti-Communist conservatives in Leipzig or the advocates of immediate working-class unity in Thuringia, had evolved their own platforms in the meantime.[90]

By late summer of 1945 it was clear to the Central Committee that the SPD's organizational weakness was critical at all levels, especially in remote areas. Party offices were small and manned mainly by volunteers, while the KPD maintained paid staffs of workers even in minor towns. Like the bourgeois parties, the SPD also suffered from the lack of communications facilities which cut off local Social Democratic groups from the party leadership and made them entirely dependent on Communist news sources. Under these circumstances they were easily dominated by their KPD counterparts. Communists—sometimes including SMA representatives—loudly characterized as "progressive" and "constructive" those SPD leaders who, by cooperating unquestioningly with KPD initiatives, demonstrated that they had "learned from the mistakes of the past." The KPD backed such leaders for top party and administration posts. Occasionally, veteran Social Democrats who applied to join the KPD were asked instead to help rebuild the local SPD, so as to influence it in a pro-Communist direction. The cumulative effect of these conditions was pitifully evident in a document of the small, isolated SPD group in Stralsund, calling for "Adoption in its entire content of the Communist Party of Germany's [founding] declaration of 12 June 1945."[91]

The KPD was the only German party to emerge from fascism and war stronger than it had been in Weimar times. The Nazi persecution had had a leveling effect on the two great socialist parties. Although both suffered tremendous personnel losses, the KPD was by its very nature better prepared to conduct underground operations, and benefited as well from the increased radicalism of determined anti-fascists. Above all, it had had the enormous advantage that its base of operations lay beyond the Gestapo's reach, in the USSR.[92]

As a result, the KPD was able to enter the occupation period with an intact leadership and a coherent program. Its strict party discipline, as opposed to the internal democracy practiced by the SPD and bourgeois groups, gave it a further tactical edge. "Democratic centralism" allowed the KPD to set and achieve concrete goals while others were still arguing over priorities. Even in the U.S. Zone the Communists' superior organization and effectiveness were noted.[93]

The KPD was not without its problems, however, particularly in public relations. It had to overcome not only its own extremist image from the Weimar period, but also the stigma of being, as the people commonly called it, the "Party of the Russians." Although relations between the German population and its Soviet occupiers were not uniformly bad (the Red Army having done much to restore humane living conditions in many areas), the inevitable resentments involved in any occupation were fanned by some specific grievances. The rape and pillage engaged in by Soviet troops during their first weeks on German soil and the dismantling of German industries created a deep reservoir of bitterness. The KPD was helpless to do anything about these problems, but its inability to distance itself publicly from unpopular Soviet actions nevertheless tended to neutralize the good will won through its coordination of reconstruction activities. The party leadership tried to avoid taking any position at all on the most sensitive matters. Even intra-party discussions that drifted onto forbidden subjects such as abortions for women raped by Red Army soldiers, or the possibility of intervention with Soviet authorities to save vital facilities from dismantling, were squelched by the iron hand of Ulbricht. Publicly Ulbricht denounced those who would blame the KPD for the inevitable evils of occupation, warning ominously:

> We are in no way responsible for the severity with which the struggle against German fascism has had to be waged or for the consequences of Hitler's war. . . . If there are people in some circles who feel a need to exploit for political purposes the unpleasantness which here and there has accompanied occupation, I have only this to say to the people concerned: such maneuvers amount to nothing other than support for fascist subversion.[94]

Nevertheless, the KPD's unique status as an agency (albeit unofficial) of the occupying power was on balance a distinct advantage. Otto Buchwitz, an old Social Democrat who went on to hold high position in the Socialist Unity Party (SED), later recorded with surprising candor that the KPD could reorganize far more quickly than the SPD because

> . . . in the entire Soviet Zone at that time, as well as in the individual provinces, the KPD had the extensive support of the occupation authorities for all its organizational efforts. The reason was only too clear, since the Soviet authorities knew that the Communist Party of Germany—despite some political mistakes—had ever been steadfastly loyal to the Soviet Union. Those with responsibility for reconstituting the Social Democratic Party, on the other hand, had first of all to prove that they had drawn the right conclusions from their earlier policies.[95]

While the emerging SPD leadership in Saxony had, according to Buchwitz, "not a single automobile with which they could visit the towns and villages," the help of the SMA enabled KPD leaders to be highly mobile—especially Ulbricht himself, who was literally everywhere. The SPD

was not able to publish its central party organ *Das Volk*
until 7 July 1945, and was thereafter under constant con-
straints from censorship, restrictions on format and number of copies printed, lack of reliable information, and
distribution problems. The CDU and LDP fared still worse,
and all three had great difficulty getting approval for provincial newspapers. The Communists meanwhile began
printing their *Deutsche Volkszeitung* on 13 June, with
sister publications appearing in the provinces in the weeks
following. These were distributed with SMA help
throughout the Soviet Zone, even to remote areas. (In
Mecklenburg, for example, twenty-eight Red Army transport planes flew the provincial KPD organ out to distant
county seats each morning.) The KPD's sources of information were also the best, since they were identical with
those of the Soviets themselves.[96]

Such special treatment went beyond favoritism, demonstrating the true relationship between the KPD and the
SMA, which was one of partnership. Unlike the Anglo-
American powers, the Soviets had no military government experts trained to undertake the social and political
reconstruction of their zone. This task was to be accomplished by the "anti-fascist Germans" themselves—that
is, by the KPD —thus giving the appearance of an indig-
enous popular movement. The SMA's political responsibility was to provide favorable conditions for Communist
hegemony and to intervene wherever the KPD program
met entrenched resistance, but otherwise to keep the lowest possible profile. Soviet authorities retained the final
word over all legislation and administrative appointments, and over the definition of "democratic" political
activity (powers which they exercised in close consultation with German Communist leaders). SMA administrative bureaus supervised the work of the German administrations at every level of government. But it was intended
from the beginning that the details of creating and running

the new regime should be left to the KPD and, increasingly, to the new institutions through which it worked.[97]

One of the most important of these institutions was to be the four-party Anti-Fascist Bloc. Establishing Bloc committees on the Berlin model throughout the Soviet Zone, and securing Communist dominance within them, was a top KPD priority during summer 1945. As part of this process, KPD-SPD Action Committees were also created to foster "unity of action" between the parties of the socialist United Front. Joint strategy meetings (normally held just before meetings of the full Bloc) and ideological "schooling" sessions were consistently used by the Communists to probe divisions in the SPD and isolate "reformists" from those who supported KPD policies. "The task of the KPD," according to GDR historian Siegfried Thomas, "consisted in leading the mass of Social Democrats to the correct class position."[98]

The Communists were always on the initiative in the Bloc committees. Because of its special relationship with the SMA, the KPD was able to prepare its own position on any issue and to inform all its party bureaus of the correct line well in advance of Bloc discussions. Typically, KPD leaders themselves would decide what legislation was needed and consult with the SMA to determine the exact nature and timing of it. Occasionally a few trusted leaders of other parties, particularly the SPD, were also consulted. All too often, however, the Communists would appear in Action Committee and Bloc meetings with a statement of the problem, some information about Soviet intentions, and a prepared plan of action which they insisted must be approved immediately in every detail. The other parties, with no opportunity to prepare positions of their own and eager to preserve harmony, tended to lay aside any minor objections and acquiesce so long as the KPD's proposals dealt with urgent matters such as food distribution or restoring public utilities. But by the end of summer 1945, issues began to arise that involved major, long-range political decisions. The Communists' unwillingness to consider compromise even on such controversial questions led to tensions in the Bloc, as non-Communist representatives realized with mounting frustration the impotence to which they were being reduced.[99]

KPD dominance of the Anti-Fascist Bloc helped strengthen in turn the Communist hold over the new administrations, whose experienced personnel were still mostly bourgeois civil servants. By the second half of 1945, though, the KPD also held its own formidable positions of power in the administrations. In conservative Mecklenburg, for example, eight Communists held posts as city mayors or rural district presidents, compared with seven Social Democrats, three Christian Democrats, and ten nonpartisans. Of eighty small-town mayors, thirty were KPD and twenty-five SPD. In Thuringia, two city mayors and nine district presidents were Communists (SPD: three mayors and eleven district presidents), while key "first deputy" positions, significantly, went mainly to Communists (five deputy mayors and fourteen deputy district presidents, compared with three and five respectively for the SPD).[100]

The KPD's monopolization of pivotal positions in many local administrative bodies became a further source of irritation in its relations with the SPD, particularly where qualified Social Democrats were overlooked in favor of less qualified Communists. SPD leaders pointed to the much-vaunted "parity principle" being applied so vigorously in the trade unions and insisted that steps be taken to equalize representation in top administration posts as well. In reply, the KPD admitted that a certain imbalance had arisen out of the tendency of Soviet commanders to appoint Communists preferentially in the first weeks, and the Communists' own seizure of the initiative in reconstruction. However it was, in Siegfried Thomas's words, "not possible now to remove from the administrations again a proportionate number of Communists who up to that time had done exemplary work." The KPD suggested instead that the matter be taken up "in comradely discussions in the Action Committees"—with the understanding that any new SPD appointees must include no "enemies of the United Front" or "anti-Bolshevists."[101]

Such language further illustrated the KPD's determination to insure that members of other parties who did attain power were those most inclined to cooperate with the Communists. The extent to which their cooperation might sometimes be expected to go is shown in the following instructions given to Otto Buchwitz (SPD) as he assumed from Communist leader Hermann Matern the crucial post, rarely held by any non-Communist, of personnel director for the City Council of Dresden:

> The new city administration, he explained emphatically, with all its offices, utilities, establishments, and institutions, was to be staffed in such a way as to guarantee maximal realization of the spirit and content of the KPD [founding] declaration of 11 June 1945, especially, he stressed, since the Soviet class-brothers regarded precisely this task as politically one of the most important and decisive.[102]

Those veteran civil servants permitted to retain their offices were given ideological schooling and individual counseling to correct their bourgeois misconceptions about the state: "The idea that the state stands above social classes was widespread. From it resulted the viewpoint that administrative expertise is more important than the teachings of Marx."[103] Only in economic departments, where such expertise remained frustratingly indispensable, were the old technicians generally free to carry on for a while in their traditional "bureaucratic" style.[104]

New provincial administrations were created along the same lines in July 1945. For the sake of form, it was arranged for "democratic organizations and public bodies" in Saxony, Mecklenburg, and Brandenburg—primarily the

Bloc parties—to unite in petitioning the SMA for the establishment of their respective provincial administrations and the appointment of preselected candidates to the top posts in them. The end result was the same here as in Thuringia and Saxony-Anhalt, however, where such administrations were appointed directly by the SMA two weeks later. In every case the new provincial president was a non-Communist, while the first-vice-president who wielded the real power was supplied by the KPD. Key ministries were controlled almost exclusively by Communists and a few reliable Social Democrats.[105]

The Trade Union System

In trade union affairs as in politics, Berlin was to serve as the model and the KPD as the agent for its propagation. The FDGB had scarcely been constituted in the capital when the KPD Central Committee there sent out a set of "Guidelines for Construction of the New Trade Unions," embodying the Communist interpretation of FDGB policy, to all provincial KPD offices. Where necessary, Ulbricht dispatched representatives from Berlin or even visited the provinces personally to guide FDGB development into prescribed channels.[106]

The speed and vigor with which the Communists acted was due to the fact that, in this area more than in any other, they were faced with a serious challenge from alternate conceptions. Already in March 1945, U.S. authorities in Aachen had approved the first postwar German trade union organization (coincidentally also under the FDGB name), thereby stealing a march on the Soviets for once—albeit unintentionally. Afterward, in keeping with the U.S. policy of discouraging all spontaneous activity of even a remotely political nature among Germans, American commanders were far more reluctant about licensing unions in other cities.[107] Nevertheless, the thirteen-point Aachen "FDGB" program had a widespread influence on emerging trade union groups throughout

Germany, who saw in it the first and brightest hope for a united, democratic trade union movement after Hitler's final defeat. Its strict rejection of all political alignments and its characterization of the unions as purely an "economic organization" had particular appeal for ADGB circles.[108]

The battle against advocates of political neutrality and of a looser, ADGB-style organization had to be fought in some form in every province of the Soviet Zone. In Brandenburg, SPD members had a majority in most union leadership bodies. Since the trade union movement was relatively weak in that largely agricultural province, however, and the Brandenburg FDGB had its headquarters in Berlin, the KPD was able to influence developments there both directly and through the Berlin FDGB. Young KPD "assistants" assigned to union executive boards helped to counterbalance, and eventually eliminate, uncooperative Social Democrats. In Mecklenburg, more rural still and farther removed from the capital, recalcitrant opponents of the new industrial unions and of the FDGB's political role delayed agreement on an FDGB platform until September, and kept up serious opposition throughout 1945.[109]

Heavily industrialized Saxony, on the other hand, with its large working class, had a much faster, more intensive and pro-KPD trade union evolution than elsewhere. In the major cities, trade union groups sprang up right after occupation and were composed almost exclusively of Communists and Social Democrats. The KPD grew faster as a party than the SPD and, with this numerical advantage plus the determined support of Ulbricht and his envoys, was soon able to bring the Saxon FDGB largely under its control. The FDGB Committee for the State of Saxony even adopted the KPD trade union "Guidelines" as its own official policy. Here too, though, resistance from old ADGB circles had to be overcome. Before a trade union preparatory committee could be set up in the capital of Dresden on 20 June, a preexisting council of "reform-oriented" ADGB veterans had to be induced to cooperate with KPD and other representatives. This group's influence was evident in the Saxon FDGB's founding declaration, which typically followed that of Berlin, but omitted any reference to the failure of the Weimar union leadership. In Leipzig, a similar group came to dominate the local trade union movement under temporary U.S. occupation. Its members could only gradually be eased out of authority after the SMA took control, and Leipzig remained for a while a vocal center of opposition within the FDGB.[110]

Inevitably, the large areas of the Soviet Zone occupied first by American troops posed the greatest problems for the Communists. In the four counties of Saxony-Anhalt (another working-class stronghold) which saw only Soviet occupation, trade union development followed the Berlin pattern. Throughout the rest of the province, however, U.S. authorities either discouraged formation of unions altogether or tried to minimize Communist influence in them, supporting the old ADGB leaders instead. Local ADGB committees, organized on the old craft union principle and sharing the apolitical stance of the Aachen "FDGB," arose in over two-thirds of Saxony-Anhalt's municipalities. The situation in conservative Thuringia was much the same, but complicated still further by a strongly-entrenched and self-willed Social Democratic leadership.[111]

Thus, while an FDGB organization had been formally established in every province of the Soviet Zone by September 1945, it was to be several more months before KPD control of the unions was secure. The process by which the Communists finally overcame the resistance of traditional trade unionism and transformed the FDGB into an instrument of KPD policy will be discussed in Chapter Four.

The Special Problem of the U.S.-Occupied Areas:
The Example of Thuringia

The presence of American troops in Thuringia, Saxony-Anhalt, and parts of the State of Saxony delayed the beginning of the "Anti-Fascist, Democratic Transformation" in large areas of the Soviet Zone until July 1945, and complicated it for some time thereafter. As the Communists were well aware, the potential for reshaping society was greatest at the moment of the old order's collapse, when all was in flux. The American Military Government's suppression of all political initiatives, and its naive attempt to create an apolitical German administration staffed by colorless bureaucrats, allowed political institutions and elite groups to begin recrystallizing in forms which the Communists saw as dangerous to their democratization scheme. For this reason among others, the Soviets pressed urgently for an early evacuation of U.S. troops from their zone.[112]

Thuringia presented the most dramatic example of the problems created by successive U.S. and Soviet occupation. Spontaneous "Antifa" activity there, much of it organized by Communists from the self-liberated Buchenwald concentration camp, soon ran afoul of the American ban on political activity. KPD and SPD organizations begun among prisoners at Buchenwald had to continue to work underground for the duration of the U.S. regime. Where this work was conducted through trade unions it had to be discreet, as shown by an incident in which Communists led a self-proclaimed "FDGB" group in a takeover of the old trade union headquarters seized by the Nazis in 1933. Within an hour a detail of U.S. soldiers arrived to haul down and burn the red flag hoisted there. Carefully-prepared May Day demonstrations were similarly squelched. Unfortunately this American reaction to spontaneous anti-fascist measures (or to KPD provoca-

tions planned to look spontaneous) was accompanied by
a failure of Military Government to take strong anti-fascist actions of its own. Removal of Nazis from office proceeded at a snail's pace, even when compared with the
U.S. Zone proper. Such American behavior nourished suspicions among left-leaning Germans that the U.S. was
more interested in preserving the old capitalist order than
in destroying fascism.[113]

Although thwarted in their own political initiatives, the
KPD and SPD did have some influence on occupation
policy through the American-appointed administrations.
At first these administrations were strictly local. On 18
April the new mayor of Weimar, the state capital, formed
a "Political Advisory Board" to take the place of the old
city council. To give his administration some democratic
legitimacy and gain control over underground political
activities, he co-opted the Advisory Board's members from
the local Antifa Committee: one representative each from
the former KPD, SPD, Center, and Democratic parties.
Meanwhile, at Buchenwald, the Social Democratic head
of the KPD-SPD "Popular Front Committee" among the
prisoners, Hermann Brill, was being consulted by U.S.
authorities for his advice on reconstituting the Thuringian state administration. Through the close contacts between Buchenwald's activists and the Weimar Antifa
Committee, Brill subsequently became the Weimar Political Advisory Board's nominee to head the new state
administration. He gradually assumed the responsibilities
of the office during May, and was named provisional president of Thuringia on 9 June. In this office he continued
to consult regularly with the Weimar Antifa Committee
and the Buchenwald Popular Front organization, particularly on personnel matters. Although the American preference for experienced civil servants made it necessary
for him to appoint mostly SPD and bourgeois candidates
to ministerial posts, Brill promised to compensate the

KPD with better representation in lower administrative positions.[114]

Brill was interested in more than mere cooperation with the KPD. He and his followers were probably the most determined advocates anywhere of immediate political unification of the working class. Even at Buchenwald the Brill group had refused to set itself up as an SPD organization, proclaiming instead a "League of Democratic Socialists" (Bund demokratischer Sozialisten, or BdS) intended to include all socialists. The Buchenwald KPD held aloof, however, "since the implementation of demands of this sort meant renunciation of the Marxist-Leninist party; of its existence and its role as leader and organizer of the working class." The Communist organization preferred to work within the looser "Popular Front" arrangement.[115]

When the Soviets finally assumed control of Thuringia on 2-3 July and organization of political parties became legal, the unification issue acquired new urgency. Branches of the BdS now existed in several larger Thuringian towns, and less formal Social Democratic groups in still more localities. Brill, elected chairman of the state organization by a convention on 8 July, once again approached the KPD about immediate union on the basis of the BdS's "Buchenwald Manifesto,"[116] and once again received a cool reception for the idea. Then the axe fell: the BdS was refused recognition by the SMA in Weimar, since it did not acknowledge the authority of the "legitimate party leadership of the SPD" in Berlin. Meanwhile, Ulbricht had (predictably) appeared in Thuringia to begin reorganizing and reeducating the Communist Party there. By August, when Brill had visited Berlin, done homage to Grotewohl and company, and received in return a license to rebuild the Thuringian SPD, the KPD had a well-run network of party organizations throughout the state, in close coordination with its Berlin Central Committee and the SMA.[117]

In the meantime, the state administration was being rearranged according to Soviet Zone standards. Not having had the opportunity, as elsewhere, of rebuilding the civil service from scratch, the Communists now proceeded to purge many officials left in place by the Americans. "Already in the first few days after the change of occupation . . . mayors and district presidents whose political attitudes did not assure an anti-fascist, democratic development were being removed from office."[118] This process went on until January 1946. Political control at the top was also changed. The first vice-president was made responsible for all state internal affairs, including personnel policy and control of the police, and the post was given to Communist Ernst Busse. Finally, the KPD decided it could no longer tolerate Brill as president. The way in which it forced his removal dramatically demonstrated the KPD's special status as a partner in the occupation regime.[119]

On 5 July, Brill submitted a "state of the state" report to the SMA and was interviewed by General V. S. Seminov, an SMA political advisor, and by Walter Ulbricht. In a subsequent reorganization of the administration, the SMA solicited resumés from leading candidates for top offices, including Brill, and interviewed the candidates on 10 July. The following day the Soviet commander for Thuringia convened a staff meeting which included the leading SMA generals in Thuringia, plus one German: Georg Schneider, Ulbricht's representative. Schneider immediately made clear that Brill was out of the question as president. When informed by the Soviet officers present that both they and the SMA in Berlin were favorably inclined toward Brill, Schneider asked that the record show "that the representative of the KPD-Thuringia spoke against the candidacy of Dr. Brill." Scenting the danger, the SPD, CDU, and LDP all wrote letters to the SMA in Brill's support—but to no avail. On 14 July, Schneider had the satisfaction of seeing his candidate chosen as president by the SMA: Dr. Rudolf Paul, a bourgeois anti-fascist.[120]

The Thuringian SPD (BdS) reacted angrily to Brill's dismissal, declaring that all responsibility for the new administration would henceforth rest with the SMA and KPD. The recriminations went on well into August. In the end, however, the Communists held all the cards. The SPD needed formal recognition and a role in government to survive; moreover, it was unable to embarrass the KPD by its noncooperation. When, for instance, the Social Democrats suddenly canceled plans to participate in an FDGB founding conference in Weimar on 13 July, the Communists replied by switching the conference to the KPD stronghold of Erfurt. There, on 20 July, a founding declaration and a trade union program based on the Berlin model were accepted and a Communist was elected chairman of the state FDGB organization. Through discussions with SMA and KPD leaders, some minor concessions on ministerial appointments, and a variety of other pressures and inducements, the SPD was gradually brought around to a more compliant posture; its troublesome leaders, expecially Brill, were progressively isolated and removed. With them went the main obstacle to Thuringia's coordination into the socio-political system of the Soviet Zone. Having now the same political and organizational advantage it enjoyed elsewhere in East Germany, the KPD proceeded to consolidate its positions in the institutions of power.[121]

THE POTSDAM CONFERENCE

The withdrawal of Western troops from the Soviet Zone and their simultaneous occupation of their assigned sectors of Berlin heralded the end of what has been called an "interregnum" in Germany. The jurisdictional boundaries agreed upon at Yalta—eventually to become the borders between East and West German states—were now in force. The stage was set for the last great conference of the Big Three powers, at which the common policies evolved during wartime were supposed to be expanded into a master plan for the reconstruction of Germany and Europe.

Down to the Potsdam Conference (16 July-1 August 1945), the Soviets had taken no sweeping or irrevocable measures to restructure the economy and society of their zone. While there had been some seizures of abandoned or Nazi-owned properties (as there had been under Western occupation as well), and considerable collection of "war booty," there had been as yet no systematic land reform or takeover of industry. The closure of the old banks and probable confiscation of their reserves was motivated by practical rather than ideological considerations. Creation of a new system of financial institutions did not begin until after the Potsdam meeting had failed to produce a common Allied policy in this area.[122] Before they tipped their hand, the Soviets wanted to see what could be gained by negotiation. In the meantime, their efforts were devoted to installing quietly the necessary machinery of control to implement their transformation program once the overall conditions of four-power sovereignty had been clarified.

One question of vital importance to Communist strategy was the extent to which the Western powers would permit the establishment of this same control machinery in their own zones—would acknowledge, that is, the supra-zonal claims of the parties and trade unions created in Berlin. Already the Soviets and KPD were encouraging the Bloc parties to extend their operations into the West.[123] When, during the Potsdam negotiations, the U.S. proposed creating some central German administrative bodies to assure uniform implementation of Allied economic policies, the Soviets eagerly pursued the idea and recommended a Central German Administration with quasi-governmental powers. Simultaneously they hurried to insure that here too, further developments would be influenced by institutions of their own creation. On 25 July, the SMA asked the Berlin party leaders to submit *by the following day* lists of nominees for key positions in a central administration for the Soviet Zone, including all of Berlin.[124]

The Soviet push to create *faits accomplis* influencing the development of Germany's future political institutions presented the Western powers with a dilemma. U.S. observers of Soviet behavior in Eastern Europe, notably Ambassador to Moscow Averell Harriman, had been aware for some months of the Soviet practice of "employing the wide variety of means at their disposal—occupation troops, secret police, local communist parties, labor unions, sympathetic leftist organizations . . . —to assure the establishment of regimes which, while maintaining an outward appearance of independence and of broad popular support, actually depend for their existence on groups responsive to all suggestions emanating from the Kremlin."[125] There was every reason to believe the same tactics were being applied in Germany. To go along with the political precedents set in the Soviet Zone thus might lead eventually to Communist domination of the whole country. To reject them completely, on the other hand, could aggravate inter-Allied tensions and risk permanent division of Germany—the western part of which, it was feared, would never be a viable economic entity.[126]

U.S. policy as demonstrated at Potsdam was to reaffirm the Allied commitment to German unity in principle, and to postpone difficult negotiations about the details of the new regime to be constructed. The final protocol declared that "So far as is practicable, there shall be uniformity of treatment of the German population throughout Germany." It included American-sponsored provisions that "free trade unions" and "all democratic political parties" be allowed throughout Germany,[127] and that elected German administrations should be introduced as soon as conditions permitted, beginning at the local level. The conference also adopted the U.S. recommendation to create "certain essential central German administrative departments." The proposed Soviet amendment granting a Central German Administration power "to coordinate the activities of the Provincial Governments" was dropped, however, on the discreet suggestion by the U.S. and U.K. that the Allied Control Council, which was to supervise the new organs, should also define their responsibilities.[128]

Likewise, the section on "Economic Principles," as framed by the Americans, stated broadly that "During the period of occupation, Germany shall be treated as a single economic unit." Common policies were to be evolved in a number of listed areas, covering virtually every aspect of the economy. Otherwise, this section was devoted largely to outlining more precisely the means by which the Allies intended to achieve the denazification and demilitarization of economic life to which they had pledged themselves at Yalta, including removal or control of strategic industries. Of particular significance for later developments in the Soviet Zone was the provision: "At the earliest practicable date, the German economy shall be decentralized for the purpose of eliminating the present excessive concentration of economic power as exemplified in particular by cartels, syndicates, trusts, and other monopolistic arrangements." This point, along with the political principle calling for removal of active Nazis and "all other persons hostile to Allied purposes" from public office and from "positions of responsibility in important private undertakings," provided the main legal underpinning for the Communist transformation program.[129]

The Soviets were under no misapprehensions about what the Western powers intended by the terms of the Potsdam accord. Obviously they aimed to weaken Germany's war-making potential, to limit its economic power to some degree (as one would expect of capitalists dealing with a vanquished competitor), and to eliminate the Nazi political elite. There was even reason to hope that in pursuing these goals they might dismantle much of the traditional power structure in their zones, at least temporarily. There was, however, no reason to expect them to undertake voluntarily the kind of deliberate social and economic restructuring which the Communists saw as the only real guarantee against renewed German aggression. The roots of the problem lay where no bourgeois power would dare to attack them: in the rule of the bourgeoisie itself.

Yet, while the Potsdam agreement predictably did not endorse a social revolution against the bourgeoisie, it also did not preclude one. Its terms could be interpreted broadly enough to cover not only the Western, but also the Soviet concept of democratization. Moreover, now that Western forces had been withdrawn from the Soviet Zone and the Potsdam Conference had resolved (more or less) the outstanding questions of "who gets what"—particularly the reparations question, which was resolved not at all to Soviet satisfaction—the Soviets had little reason to hesitate further in pursuing their real intentions in Germany. If the West feared a Communist attempt at "Bolshevization," the Communists equally feared a new "restoration" of the sort the Western Allies had engineered after World War I. They now prepared to take steps they had long planned to make such a restoration impossible, at least in the Soviet Zone. In so doing, they gambled that the West, with its demonstrated concern for maintaining Germany's unity, would see no alternative but to follow suit.[130]

THREE

The Land Reform

Land reform was the first priority of the Communist transformation program. KPD policy dictated that preparations for it should start as soon as the Communist Party was reestablished and could begin schooling its cadre. The land reform itself was to be initiated before the end of summer 1945.[1]

The Economic, Political, and Ideological Rationale

Although no specific provision for a land reform existed in Allied agreements, including the Potsdam accord, the economic and political necessity of such a measure was acknowledged by East and West alike. A number of U.S. government studies and policy directives on German agriculture produced in the period 1944-1946 document this fact. American planners recognized as well as the Soviets the reactionary nature of the "Junker caste" and the need to break its grip on German rural life by eliminating the great latifundia of central and eastern Germany. Even at the cost of some temporary disruption in food supply, the great landowners had to be prevented from retaining the social and economic power which they had used to sabotage the Weimar democracy. Like industry, German agriculture had to be decentralized, and the land settled by poor peasants and refugees from the East to form a new class of independent freeholders with a stake in democratic government. Clearly the problem was nowhere more urgent than in the Soviet Zone, where private estates of

100 hectares (250 acres) or more accounted for nearly a third of the total land area (versus about 11 percent in the Western zones), and the flood of uprooted immigrants to be resettled rose to about a quarter of the total population in the first postwar period.[2]

The Communists' sense of urgency had still another and deeper source, however, in Leninist theory and Soviet revolutionary experience. In his "Preliminary Draft Theses on the Agrarian Question" of 1920, Lenin drew conclusions from the revolutionary movements of the preceding three years that were to guide Communist strategy toward the peasantry for the next three decades. He attributed the failure of such promising experiments as the Bavarian and Hungarian soviet republics largely to their doctrinaire insistence, still typical of the parties of the Second International, that the proletarian revolution must express the power and the interests of the proletariat alone. "The proletariat," Lenin admonished, "is really a revolutionary class . . . only when it comes out and acts as the vanguard of all working and exploited people. . . ." Specifically, the Russian Revolution had shown that, while the working class must seize power on its own initiative, it could only hold on to power if it immediately carried the class struggle into the countryside, becoming the champion of land-poor peasants against the wealthy proprietors. "The revolutionary proletariat must immediately and unreservedly confiscate all landed estates, those of the big landowners who . . . systematically exploit wage labor and . . . are in the main descended from the feudal lords . . . or are rich financial magnates, or else a mixture of both these categories of exploiters and parasites." At least a portion of the land thus seized would have to be distributed to the peasants themselves. Only if the small peasants could see an "immediate and considerable improvement in their conditions at the expense of the exploiters" would their support be forthcoming—and with it, food for the urban proletariat.[3]

In the course of the 1920s, increasing Soviet influence over the KPD was reflected in the latter's evolving agrarian policy. Beginning with an orthodox Marxist theoretical stance—solidarity with the rural proletariat (landless farm workers) but disdain for peasant smallholders as a doomed class—the KPD graduated to an ever more forthright and active bid for the support of small and "middle" farmers. By the early 1930s, Stalin advocated Communist cooperation with any peasant movement "which in one way or another brings grist to the mill of the proletarian revolution and which facilitates the transformation of the peasantry into reserves and allies of the working class."[4] Consistent with this supple policy, the KPD finally made satisfaction of peasant land-hunger an explicit part of its program, calling for "uncompensated expropriation of large estates and gratuitous allocation of land for land-poor peasants and sons of peasants."[5]

The part played by this peasant policy in the United Front strategy of the fascist era has been discussed in Chapter One. With the end of the war and the advent of Soviet hegemony in Eastern Europe in 1944-45, each of the national Communist parties there began implementing a land reform ostensibly aimed at redistribution of land to the peasantry, rather than the collectivization that was widely feared and expected. Although details varied to suit the economic, social, and political conditions in each country, the underlying pattern was everywhere the same—including the general rule that land reform was not to be associated with socialism, but with popular liberation and national revival. In countries recently freed from Nazi domination, it was identified with a nationalist movement to rid the land of Germans and pro-German collaborators: all who had enjoyed wealth and power under the Nazi regime. In Germany itself it was incorporated, like all Communist transformation measures, into the campaign against fascism.

THE POLITICAL STRUGGLE

To disarm political opposition and win genuine popular support, the land reform had to appear as a movement of the peasants themselves, with the KPD acting merely as an instrument of their righteous zeal. The Communists thus sought throughout the spring and summer of 1945 to encourage spontaneous peasant seizures of "Junker" land. Much of their work had already been done for them by the Red Army, since many estates whose owners had fled were now de facto in the hands of the farm workers. To further whet the peasants' appetite, the SMA newspaper *Tägliche Rundschau* printed glowing accounts of successful land reform movements in Eastern Europe, and of the millions of hectares being divided up among the peasants there. On 25 June, Ulbricht told a KPD convention that expropriation of the great landowners and redistribution of their lands should begin immediately, with local peasant commissions taking the initiative and higher-level administrations backing them up. Shortly afterward, Ulbricht and his colleagues were abroad in the countryside themselves, advising local officials to assemble the peasants and occupy nearby estates without waiting for explicit legal sanction.[6]

By August, KPD organs all over the zone were filled with anti-Junker articles and peasant petitions calling for immediate land reform. The latter, obviously of KPD origin, were mostly the product of hundreds of village rallies being drummed up by Communist agitators. Under their supervision, peasant commissions were also formed to seize and partition the land. Yet despite all these Communist efforts, the overwhelming mass of the peasantry remained impassive and suspicious. The ingrained conservatism of centuries did not yield overnight to a good propaganda campaign.[7]

Although the Communists had apparently hoped for more enthusiasm and initiative on the part of the peasants, it is unlikely that they ever intended a truly spontaneous land reform. Experiences in Poland had already shown the need for close central supervision to insure politically correct implementation of the Communist land reform program.[8] The KPD aim was rather to create an apparently irresistible groundswell of popular support for its program; to put on a good show for the West and grease the rails for land reform legislation in the East. With the Potsdam agreement concluded, the time for such legislation was deemed ripe by mid-August. The propaganda barrage reached a crescendo, and the Communists prepared to put the Soviet Zone's new political system to the test.[9]

The German parties, like the Allies, all recognized the need for land reform. The challenge facing the KPD was to gain universal acceptance of its own program as the only truly effective and democratic solution. Although none of the other parties had as yet had a chance to formulate a detailed agrarian policy, the CDU and LDP both envisioned a long-range resettlement program rather than a sudden rural revolution. Private latifundia were to be bought up and, supplemented by land confiscated from convicted war criminals, used to provide homesteads for refugees and landless peasants. In any case, the bourgeois parties opposed any fundamental reforms until the present food crisis was stabilized and a Reich government formed which was competent to decide issues of this magnitude for the entire nation. The SPD formally called for outright seizure and partition of large land holdings for resettlement, but Social Democrats generally favored retention of large-scale agriculture and introduction of collective farming as soon as possible. Their orthodox Marxist position thus contradicted the KPD's plans for direct transfer of the land to a maximum number of land-hungry peasants.[10]

In reply to the admonitions of socialist and bourgeois experts alike about the economic superiority of large farms, the KPD was ready with its own economic arguments in favor of small ones.[11] But the real issue was one of political strategy. The land reform could not be delayed, lest the moment for achieving it be lost forever. The threat of collectivization might stampede the peasantry into a reactionary alliance with the great landowners. A swift and violent seizure of "Junker" land by the mass of peasants themselves, on the other hand, would signify a revolutionary break with the past on their part. Henceforth, the peasantry would be bound to the new order by its complicity in the destruction of the old.

Notwithstanding the hitherto compliant behavior of the Berlin Bloc parties on less momentous issues, the Communists anticipated a real battle with them over land reform. They therefore decided to circumvent the central party leaderships and seek acceptance for their program first in the provinces, where the opposition would be relatively weak and ill-prepared. In mid-August 1945 the KPD provincial leadership in Halle, capital of Saxony-Anhalt, received from the Central Committee in Berlin a copy of the party's draft for a land reform decree, with instructions to insure its passage into law by the beginning of September. To oversee the effort, the Central Committee also dispatched its senior official for economic and political affairs to sit in on the negotiations: Ulbricht.[12]

The Halle KPD leaders submitted the proposed decree to the other parties at the first meeting of the political committee of the provincial administration on 29 August, with the statement that its immediate acceptance was a political and economic imperative. It provided for expropriation of all land belonging to war criminals and leading Nazis or supporters of Nazism, of all estates comprising more than one hundred hectares, and (with certain exceptions) of lands belonging to the state or its institutions. These properties, including buildings, livestock, and equipment on them, were to be redistributed to peasants with less than five hectares of their own land.[13]

The representatives of the other parties, somewhat taken aback, asked for an adjournment until 3 September to give them time to consider the KPD proposal. Bernard Koenen, leader of the KPD delegation, at first resisted any delay, but finally agreed reluctantly to recess only until 1 September. When the committee reconvened on that date, CDU and LDP spokesmen declared their parties ready to support immediate confiscation of land belonging to war criminals and Nazis, and of any land not being cultivated productively, for settlement by landless peasants. They went on to stress, however, that they did not consider a provincial committee competent to enact a land reform that would affect all of Germany, and recommended that the question be referred to the new Allied Control Council in Berlin. In addition, all three non-Communist parties were agreed that the present tenuous food supply must not be further endangered by a breakup of the large estates into smaller, less economical parcels. The SPD, while accepting the KPD plan for expropriation, advocated collective farming where feasible.

The KPD representatives reacted with astonishment, then anger at the other parties' objections. Koenen accused the CDU and LDP delegates of fascism since, he claimed, they wanted to protect the latifundia and the Junker class which had helped to breed fascism. Economic arguments were dismissed with the comment, "We are not an economic committee, but a political committee." The issue, according to Koenen, was very simple: "Do we or do we not want to retain the great landed estates . . . and thereby the source of fascism itself?" After further heated debate, a short recess was called during which the Communists and Social Democrats conferred privately.

Whatever was said in this hasty conclave, the SPD representatives were obviously persuaded of their overriding duty to uphold socialist unity. When the session resumed, they declared themselves in agreement with the KPD proposal. Furthermore, the political advisor to the Soviet commandant of Halle, Major Dimisov (who had been present throughout the proceedings), informed the CDU delegation leader that any plan to refer the land reform question to the Allied Control Council would be interpreted as a lack of confidence in the SMA. Hoping to save something, the bourgeois parties tried to extract a guarantee that large landowners not implicated in Nazism or war crimes would be exempted from expropriation. Finally they settled for a promise that anti-fascists would not be expropriated, and signed the KPD resolution.

The following day, 2 September, the proposed legislation was submitted to the presidium of the provincial administration. The president of Saxony-Anhalt, Professor Erhard Hübener (LDP), at first tried to amend it so as to allow expropriated landlords to retain a portion of their land, but (in Ulbricht's words) "soon let himself be persuaded by the arguments of the workers' and peasants' representatives." On 3 September, the KPD draft appeared in virtually its original form as the "Decree of the Provincial Administration of Saxony on the Democratic Land Reform."[14]

During the negotiations, the Communists exploited their communications monopoly to the fullest to isolate and demoralize their opponents. While the provincial KPD was reinforced by the presence of Ulbricht and Dimisov, the other parties were unable to make contact with their own headquarters in Berlin, let alone with the other occupation powers. The Berlin leaders of the bourgeois parties were not even aware of the confrontation in Halle until after their colleagues there had capitulated. Within Saxony-Anhalt itself, mass meetings, leaflets, and the press continually exhorted the people to join in expropriating the "fascist and militarist Junkers":

Daily one could read in the *Volkszeitung* resolutions of peasants and farm workers from all areas demanding the immediate, unconditional implementation of the land reform. "All land to the peasants—smash the great estates" was the slogan of the day. Since there are presently no other newspapers in Halle, there was no opportunity for the [Christian Democratic] Union or the other parties to take any action against this propaganda campaign.[15]

On 27 August Marshal Zhukov's deputy, a General Bokov, requested the FDGB to take a position on the land reform. The following day—one day prior to the beginning of the debate in Halle—an FDGB organizing conference there was induced by Ulbricht and other Communist participants to endorse the KPD's land reform demands.[16]

The Communist victory in Halle at once became further grist for the KPD propaganda mill, which now began publishing letters and resolutions in each province calling for immediate passage of land reform legislation "as in Saxony-Anhalt." In every provincial administration the political battle was fought along much the same lines as in Halle, and always with the same result. Occasionally, a particularly stubborn opposition was able to extract minor concessions, such as an amendment finally agreed to in Thuringia permitting proven anti-fascists to retain up to one hundred hectares. In practice, however, such anomalies were without real effect. By 10 September, all five states and provinces of the Soviet Zone had passed essentially the same land reform law.[17]

Having removed the Berlin party leaders from any real influence in the land reform question, the KPD finally approached them, too, for their support. This it did with less overt pressure than in the provinces, apparently expecting that news of the Communists' quick victories there would discourage further useless wrangling and thus avoid an ugly scene under the noses of the Western powers. At a meeting of the Bloc parties in Berlin on 30 August, Wilhelm Pieck suggested forming a special commission to study the question of land reform, particularly with respect to two issues: removal of the power of the landed gentry, and a just redistribution of land to poor peasants and refugees. The other parties agreed and the commission was created. When it convened, however, the CDU and LDP leaders insisted, as the main condition for their approval of so radical a land reform plan as the KPD now put before them, on the payment of compensation for land expropriated for any reason other than as punishment for war crimes. The Communists would not meet this condition, and the talks stalemated.[18]

As in Halle, the SMA finally felt compelled to step in. On 5 September, Marshal Zhukov summoned CDU chairmen Andreas Hermes and Walther Schreiber and LDP chairman Waldemar Koch to his headquarters at Karlshorst. Accusing them of insufficient support for the Anti-Fascist Bloc, Zhukov advised the party leaders (in the presence of Ulbricht) that speedy elimination of the "Junkers" was a necessary step toward destroying the fascist ideology, and that the land reform would be brought about in any case "from below." The people "on top" were not to interfere; they must be prepared to make concessions. Zhukov reminded the CDU and LDP chairmen that the SMA had the power to dissolve their parties, and indicated that he regarded their behavior in the land reform question as a test of their good faith.[19]

Despite Zhukov's warning and continued pressure from the KPD, the bourgeois parties remained adamant on the issue of compensation. Finally, at a meeting of the land reform study commission on 13 September, the Communists offered to omit any reference to compensation from the proposed four-party resolution, leaving the question completely open as had been done in the provincial land reform laws already passed. The CDU and LDP representatives accepted this apparent compromise and signed. The Communists, however, had by this time already begun the land reform they had originally planned—without compensation.[20]

Notwithstanding their defeat on the legislative front, and particularly in view of the way in which that defeat had been accomplished, the bourgeois party leaders felt no obligation to support the sort of land reform the KPD was trying to implement. In Brandenburg, CDU and LDP refused to participate in land reform actions until late November 1945. Andreas Hermes, for his part, immediately made an official statement explaining that the CDU's signature on the Berlin Bloc resolution was not to be construed as approval for the form that the land reform was already taking in some areas. During the following weeks, he and other CDU and LDP leaders continued their opposition in speeches and letters and through the press. On 20 and 22 September, Hermes disregarded the warning of the SMA in Halle and sent each of the four Allied commanders in Germany a copy of a letter outlining the CDU's objections to the Communist land reform. At about the same time, he wrote to the administrations of all Soviet Zone provinces but Thuringia, warning of the legal and economic repercussions such a land reform would have. All these letters went unanswered. Another sent to the head of the German Central Administration for Justice, Dr. Eugen Schiffer (LDP), produced a short reply to the effect that Schiffer's office did not consider itself competent to take a position on the land reform question.[21]

The behavior of Hermes and his colleagues indicated that they had not yet grasped the full significance of the Communists' actions. The question at issue was not merely land reform and its modalities; it was whether the Communists were willing to negotiate on their basic program of social and economic restructuring. The answer was that they were not. The compromises they were prepared to make had already been made in their decision to accept bourgeois-democratic political forms for Germany. Any attempt to obstruct the KPD's rearrangement of actual social power would be interpreted as pro-fascist, in effect if not in intent. The interventions of Dimisov in Halle and Zhukov in Berlin were to serve notice of this fact on the bourgeois parties.

The political battle over land reform was a test both of the parties themselves and of the individuals who composed them. Not that the Soviets had any real intention of dissolving uncooperative parties (as Zhukov, despite his threat, himself admitted), since this would have meant abandoning the whole "Popular Front" idea and all the benefits the Communists hoped to gain from it, particularly in the West.[22] Rather, the parties had to be educated and molded to their proper role in the new "people's democracy." The Communists' strategy was to identify and encourage those individuals and factions who would support the KPD program, to intimidate their less tractable colleagues (especially in the provinces), and to isolate and eventually eliminate those whose opposition was adamant and dangerous.[23]

Hermes, Schreiber, and Koch had placed themselves in the last category. Koch's claim to leadership was already being challenged in any case by the more dynamic Wilhelm Külz, who was on much better terms with the SMA. In retaliation for Koch's attacks on the land reform, the Soviets forbade him from publishing or making any public speeches and stopped distribution of the LDP daily *Der Morgen* outside Berlin. They also made it known that Koch's resignation might speed the licensing of some provincial newspapers the LDP badly wanted. This pressure proved sufficient to force Koch to step down on 29 November 1945.[24]

Shortly afterward the final showdown came for Hermes and Schreiber. The KPD submitted a resolution to the Bloc calling for an all-out effort to aid the many "new farmers" who were finding it impossible to make a living on the tiny plots distributed in the land reform. The LDP agreed to sign, but the CDU leaders saw the move as an attempt to involve their party in responsibility for the economic disaster they had predicted. They said they would join in helping the peasants, but would not sign the resolution. Personal contacts between Pieck and Hermes failed to budge the latter. On 8 December, the resolution became the first to be issued over the signatures of only three of the Berlin Bloc parties.[25]

On 11 December, the leaders of the Halle CDU were summoned to local SMA headquarters. Soviet officers there informed them that recent positions taken by the CDU in Berlin represented a continuing policy directed against the land reform, the democratic measures of the Anti-Fascist Bloc, and the SMA itself. The officers then asked them where they stood on the actions taken in Berlin. Before leaving the interview, the provincial CDU leaders had signed two resolutions: one supporting the KPD program to help the peasants, and one condemning the party leadership in Berlin. In return for a promise to print these resolutions, the Halle CDU was granted a long-standing request for a newspaper license. Within the next few days, similar resolutions appeared over the signatures of every provincial CDU leadership in the Soviet Zone. On 19 December, the SMA assembled fifty CDU representatives from all parts of the Zone in Berlin-Karlshorst, and demanded that Hermes and Schreiber present their resignations to this group. They refused. SMA political advisor Colonel Tjulpanov thereupon produced an order signed by Marshal Zhukov, relieving both men of their party offices and forbidding them to engage in any further political activity in the Soviet Zone.[26]

Although the bourgeois parties continued their efforts to exert a moderating influence on KPD policies (for example by calling for review boards to rectify mistaken land expropriations), they never again dared to challenge openly any aspect of the Communist transformation program. The Communists' success in playing off provincial party organizations against their nominal superiors in Berlin, plus the example made of Hermes, Schreiber, and Koch by the SMA, demonstrated clearly enough who had the whip hand behind the parliamentary façade. CDU-Halle chairman Leo Herwegen, soon to be promoted to his party's Central Executive Committee to help fill the newly-created vacancies, recorded his conclusions as follows:

> At stake here was not the land reform, but the continued existence of the Anti-Fascist Bloc and thereby the continued influence of the bourgeois parties on the direction of politics in general.
>
> The Christian Democratic Union is aware that this influence can be, in the main, only a monitoring and guiding one; nevertheless, the Executive Committee of the provincial organization is of the opinion that even this limited influence is better than the renunciation of all influence.[27]

THE CAMPAIGN FOR SUPPORT

The deluge of propaganda unleashed by the KPD in late summer of 1945 was intended not only to expedite land reform legislation, but to excite active popular support for the land reform itself and for the KPD as the savior of the peasantry. Typically, KPD speeches, articles, and pamphlets began by recounting the suffering and betrayal that Hitler's regime had meant for the peasants. Instead of their promised land redistribution, the Nazis had introduced repressive agrarian legislation and high tariffs which had enriched the large landowners and raised the cost of fodder for the peasants' livestock. To protect the Junkers and divert attention from his unfulfilled pledge of land reform, Hitler had then duped the peasants with the lie that Germany was overcrowded and needed "living space in the East." The result was a war that had cost millions of common people their lives and brought devastation, defeat, and the loss of much land that had once been German. Yet through it all the great landowners had flourished, their numbers even increasing with the addition of the Nazis' own "aristocracy." By 1939, after six years of fascist rule, their share of German soil had risen from 36.4 percent to 38 percent.[28]

The Nazis were thus the modern agents of the peasant's ancient enemy, the reactionary landowning class. The "Junkers" (a term used synonymously with "large landowners") had, to begin with, stolen their lands from the peasantry when feudalism was becoming established. They had brutally crushed the peasants who rebelled at aristocratic injustice in 1525, had reneged on promises made to the peasantry during the Napoleonic Wars and in the Revolution of 1848, and had remained down to 1918 the main source of Germany's militarist officers and antidemocratic bureaucrats. Finally, because after World War I the broad mass of Germans had failed to heed the call of the working class to eliminate all reactionary forces along with the Kaiser himself, the Junkers were able to join the monopoly capitalists in provoking the latest war.[29]

Such, then, were the oppressors and parasites whom the land reform would sweep away forever. To this dark history the Communists contrasted their own record of friendship for the peasant. The KPD pointed to its Peasant Aid Program of the Weimar era, as well as to recent appointments of peasants to positions of power in local government. It also sought to gain maximum political advantage from the SMA's repeal of Hitler's most unpopular agrarian legislation: the entailment of land under the Hereditary Farms Law and the confiscation of all farm produce by the Reich Food Estate. KPD leaders explained the advantage of the fixed production quotas introduced by the Soviets, which allowed farmers to sell essentially at black-market prices the so-called "free peaks" of their production over and above assigned quotas:

> After delivering your obligatory contribution to the people's food supply, you, the peasant, have a legally-

protected right to free disposition over the remainder
of your harvest. You can sell it on the open market or
to cooperatives, as you please. No one has the right to
interfere with your doing so.

So you see, things are different than they were under
the Nazis, who took absolutely everything from you.
Yes, this new agrarian policy of the new democratic
Germany is a policy of social justice.[30]

The land reform the KPD now called for was to be the
culmination of its campaign to emancipate the countryside, embracing the centuries-old desire of the peasants
themselves to stand as free farmers on their own soil.[31]

The success of KPD policy in the countryside, including
land reform, did not depend on the peasant alone, however, but rather on the "alliance of city and country," in
which the industrial workers of the city were to be the
dominant force. Communist propaganda sought to persuade the peasants that they needed the products manufactured by the workers as much as the latter needed food
from the farm: "What is the peasant without equipment,
without machinery; what is the peasant without the necessary fertilizer?" But an equal effort had to be made to
involve workers in the economic and political reconstruction of rural areas, so that they might establish their class
leadership in fact as well as in theory. In a letter of mid-
August 1945, the KPD Central Committee advised its
regional bureaus, "The land reform will give the Party
great opportunities to expand its influence over the peasant population and to establish close cooperation between
workers and peasants, in which the worker must prove
himself to be the peasant's true friend and helper." To
achieve this ideal, the KPD had to battle against long-
standing mutual prejudice: the peasant's mistrust of the
city-dweller, and the urban proletarian's ill-concealed
contempt for his bucolic brother.[32]

The first real opportunity to put the worker-peasant

alliance into practice was the mass mobilization to help with the harvest beginning in July 1945. At KPD instigation and with Soviet logistical support, the FDGB dispatched armies of factory workers into the countryside with great fanfare, to work side-by-side with peasants in the common interest. Wide publicity was given to ostensibly spontaneous workers' campaigns to repair and replace farm machinery and equipment for the peasants. As a special public relations effort, trade unions, factories, and even the KPD itself organized a few mobile repair stations to tour farm areas.[33]

Of course, the workers' help extended to the political realm as well. KPD and SPD functionaries used the opportunity to instruct the peasants about their class situation and to persuade them of the need to expropriate the "Junkers" immediately. Soon they were also helping to set up and supervise local land reform commissions, inventory "Junker" properties, and lay out new farmsteads. Trade union proclamations in support of the harvest action gave way to resolutions, still under the banner of worker-peasant solidarity, calling for land reform; and the FDGB established a special secretariat for land reform questions. Meanwhile, factory workers were being installed as village mayors and in other important local and county administrative positions. In all about 25,000 urban workers were involved in the "struggles in the village" to achieve the KPD program, according to East German accounts. If the land reform was indeed to be consummated by the peasantry itself, as KPD propaganda had it, it was clearly to be orchestrated by the Communist-led proletariat.[34]

IMPLEMENTATION

The implementation of the land reform followed a pattern already tested in other parts of Soviet-occupied Europe.[35]

The Province of Saxony-Anhalt's land reform decree of 3
September 1945 stated:

> The distribution of the land is to be decided upon in
> assemblies of the landless and land-poor peasants of the
> community concerned. . . . The resolution of the peas-
> ants . . . has the force of law once it has been confirmed
> by the County Commission for Implementation of the
> Land Reform.

The decree called for an assembly of all local peasants
owning less than five hectares and all new settlers in the
area, exclusive of former Nazi party members, to be convened in each village by 15 September. This assembly
would in turn elect a local land reform commission of
five to seven members. By 25 September, the local commission was to submit two lists to the German administration of its county: one designating the properties slated
for confiscation in its jurisdiction, and a second naming
the eligible candidates for receipt of land. The county or
provincial administration would notify each locality by 1
October of any estates that were not to be broken up, after
which the local commission could submit its recommendations to the peasant assembly for a final vote. Once the
county land reform commission had ratified the peasants'
decision, the local commission and the peasants themselves would perform the actual confiscation of the old
estates, eviction of the former owners, and distribution
of the land.[36]

The entire process was to be completed by the end of
October 1945. This emphasis on speed was for two reasons, one economic and the other political. First, the land
reform had been timed to fall between the harvest and
the autumn planting, and any extended period of disorder
and uncertainty could adversely affect the latter and thus
aggravate the food shortage. Secondly, the Communists
deemed it essential to keep opponents, particularly the
landlords themselves, off balance, so as to give them the

least possible opportunity to organize any effective resistance or to remove large amounts of livestock and equipment to the West. A firm 100-hectare limit on estate size facilitated quick expropriation. As Ulbricht later observed, "The land reform commissions could determine which properties were to be confiscated merely by glancing at the land register."[37]

In the partitioning of the estates, each eligible peasant family was to receive a maximum of five, or if the land was very poor ten, hectares. The land was to be transferred to the peasants free of all prior debts and obligations at a cost equal to the value of one year's harvest, payable in money or in kind over the next ten to twenty years. It could not be resold, leased, or mortgaged. These terms, while generous, were a retreat from the KPD's prewar promise of free land to the peasants. Several considerations lay behind the decision to charge a nominal fee. One of the more important was that it gave the transfer of property the legal character of a sale, thus strengthening the recipient's claim to ownership and discouraging any future challenge to the land reform. To illustrate this point and emphasize the finality of the transaction, the old land registers were burned and provincial administrations issued certificates of title for the peasants' new plots. These gestures indicate another, even greater concern, though; that being the peasants' *perception* of their proprietory rights. Soviet historian Grigori Kotov has summarized Communist thinking as follows: "Someone who had bought a parcel of land, paid money for it and had his purchase of the property officially recorded had a much stronger feeling of owning that parcel. This psychological factor definitely had to be taken into account."[38]

The KPD relied on its strong representation in the land reform commissions and its control of key posts in the German administrations to hold the "spontaneous" land reform on course. Where KPD and SPD agitators had not already created land reform commissions before the expropriation decrees, the administrations founded them in the weeks following. The makeup of the commissions reflected the huge political advantage the two socialist parties had already secured for themselves in the countryside. Of a total 54,300 members of these bodies, 24,700 belonged to the KPD or the SPD (whose cooperation with one another was generally very good), 28,000 had no formal party affiliation, and only 1,600 belonged to the bourgeois parties.[39] The membership of the local commissions, and of the county and district commissions that reviewed their decisions, each had to be ratified in turn by the German administrations at the next higher level, with the highest commission at the provincial level being named by the provincial administration and chaired by its Communist first vice president.[40]

Higher-level land reform commissions and representatives of the provincial administrations—particularly of their heavily-Communist Interior Ministries—monitored and directed the work of the local peasant commissions. Their task was to see that these local bodies were quick and thorough in their work, and that they adhered to KPD standards for the land reform. Where necessary, county or district commissions intervened to direct local authorities to divide up an estate or correct any steps deemed inconsistent with land reform laws and objectives. Higher commissions also took upon themselves the resolution of any unusual or difficult problems. These included cases where the nature or extent of land ownership was unclear, as well as hardship cases where petition was made for compensation or a residual plot to save the livelihood of some expropriated widow or anti-fascist.[41]

By far the greatest source of difficulties was the expropriation of alleged fascists. In contrast to the clear 100-hectare criterion defining large landowners, political liability was easy to allege and hard to prove. All too commonly, peasants denounced a neighbor as an active fascist merely because they disliked him. Formal policy was to review political cases at the county level and, if guilt was not immediately evident, to invite the accused to a hearing before county land reform authorities. A final review and determination was to be made by the provincial commission on all decisions to expropriate. In practice, however, this elaborate procedure was hardly compatible with the sort of swift and sweeping purge the Communists demanded. Many properties were mistakenly confiscated, particularly in the early weeks and at the local level. While some attempt was later made to restore these to their rightful owners, efforts of the bourgeois parties to arrange for a full-scale review of all doubtful expropriations were fruitless, and many injustices were certainly never rectified. The Communists' overriding priority was to avoid arousing doubts among the peasants as to the legality of their claim to their new plots.[42]

In general, the expropriation reflected the Communists' conception of it as an act of class warfare in which a certain amount of harshness and suffering were inevitable, even desirable, in the interests of quick and dramatic change. Although later implementation instructions supplementing the land reform decrees permitted expropriated landlords to take some personal possessions with them, these instructions often arrived too late or were ignored in the field. Thus in practice, the relative cruelty or humanity of eviction depended largely on the character of the local official in charge, and varied greatly. Many peasant committees, encouraged by KPD activists who were concerned far more with goading on the timid than with restraining the overzealous, gave landlords and their families less than an hour to pack a single suitcase before literally running them off their estates. Manor houses were frequently looted. Some landlords were treated brutally, and many were transported off to do forced labor on estates retained as experimental farms, or to fend for themselves without food or shelter on the Baltic island of Rügen.[43]

On the other hand, the KPD and administrations did make an effort to confine peasant violence to the class enemies of the moment. The arbitrary limit of 100 hectares was scrupulously observed, and Communists condemned the actions of some peasant groups who confiscated farm machinery from those classified as wealthy peasants, thereby jeopardizing the worker-peasant alliance. The *Deutsche Volkszeitung* admonished:

> Peasant property—as opposed to that of the militarist Junkers—must not be touched. . . . Mistaken actions are apt to disrupt the close friendly relations between town and country and between the rural population and the authorities.

Nor were former overseers on great estates necessarily to be treated the same as their "Junker" masters:

> If they were active members of the Nazi Party, if they were slavedrivers, then they must disappear. But there will also be quite a number of decent, capable people among them. Since trained personnel are needed, the county commissions will have to take care to make the best possible use of the latter.[44]

Responsibility for coordinating land reform activities throughout the zone lay with the newly-created German Central Administration for Agriculture and Forestry, headed by Edwin Hoernle and including a separate department for land reform under another Communist, Hermann Dölling. Hoernle's staff conducted an extensive inspection of the work of the commissions at all levels, to find and correct irregularities.

Ultimate control, however, was exercised behind the scenes by the KPD and SMA in Berlin. Major policy decisions and supplementary land reform legislation were hammered out by the KPD central leadership in consultation with Zhukov and his staff. They were then passed downward through subordinate levels of both the KPD and SMA organizations (Hoernle's office being included in the latter, since the German Central Administrations worked as mere adjuncts to their Soviet counterparts). KPD representatives in the administrations saw to the details of formal promulgation by the provincial authorities and implementation in the field. Meanwhile, Red Army commanders at all levels received the same instructions as the corresponding German authorities, and were thus in a position to intervene when necessary to enforce compliance.[45]

As a rule the Soviets avoided overt intervention. The land reform was after all supposed to be an affair of the German people. The Soviets much preferred to work through the German administrations, thereby reinforcing the legitimacy of these organs. Soviet officers met frequently with provincial, regional, and local authorities, Bloc representatives, etc., to advise and instruct them. The SMA carried out repeated field inspections and required regular reports on land reform progress both from the German provincial administrations and from its own regional commanders (as did the KPD from its provisional party leaderships). When problems began mounting up after the first few weeks, the Soviets sought to remedy them where possible by ordering the administrations to take specific corrective actions and by counseling KPD functionaires on proper revolutionary tactics. Nevertheless, when all else failed, the SMA was prepared to reveal its mailed fist.[46]

PROBLEMS IN PRACTICE

By the end of the first month the land reform was mired in difficulties. The resistance of the landlords, for one thing, was proving stubborn and resourceful. Many misrepresented the extent of their holdings. Other, more imaginative souls transferred titles to friends and relatives or even changed their nationality to avoid expropriation (foreign-owned properties being temporarily exempted due to the legal complications involved). Companies with interests in several zones appealed to the Western occupation powers for protection. And from all sides a flood of letters inundated the already overburdened administrations: appeals for exemption, legal challenges, statements by peasants attesting the anti-fascist loyalties of this or that landowner, and so forth. Meanwhile, "sabotage" by those anticipating expropriation—neglect of their crops and smuggling out of farm equipment from their condemned estates—further upset food production.[47]

The SMA and KPD tended to blame the administrations and land reform commissions for much of the trouble, accusing them of "bureaucratic procrastination," and exhorting peasants to compel faster action. The criticism was not entirely misplaced. The civil service, particularly the judiciary, was still heavily laced with bourgeois bureaucrats inclined to sympathize with the landowners. In Thuringia (a problem area), 32 percent of civil servants were still former Nazis in October 1945. Some of these people did try to thwart the land reform, and many others were no doubt unenthusiastic in their cooperation—especially in view of the opposition currently being voiced by CDU and LDP leaders. Even Communist officials were taken to task for being too willing to grant exceptions in cases of personal hardship. They must, one SMA colonel admonished, show "greater firmness of principle" in this "revolutionary class battle."[48]

Yet with the best of intentions, the administrations would have been hard pressed to consummate an agrarian revolution, including all the review procedures called for in land reform legislation, in the space of a few weeks. In Mecklenburg and Brandenburg, bastions of the landed gentry, urban workers and the socialist parties were still a weak force in the conservative countryside. Thuringia, on the other hand, had few large landowners but many small and middle-sized proprietors with fascist backgrounds. Careful judgments had to be made to insure that only the guilty were expropriated, lest the entire peasantry be stampeded into opposition.[49]

In any case, the main problem was really the reluctance of the peasants themselves. From the upper and middle peasantry, which had nothing to gain, the KPD had never hoped for much more than neutrality. But even the poor peasants and farm laborers who were the intended beneficiaries of the land reform were ambiguous in their attitudes toward it. They generally wanted the land, but were suspicious of the Communists. Particularly in more backward areas, they hesitated to seize outright the property of local suzereins whose traditional authority they had hitherto never dared to question, and whom they feared would one day return with a vengeance—a fear the landlords did their best to cultivate.[50] Their hesitation also reflected a well-founded modesty about their own ability to manage an independent farm. Many estate workers preferred the relative security of their present positions to the risks of entrepreneurship, particularly in the present unsettled times. Finally, in areas where prosperous peasant farms predominated, neighbors would help each other to conceal facts that might lead to expropriation. Not all the old land registers survived long enough to be burned by the land reform commissions; some were burned beforehand for much different reasons.[51]

The KPD's policy was to try first and foremost to arouse the peasants to more radical action on their own, through the grass-roots work of Communist agitators:

> We Communists and friends of the working peasants leave it to the locally-elected, responsible peasant commissions to implement the land reform as they see fit. But we shall give them pointers; make them aware of mistakes and deficiencies. . . .[52]

Conferences were held for commission members to warn them against a "soft" attitude toward the many Junkers and Nazis seeking exceptions to land reform laws. The Communist press lamented the foolishness of peasants and villagers who let themselves be duped by wealthy landlords into signing certifications of their political rectitude or pleas for clemency on their behalf. In addition, though, the KPD did sometimes take matters into its own hands. One KPD county organization reported to the SMA in Weimar that it had itself done the work of the peasant commissions in drawing up a list of landowners to be expropriated—probably a common occurrence. In a mining area in Saxony, a Communist-led team of miners allegedly confiscated nearly a hundred estates in forty-eight hours.[53]

As a last resort, recalcitrant landowners and fascists were declared to be committing "sabotage of the land reform," and the problem was turned over to German police or the SMA for "administrative measures." These mainly involved arrest or forceable expulsion of landlords from the neighborhood of their expropriated estates. Thuringia's First Vice President Ernst Busse stated on 30 September that he had already had to order such removals personally in various parts of the state, due to the inaction of the commissions. At about the same time, word went out to all five provincial administrations from the SMA that, because of the high incidence of sabotage and persistent efforts by "reactionary forces" to sow confusion among the peasants, expropriated landowners and their families were henceforth to be evacuated from their home communities as a matter of policy. Where resistance was especially tough, measures were correspondingly harsher. In Thuringia, 115 landowners were under detention for sabotage by October 1945; and by the end of the land reform period in 1949, 1,028 Thuringian landowners, 259 tenant farmers, and 258 overseers had been removed fifty kilometers or more from their former homes.[54]

This policy of expulsion had proven effective in resolving similar problems in the Polish land reform a year earlier, and it proved itself again in Germany. The peasants, impressed with the regime's show of determination and relieved of the intimidating presence of their erstwhile masters, soon lost their inhibitions about taking land that was now manifestly ownerless. By late October, problems of expropriation were giving way to problems of redistribution.[55]

The first estates were partitioned with great ceremony beginning in late September 1945. The real work of dividing up the land, though, only got under way about mid-October, and lasted several months. One difficulty which quickly arose was a shortage of equipment and personnel to accomplish the enormous task of resurveying; a shortage aggravated by the recent purge of many fascists from the land offices. To avoid letting the tempo of the land reform bog down on this relatively minor point, the administrations arranged to send out a county land commission member and whatever technical assistance was available to help local commissions and peasants stake out new parcels as best they could for the time being. This stopgap solution really satisfied no one, however: peasants and land office personnel objected to the crudity of the hasty surveys, while the central authorities repeatedly criticized local officials for dragging their feet and for neglecting to provide new settlers with proper deeds. Finally, a more careful resurvey was undertaken beginning in early 1946, for which the regime found itself forced to rehire qualified surveyors regardless of their political past.[56]

But the most serious obstacles to partitioning the land were not technical but, again, human ones. Many Social Democrats—and not a few Communists—in the administrations remained convinced that five hectares was too little for a viable farm and that collective farms were after all, as socialist parties had hitherto always maintained, the logical successors to the great private estates. Doubts about the small peasants' ability to manage their own farms were also universal. Inspections consequently exposed numerous local commissions that were experimenting with various cooperative farming arrangements on the old estates instead of breaking them up. KPD leaders worked doggedly to convince well-meaning officials that such deviations were playing into the hands of the former landlords, who were only too happy to see their holdings kept intact pending some future change in their political fortunes.[57]

For similar reasons, governmental agencies of all sorts and at all levels were managing to keep as much property as possible in their own hands. The land reform decrees had provided for tractors, reapers, and other large farm machinery from confiscated estates to be turned over to new Peasants' Mutual Aid Committees for common use. These committees were soon found to be withholding also small plows, harrows and similar equipment, livestock, and supplies of fodder and seed intended for the peasants. Cities and rural communities took advantage of the land reform to gain control of extensive tracts. Meanwhile, economic experts in the provincial administrations tried to preserve as many estates as possible in the form of state breeding stations, seed farms, experimental farms, and the like. Officials at all levels were especially loath to break up large stands of forest, despite specific directions to do so, in the firm conviction that peasants would soon do irreparable damage by indiscriminate felling of trees.[58]

In light of the above it was inevitable that spot inspections performed by the Central Administration for Agriculture and Forestry toward the end of 1945 revealed conditions like the following, found on a sampling of Saxon estates:

> On 15 of the 17 estates, the division of the land and inventory and the transfer of residential and farm buildings to the peasants had been accomplished only in part, or not according to the law, or only on paper.
> On a few estates, the land ostensibly partitioned among

the peasants still had absolutely no fixed, marked boundaries. . . .

Distribution of woodlands . . . had sometimes not even begun. The woods had been handed over to the community, but not to the peasants. . . .[59]

Reports from remote areas of Brandenburg and Mecklenburg included cases in which trustees, appointed by county and district administrations to manage expropriated estates and protect against "sabotage" and looting until new farms could be carved out, were in fact perpetuating the old rural regime. They treated the "new farmers," to whom the land theoretically belonged, as farm hands, paying them a wage and perhaps a share of the product from "their" livestock. Milch cows, for example, were kept and milked by estate dairy workers, and their "owners" received an allotment of milk.[60]

Some of the discrepancies uncovered were obviously due to honest misunderstandings or to economic necessity. Many estates could not effectively be broken up for a year or more because there were simply no buildings to house the "new farmers" and their livestock other than the manor house and its outbuildings. On the other hand, a fair number of problems arose out of corruption and apathy among the peasants themselves. Chairmen of land reform commissions saw to it that they and their relatives received the best land, sometimes in portions of twenty or thirty hectares, and as much as possible of the available livestock. Laborers on condemned estates divided farm animals among themselves to avoid having to share them with the rest of the community. The *Deutsche Volkszeitung* complained:

Sabotage was often made possible by the inactivity of the very people with an interest in the land reform. Land was distributed either improperly or not at all, no certificates of title were given out, entry in land registers was prevented or delayed, no payment was received for the lands transferred, etc.

The Communist press exposed numerous cases of former Nazis serving on land reform commissions and receiving land, and of former landlords returning to their old estates to claim generous parcels. As in the expropriation phase, the SMA occasionally intervened forcefully to correct cases of "sabotage" in redistribution which came to its attention, when KPD pressure on the administrations seemed ineffective. The problems themselves were widespread, however, and resisted a quick solution.[61]

The peasants' lack of interest in the broader social aims of the land reform was most evident in their treatment of refugees from the East. The resettlement of these masses was, as has been seen, a major goal of the agrarian policies of all the Bloc parties, but particularly of the KPD. The Communists felt that only complete absorption of the refugees into the society and economy of the remainder of Germany would prevent their becoming a breeding ground for irredentism and future aggression. To the native peasants, however, the refugees were interlopers. The more of them who came into the neighborhood to claim a share of the land, the less land would be available for older residents. Despite warnings from the Communists that the size of new parcels prescribed in the land reform laws must not be exceeded and that excess land must be made available to settlers from other areas, local peasants resorted even to beating up refugees to drive them off. Since native peasants generally controlled the land reform commissions, they made sure that new settlers who remained received smaller plots and poorer land than older residents and that the latter were heavily favored in the distribution of livestock.[62]

Those refugees who could find land nowhere else were transported by the thousands to war-ravaged areas in the eastern part of the zone. There, often living in cellars and temporary shelters miles from the nearest town or railway, they tried to restore to cultivation derelict farmland still scarred with trenches and strewn with barbed wire, land mines, and other debris of battle. Shortages of buildings, equipment, livestock, seed, and every other necessity were severer here than elsewhere in the zone, and not surprisingly, many of the new farms in this region failed.[63]

Even in more fortunate areas, however, many peasants soon found they were unable to survive on their little plots. Lack of proper shelter and equipment was in some degree a problem everywhere. In January 1946, for example, it was reported that 70 percent of "new farmers" in Saxony-Anhalt (a comparatively untroubled area) would require complete outfitting with tools and livestock before they could begin farming. Moreover, the equipment available was not always usable on a small farm, since much of it was horse-drawn and relatively few peasants had received—or could have supported—horses or oxen. Finally, as a "leading agricultural authority in the Soviet Zone" confided to U.S. farm expert Philip Raup, "two-thirds or more of the new settlers were incompetent to operate a farm at the time of their selection."[64]

Confusion and inequities in the production quota system created further hardships. Inexperienced officials working in haste and without necessary documentation had trouble setting equitable quotas. At collection time, overzealous food authorities often seized supplies of seed grain and fodder or breeding animals if normal production did not meet fixed quotas—thus undoing the work of the agricultural authorities who had labored mightily to provide peasants with these necessities. In winter 1946, a wave of arrests for nonfulfillment of mandatory deliveries resulted in punishment of many peasants who, despite honest efforts, had simply failed to produce enough.[65]

The result of all these hardships was the flight of many "new farmers" from their land. By early 1946, the tide of farm abandonments began to reach proportions that clearly alarmed the SMA.[66] Production quotas for "new farmers" were suddenly slashed for 1946 and 1947, and land taxes for those years were completely remitted on all new farmsteads valued at up to 8,000 marks. In February 1946 the SMA instructed the German administrations to organize a program, administered by the new provincial, county, and city banks, of long-term, low-interest loans to peasants who had received land grants, giving them the means to purchase necessary supplies and equipment. In addition, these peasants had priority in deliveries of scarce fertilizer, seed, fuel, and building materials. Efforts begun in late 1945 to relieve the desperate rural housing shortage culminated in 1947 in a crash building program. Authorities also imported livestock from the Western zones and from more prosperous areas of the Soviet Zone to new farmsteads in barren regions, and encouraged older, established peasants to offer material help and advice to "new farmers" who settled nearby. All these measures were only moderately effective, however, and the problems mentioned above continued to plague Soviet Zone agriculture through the rest of the decade.[67]

RESULTS OF THE LAND REFORM: SUCCESS OR FAILURE?

The work of the land commissions was largely completed by the middle of 1946. While retroactive expropriations of alleged fascists, "saboteurs," and evaders of the land reform continued to occur on into the early 1950s, the principal remaining concern after 1946 was the legal and administrative consolidation of the achievements of the first turbulent months. When final results were tallied in January 1949, a total of 13,699 properties with an average size of 235 hectares and a combined land area of 3,225,364 hectares had been expropriated: about a third of all agricultural and forest land in the zone. From this "land fund," 209,000 new peasant farms with an average size of 8 hectares had been created, and 120,000 grants of additional land averaging 2.8 hectares each had been made to existing farms. Still undistributed were 90,755 hectares or 2.8 percent of the land fund, including 1 percent still in Red Army hands which later was gradually transferred to German control.[68]

Notwithstanding Communist arguments that small-scale intensive farming would prove more efficient under postwar German conditions, the land reform was a disaster from a purely economic standpoint. Farm production in the Soviet Zone had dropped by 1946 to a fraction of prewar levels: wheat, rye, potatoes, and sugar beets were down by about half; livestock products by considerably more than half. Most of this decline was undoubtedly due to the effects of war and occupation, including Soviet removals of livestock and farm machinery in spring and summer 1945. Postwar shortages of equipment and (especially) fertilizer also took a heavy toll. Yet yields per hectare remained about 15 percent below those of the U.S. and British zones, which had suffered from at least some of the same problems. A considerable part of the Soviet Zone's shortfall—Philip Raup has put it at up to 10 percent of the total decline in output—must have been caused by the land reform: by the disruption of fall planting, the expulsion of capable landlords and overseers, widespread looting, bureaucratic mismanagement, the decreased efficiency of small farms, and the general incompetence of the "new farmers."[69]

Nor was there much improvement in the overall condition of the peasantry. The enormous difficulties of the "new farmers'" existence were only part of the picture; many peasants received no land at all. This was particularly true of refugees from the East, most of whom arrived too late to participate in the redistribution. Refugees accounted for only 17 percent of peasant land recipients, and received only 23 percent of the available land. Since the haste of the land reform also precluded a careful screening of applicants, many an experienced farmer from East Prussia or the Sudetenland must have been left landless in favor of an otherwise unqualified native who happened to be in the right place at the right time.[70]

Part of the problem was that there simply was not enough land to go around. On the other hand, much of what entered the land fund, particularly after 1946, was never redistributed to the peasants, but remained instead under state control. In the end, despite the KPD's early insistence that nearly all expropriated land was to be partitioned, about a third of it was in fact retained as model farms, Machine Lending Stations, and other state facilities, which according to one later East German account were deliberately intended as "germ-cells of socialism in the countryside." On these state farms were employed, under what Communist Karl Mewis described in 1950 as "almost feudal working conditions," a mass of landless farm workers whose numbers had actually risen since prewar times. In Mecklenburg, mostly because of the influx of refugees and the shortage of jobs in industry, 140,612 wage laborers were working on state and larger private farms in 1946, as opposed to 84,030 in 1939.[71]

Even those fortunate enough to obtain land had little more than token independence. They could not sell, lease, or mortgage their land; and if they abandoned it, it reverted to the state. Credit was only available through the state and its agencies. Ostensibly these restrictions were to prevent reconcentration of land in a few private hands. At a more fundamental ideological level, they aimed at discouraging "capitalist forces and tendencies" among the peasantry itself: reinforcing the peasant's self-perception as a worker and producer rather than as an owner of means of production. Nevertheless, the effect was to achieve de facto what the Communists had so emphatically forsworn as an overt goal: nationalization of the land. The "new farmers" were essentially mere usufructaries.[72]

For all its evident shortcomings as an economic measure, the success of the land reform must be judged finally in terms of the political goals of KPD agrarian policy. In these terms it was indeed a success. Edwin Hoernle summarized KPD goals in 1944 as follows:

1. Liquidation of every form of fascism in the villages (organizational, ideological, personal);
2. Creation of firm personal and organizational bonds between country and city, and above all between the industrial workers, the laboring peasantry and the farm workers;
3. Securing of essential food supplies for the people.

According to Hoernle these objectives were interdependent, each being attainable only in conjunction with the other two.[73]

The land reform not only succeeded in stripping the last vestiges of power from fascists in the countryside, it demolished the whole structure of the old rural regime. The dominant class of great landowners was completely swept away along with the system of land tenure that had supported it. In its place, the once supine mass of poor peasants was given land and a limited sort of political power—power, that is, to play an active role in the Communist transformation program. Indeed, the Communists deliberately thrust the peasants into the position of executing the land reform themselves in order to break down their traditional conservative loyalties and involve them directly in the class struggle against the old elites. The village was politicized. The combination of this political and social revolution with an immense influx of new settlers from the East, all within a few short months, exploded the rigid patterns of the old village life and cleared the ground for a new order.[74]

The foundation of this new order was laid by the establishment of "personal and organizational bonds between country and city," or more bluntly, consolidation of the Communist control apparatus in the countryside.

This meant in part the buildup of the party organization itself. In October 1945 Wilhelm Pieck advised KPD leaders in Mecklenburg, "It is especially necessary to see to it that, in conjunction with the implementation of the land reform, local KPD groups are formed in all communities." Communist agitators succeeded in founding hundreds of such groups through the enrollment, in particular, of many "new farmers." Moreover, the KPD's position with regard to the other Bloc parties was strengthened in the confrontation over land reform. Not only were the bourgeois parties cowed into submission, but the SPD, impressed with the need for socialist unity on this critical issue, began cooperating more closely with the Communists at all levels.[75]

KPD influence was also extended by subtler means, however. One frequent Communist accusation against Nazi agrarian policies, particularly the Hereditary Farms Law, was that they deepened social divisions among the peasantry. But the KPD land reform, while it shortened the social spectrum by eliminating the great landlords and uplifting much of the poor peasantry, was not intended to obliterate social distinctions—quite the contrary. Its aim was rather to stand the old order on its head: to establish as the new dominant class a broad stratum of small peasants firmly allied with the proletarian regime. The KPD's Leninist strategy was to neutralize the "middle peasants" (proprietors of five to ten hectares) for the time being by granting them some forest land. The "great peasants" (up to one hundred hectares), on the other hand, it always regarded as capitalists and potential enemies. Taxes and production quotas were made steeply progressive to limit the economic strength of larger farms, and in 1948 the regime launched a new campaign against the "great peasants" aimed, as Lenin had once put it, at "liberating the toiling and exploited majority of the rural population from the ideological and political influence of these exploiters."[76]

The inherent economic weakness of the "new farmers," far from being a drawback of the new agrarian order, was one of its main advantages from the Communist perspective. The last of Hoernle's stated goals, the securing of reliable food supplies, was as much a political as an economic consideration. Soviet experience had taught that abundant food production was of no help to a proletarian-based regime if the supply of food to the cities could be withheld at any time by recalcitrant farmers. Yet socialization of agriculture was impossible at this stage, both for political reasons and because of a lack of proper equipment and of reliable farm experts to operate collectives. The promotion of the small peasants was an ideal transitional solution. By carving out a maximum number of minimum-sized farms, the Communists created a large class of peasants who were indebted to the regime for their economic existence and dependent on it for their future survival. The "new farmers" were, moreover, dependent on one another—on cooperative use of large machinery, draft animals, and other resources beyond the means of individual small farms. The KPD had anticipated this need for cooperation and encouraged it, providing in the land reform decrees for Peasants' Mutual Aid Associations to promote and coordinate common efforts. These organs were intended to educate the peasants toward an eventual transition to collective farming. In the short run they became as well the prime instrument of Communist control in the countryside.[77]

FOUR

New Institutions for a New Order

Karl Marx himself coined the maxim that "the working class cannot simply lay hold of the ready-made state machinery and wield it for its own purposes." The old institutions were an embodiment of the class despotism of the old elite, and had to be replaced with institutions expressing the power of the proletariat.[1] If this was true of the nineteenth-century state about which Marx wrote, the Communists considered it doubly true of an all-pervasive modern fascist state. "In Germany," observed SMA political expert Sergei Tjulpanov, "the task of smashing the machinery of the state was significantly more complicated and had to be carried out more radically than in other countries." Nazism and individual Nazis had insinuated themselves into all institutions of German life and society. The destruction of the Nazi government apparatus thus had to be supplemented by the elimination of organs such as the Reich Food Estate and the German Labor Front whose political character was less overt, but equally malign.[2]

Liquidation of the existing institutions, while carried out under the banner of denazification, had the added advantage of clearing the ground for the Communists. The KPD planned to replace the "fascist economy of coercion" with a subtler system of economic "influence" based on state control of key industries, manipulation of credit, expansion and political domination of cooperatives, and above all mobilization of the masses. The new economic "organs of the people"—in particular the FDGB and the Peasants' Mutual Aid Association—were to play a critical role as what Lenin called "transmission belts," conveying the doctrines and policies of the Communist vanguard to the broad mass of working people. Like the corresponding organs of the Nazi regime, these organs were expected to help with the economic tasks of fostering and coordinating development and allocating scarce resources. In the process, however, they also had the new task of advancing the class struggle by assuming, under KPD guidance, much of the economic power hitherto exercised by private entrepreneurs. They would help organize popular support for the KPD and its programs and against its designated class adversaries. In the long run, the new organs shared responsibility with the party and the state for both technical training and political reeducation of workers and peasants, to prepare them for their roles of leadership in the new society.[3]

THE PEASANTS' MUTUAL AID ASSOCIATION

The Peasants' Mutual Aid Association (Vereinigung der gegenseitigen Bauernhilfe, or VdgB) was a valuable innovation purely from an economic standpoint. Some sort of farmers' organization was needed to cope with the problems of agricultural management in postwar Germany. Anglo-American occupation authorities planned to retain and democratize the Farmers' Associations of the Reich Food Estate. In the Soviet Zone, the Food Estate's responsibilities for supervising the production, collection, and distribution of farm products had to be temporarily assumed by agricultural departments of the German administrations, but only "pending creation of new representative agencies" for the peasantry which had been promised by the KPD in its Action Program of 1944.[4]

It was likewise a matter of sound economics that these new agencies include some arrangement for cooperative use of farm machinery. Such cooperation had long been advocated by farm management specialists throughout

Germany, and was all but dictated by conditions in the Soviet Zone in 1945. Machine and tractor cooperatives were in fact being organized by local peasants all over the zone in spring and summer of that year. A U.S. intelligence report noted that Soviet Zone authorities were encouraging this approach "on the ground that it is the most efficient way of utilizing the limited available skilled agricultural labor"—not to mention the limited supply of machines. "It seems likely," the report added, "that the reason advanced by the Russians is the real one."[5]

Nevertheless, the origins of the VdgB were also political, and were rooted once again in Soviet theory and experience. Lenin had advocated in 1920 that Communist parties in power move quickly to establish peasant "soviets" in the countryside "in which proletarians and semiproletarians must be ensured predominance." The rural soviets were to guarantee close peasant cooperation with the urban proletariat and to overcome the resistance of the "Kulaks," or wealthier farmers. In the early 1930s, Stalin had introduced a centrally-directed network of Machine Tractor Stations to aid in the collectivization program. These stations served as a framework for extending Communist power into the countryside. When the prospect of a Soviet-dominated Eastern Europe began to emerge in the latter stages of World War II, Communist strategists set about adapting Soviet tactics to the problems of cementing a worker-peasant alliance and easing the transition to collective farming in the societies there. The resulting Peasant Mutual Aid organizations, of which the VdgB was but one example, became a classic feature of the "People's Democracies" of Eastern Europe in the late 1940s.[6]

The various informal peasant cooperative arrangements which the KPD had been encouraging since spring 1945 finally acquired an official status during the land reform when, as the Communists enthusiastically pointed out, such cooperation became indispensable to the survival of the tiny new peasant farms. The provincial land reform decrees assigned tractors, threshing machines, reapers, and similar equipment which could not be employed rationally by the individual farms, to the custody of Peasant Mutual Aid Committees, who were to use them primarily to help the "new farmers." Subsequent implementation instructions further spelled out the duties of these committees and the proper procedures for founding them. Village land reform commissions were responsible for calling an assembly of all land recipients as well as any other "laboring peasants" who wished to belong to the local VdgB. Those present thereupon constituted themselves as an association, drafted bylaws, and elected by open ballot an executive committee of five to seven members, which was henceforth responsible to the general membership for the conduct of VdgB affairs. Pending the formation of this committee, the land reform commission itself was to act in its place.[7]

In the ensuing drive to establish the peasant committees in every village, the VdgB's Communist promoters stressed its democratic form as opposed to the "bureaucratic" methods and compulsory membership of the Reich Food Estate. Yet despite the committees' formal accountability to their members, their character as an agency of the regime became increasingly clear. The land reform implementation directives established them officially as corporations of public law in October 1945, thereby making them quasi-governmental organs. At about the same time, county and district VdgB committees were formed to supervise the local bodies. Provincial committees were added in spring 1946, and a Central Peasants' Secretariat was established in Berlin about the middle of that year as a nucleus for a future zonal VdgB headquarters.[8]

Parallel with this centralization process came an intensification of Communist control. As early as October 1945 the KPD Central Committee was admonishing provincial party leaders to pay more attention to creating local Mutual Aid Committees, since these were "the footholds of the party in each village." In conjunction with the spring planting in 1946, the Communists launched a crash campaign in which thousands of KPD and SPD functionaries sallied forth once more into the countryside to found new peasant committees. As a result, VdgB membership jumped from 52,031 to 255,369 by 1 June. Elections were also held at that time for new county, district, and provincial committees, and the organizational structure in the villages was tightened up in order to strengthen the Communist political hold. "Care must be taken," Ulbricht instructed his provincial colleagues, "that good peasant elements who have proven themselves in the land reform are elected. . . ." The bourgeois parties stood by helplessly in the face of this politicization, although the CDU did protest feebly and tardily against "external influence" in VdgB affairs. While the VdgB still consisted mostly of politically unaligned peasants by the time of the KPD-SPD merger in April 1946, the socialist parties' representation in it was so strong as to give the new Socialist Unity Party clear political control.[9]

The growth in Communist power within the VdgB was accompanied by a growth in economic influence of the Mutual Aid organization itself. By early 1946 Ulbricht could boast:

> We have achieved a fundamental change in the village: the command of the old landowners has been replaced by the organs of the Peasants' Mutual Aid. . . . They are becoming the strongest economic force in the village.[10]

The peasant committees were at first the designated custodians (later the proprietors) of all large machinery, breeding stock, repair stations, and similar technical facilities, and of the small mills, distilleries, dairies, and food processing plants that belonged to many of the old estates. Soon they also took over the administration of seed farms, experimental farms, etc., on behalf of the state.

To operate these facilities, the VdgB received 39,000 hectares from the land fund—an allotment that even the KPD's Hermann Dölling found excessive. Almost all new production of agricultural machinery went to the VdgB. Aside from machines and breeding animals, the Mutual Aid organization also controlled local allocation of seed, fodder, and fertilizer. It was, along with the older credit cooperatives, the official channel through which credit was available to peasants, and it functioned as a sort of housing office to find quarters for "new farmers" and arrange for new housing construction. VdgB experts advised peasants on farm management and trained them in modern agricultural methods.[11]

As an institution designed primarily for the poor peasantry, the VdgB tended to be scorned by the better-established peasants who had little to gain by a pooling of resources. Indeed, even many "new farmers" encountered by Philip Raup in Saxony and Thuringia expressed pride in their independence from the VdgB's Machine Lending Stations and contempt for neighbors who relied on them. The VdgB, for its part, made a conscious effort to preserve the appearance of a democratic, strictly voluntary organization. Nonmembers were merely charged a fee for the use of its facilities. Nevertheless, its growing powers and responsibilities as an official organ gave it an increasing sway over the fortunes of members and nonmembers alike, to the disadvantage of the latter. Its task of managing cooperative use of machines for planting and harvesting led the VdgB to be charged with overall supervision of agricultural production in the community. Beginning with the spring planting in 1946, it was the peasant committees who assigned and enforced the crop-planting goals and production quotas of local farmers. To meet production targets for the community as a whole, the VdgB needed the cooperation of all farmers, particularly those with equipment and expertise to contribute. The uncooperative could find themselves burdened by disproportionately heavy production requirements and a meager share of seed, fertilizer, and other necessities. In spring 1946, the peasant committees and local administrations also received the authority to commandeer, or if necessary confiscate, all tractors, regardless of ownership, for community use in the planting campaign.[12]

The VdgB's role as a social and economic equalizer in the countryside was nowhere more evident than in the livestock redistribution program. Originally the peasant VdgB committees were called upon to help rectify local inequities in land reform implementation by insuring that each peasant got a fair share of confiscated livestock and equipment, and no more. County committees were to see that the local organs passed on any surplus animals to neighboring villages that needed them. By early 1946, however, the VdgB's redistribution function was assuming a broader dimension. A convention of provincial VdgB committees concluded: "The spring planting has proven that the Peasant Mutual Aid must by no means restrict itself to the help of one farm for another or at best of one community for another, but must extend far beyond that to mutual aid of counties for other counties, and even of provinces for other provinces."[13] As the official representative of the "new farmers' " interests, the VdgB had taken on the task of settling landless peasants where land was still available, particularly in the devastated eastern counties of Brandenburg and Mecklenburg, and of trying to secure for them the bare necessities of survival. In cooperation with the provincial administrations, it assembled livestock and equipment from western parts of the zone, particularly Thuringia and the two Saxonies, for shipment to these regions. Some of these supplies were drawn from local land reform "surplus," some purchased from wealthier peasants with Soviet credits (and no doubt a bit of arm-twisting); and the Red Army also chipped in with 10,000 horses and varying quantities of other farm inventory seized earlier for its own use. Minimum goals set by the SMA for redistribution to Brandenburg were: 25,000 cattle, 10,000 horses, 6,000 hogs, 20,000 sheep, and 15,000 goats. The figures for Mecklenburg were nearly identical.[14]

While material aid for "new farmers" was necessary for its own sake, the VdgB was pursuing a broader political and social aim as well. An important function of the Peasants' Mutual Aid was to cultivate a new community spirit among the peasants: to educate them away from the self-centeredness and provincialism fostered by the old village life, and toward a greater sense of responsibility for each other and society as a whole. Communist propaganda presented the redistribution program as a spontaneous act of humanity and class solidarity rather than an administrative measure. It called upon peasants to donate voluntarily as much as they could spare to help the "new farmers." Beyond supplying settlers with material necessities, the VdgB also intervened to smooth over frictions between native peasants and newcomers. In the villages it involved women in the mutual aid effort through community activities such as washing and mending centers, children's day-care facilities, and care for the old and infirm. It urged its youth cadre, the Young Farmers, to take an active part in the "vocational and ideological education" of their peers.[15]

The political goal of the Mutual Aid Association was not only to build peasant solidarity, but also to define the "laboring peasantry" as a class and awaken it to its proper class role in the new order. In part, this involved a process of ideological clarification. Like all KPD-sponsored organs, the VdgB used its expanding social and economic power to combat the remnants of fascism. In time, though, its reeducation efforts turned increasingly toward creating support for the new regime, and particularly for the SED. Politically intractable peasants could be subjected to a wide range of pressures from an organization that controlled so many vital resources. Should they fail to meet their quotas or otherwise expose themselves to a charge of "sabotage of the people's food supply," the VdgB could even have their farms confiscated under the land reform law. Finally, beginning in 1948, the VdgB played an important part in the campaign against the "Kulaks," who hitherto had been tolerated as part of a KPD policy of avoiding unnecessary class conflicts in the countryside until the new order was secure. One leading SED official called upon "working class representatives" in the VdgB to expel large farmers "not only from the leadership, but also from the organization of the Peasants' Mutual Aid; let us say in a democratic manner."[16]

Like the trade unions of the urban proletariat, the VdgB was also to express the class interests of the peasantry within society at large. As of spring 1946, all legislation affecting agriculture required prior consultation with the VdgB. Later that year the Mutual Aid Associations, like the FDGB, were permitted to nominate candidates in municipal elections. The character of this representative function, however, as defined by Walter Ulbricht, was the same as that assigned to the trade unions:

> The VdgB represents the interests of laboring peasants in that it mobilizes the peasant masses for implementation of the resolutions of the workers' and peasants' government, contributes to a constant increase in agricultural production, draws the laboring peasants together to work in permanent communal associations, and helps to organize a new cultural life in the villages.[17]

Another primary responsibility of the VdgB was to promote the class alliance of the peasantry and the workers. In practical terms, this chiefly meant cooperating as closely as possible with the FDGB, factory councils, and consumers' cooperatives to regulate and encourage the exchange of farm produce for the goods and services of the cities, and thereby to inhibit the black market. To do this job effectively, the VdgB had to extend its influence in the countryside to encompass the older and politically less reliable farmers' cooperatives.[18]

THE COOPERATIVES

The farmers' and consumers' cooperatives were prewar institutions which lent themselves well to the aims of the postwar Communist regime. For both peasants and workers they were familiar organs of solidarity, a vehicle to gain economic leverage and bypass the middlemen of the capitalist marketplace. Their progressive social character had been, so to speak, "ratified" by the Nazis, who had suppressed them or absorbed them into Nazi institutions; and bourgeois anti-fascists as well as socialists favored their reestablishment and expansion after the war. In the immediate postwar months, the cooperatives offered a partial solution to the problem of getting the mechanism of food collection and distribution out of the hands of private traders and the old Food Estate apparatus and into hands more amenable to the new regime. They helped keep farm products in approved channels and off the black market. In the longer view they also seemed by their very nature to be well suited, like the VdgB, to the political aims of fostering habits of communal enterprise, strengthening class bonds between peasants and workers, and training new cadre of both these classes for positions of economic and political leadership.[19]

For the most part, the various credit unions, animal breeders' cooperatives, fruit and vegetable growers' associations, etc., which had comprised the old Raiffeisen farmers' coops had not been destroyed by the Nazis, but merely "coordinated" into the Reich Food Estate. With the coming of Soviet occupation, they were controlled for a time by the agricultural authorities of the new German administrations. Their rehabilitation finally came in the course of the land reform, as the economic weakness of the "new farmers" became a leading Communist concern.

In late October 1945 the KPD began calling on peasants and their Mutual Aid Committees to rebuild the farmers' cooperatives in every village. On 20 November the SMA decreed the formal reestablishment of farmers' coops in view of their "important role . . . in maximally increasing agricultural production, supplying the peasants with the means of production, and helping to organize the processing and marketing of agricultural products." The SMA order restored control over their financial reserves to them and replaced their old leaderships with "organization bureaus" appointed by the German administrations, pending new elections. These bureaus were instructed to give special priority to enrolling new land recipients in coops.[20]

The agricultural cooperatives were intended from the beginning to work closely with the VdgB, and the assigned functions of the two institutions overlapped considerably. In their new incarnation, the coops were expected to help in procuring fertilizer, seed, equipment, and similar necessities for the "new farmers"; and especially to serve as the authorized channels for funneling state credits to them. These duties led the coops to play a supporting role in the VdgB's redistribution program for livestock, equipment, and other resources. They also assumed a particular responsibility for developing and operating technical facilities in the villages, as evidenced by the appearance of many electricity coops, dairy coops, and the like. Cooperatives took over and ran a variety of repair stations, storage facilities, and especially food processing plants confiscated from private owners.[21]

A prime function of the farmers' cooperatives was to help squeeze private enterprise out of the food business. Wherever possible, therefore, they became the official agencies for collecting mandatory food deliveries from the farms, although some selected wholesale firms also continued in this capacity for a while. In addition, the coops came to be the focal point for the regime's efforts to get control of the so-called "free peaks," the production in excess of mandatory quotas, which tended to flow into the black market. To stimulate production, peasants had been granted the right to dispose of this surplus however they chose and at whatever price they could get.[22] In practice, though, the authorities tried hard (if not too successfully) to induce them to sell it for a "decent price" to the coops, or in officially-sanctioned "free markets" in the towns where only private citizens and authorized organizations such as coops could legally buy. Private purchase of farm produce for resale was forbidden and was punished as black-marketeering. In 1946, it finally became illegal for peasants to sell privately anywhere but in the free markets. Since most peasants had no way to get their goods to town, the KPD exhorted them as good citizens to deliver their "free peaks" to the farmers' cooperatives, who would act as their marketing agents. Unlike the "racketeers and speculators" to whom, the KPD admonished, peasants all too frequently were drawn, the coops would see to it that the food found its way to workers who needed it. In return, they would procure from the workers the industrial goods needed on the farm.[23]

The urban counterparts and principal trading partners of the farmers' cooperatives on behalf of the workers were to be the consumers' cooperatives. Unlike the Raiffeisen organizations, the consumers' coops had ceased to exist under the fascist regime. The Nazis had first "coordinated" them, then later eliminated a number of the larger ones and absorbed the rest into a system of "Supply Rings" administered by the German Labor Front. After the war, many of these Supply Rings were taken over by local food supply authorities and a few were broken up in isolated efforts to revive the old cooperatives, but most were merely purged and left to carry on pending the creation of entirely new institutions.[24]

In fall 1945, representatives of the KPD, SPD, and FDGB met in conferences in Berlin and several provincial cities to agree on a policy regarding new consumers' coops and to rally working-class support for them. Soon after, Communists and Social Democrats began setting up multiparty committees all over the zone to direct the reorganization and recruitment process. By 18 December this process had advanced sufficiently to permit publication of SMA Order No. 176, reestablishing consumers' cooperatives and claiming for them an important role in "developing trade, procuring food supplies directly from the farmers, and increasing deliveries to the cities." As before with the farmers' coops, the order recognized the "organization bureaus" being formed by the KPD and SPD as provisional management organs, and directed that remaining properties of the old cooperatives and the Nazi Supply Rings be transferred to them.[25]

In January 1946 the KPD and SPD issued their own more detailed guidelines for reconstituting the consumers' coops and launched a new campaign, together with the FDGB and provincial administrations, to found organization bureaus for them everywhere. By April the job was nearly complete. As of late 1946, 247 cooperatives were in operation, and a year later they were supplying 32 percent of the Soviet Zone population with consumer goods. Unlike their prewar predecessors, the new coops were permitted to sell not only to members, but to the public at large. Their line of merchandise was also expanded to include shoes, textile goods, office and school supplies, and a variety of other items in addition to food. Independent merchants who had at first accepted the new coops calmly as a restoration of the Weimar status quo grew increasingly resentful as they saw their livelihood being threatened by the competitive advantages of these favored institutions. While the regime aided the consumers' organizations by securing them access to inexpensive sources of food and other goods, providing them with transport, storage, and sales facilities, and giving them (as well as the farmers' coops) control of confiscated food processing plants, it simultaneously burdened private shopkeepers with unrealistically low fixed prices and spoilage allowances that reduced or eliminated their margin of profit.[26]

Some independent traders tried to remain competitive by creating private cooperatives of their own. The KPD condemned such combinations as attempts to cloak capitalist profit-seeking in cooperative forms, and urged that they be denied legal status by excluding them from the Audit Associations to which all coops were required to belong. It was through these Audit Associations that the Communists intended to control the cooperative movement and develop it into yet another instrument of social and economic transformation.[27]

The SMA directives creating both farmers' and consumers' coops had immediately provided for them to be unified in central associations, and the KPD had quickly set about establishing these organs. Like similar institutions of the Weimar consumers' coops and the old Raiffeisen Association, the new associations were to oversee the financial operations of individual cooperatives. Their power was amplified, however, by their assumption as well of responsibility for "organizational leadership"; and for maintaining common processing, storage, and transportation facilities and other services on which local coops depended. To protect the associations' leverage, the KPD battled reformers who wanted to retain the extensive Supply Ring structures or found new consumers' coops covering several counties. The individual cooperatives were to be kept small and dependent, so as to insure that they remained under the influence of the associations, and hence of the "working class."[28]

As usual, centralization was accompanied by politicization. In constructing the administrative machinery of the new cooperatives the KPD and SPD secured key positions for themselves, particularly in the coop associations. They further declared in their joint policy guidelines that administrative posts in the consumers' coops were to be open only to "reliable anti-fascists," defined as members of the four recognized parties. Former Nazis were in any event banned from joining either type of coop; a stricture that the KPD extended, in the case of the farmers' organizations, to include opponents of the land reform and other "public nuisances of all kinds." During 1946, a total of 38,400 members were purged from farmers' coops for political reasons. While accepting as "self-evident" the principle that cooperatives should be nonpartisan organizations, the KPD and its allies nonetheless warned (in an FDGB pamphlet) that unqualified political neutrality would amount to "active support for the enemies of the working class." One purpose of cooperatives, moreover, was to help attain a "higher economic order." Consequently the coops, like all Communist-sponsored institutions, had additional responsibilities as agents of political reeducation: "to support the struggle of the anti-fascist parties and trade unions against the war criminals and warmongers, and to contribute to the awakening of proletarian class-consciousness and the propagation of the socialist idea."[29]

The farmers' cooperatives were assisted in their political tasks by the Peasants' Mutual Aid Association. There is in fact ample evidence to suggest that they were intended from the first as support organizations for the VdgB, to give this new Communist construct access to a broader segment of the peasantry and to the technical facilities and expertise of established popular institutions. By late 1946, farmers' coops claimed 788,000 members, which must have included a solid majority of independent farmers in the Soviet Zone.[30] Communist policy called upon the Mutual Aid Committees not only to foster and support the coops at every turn, but to join them as a group in order to secure a leading role in them for the small peasants and to work for their democratization.[31]

Despite these efforts, the farmers' cooperatives remained too heavily under "kulak" influence and too reluctant in their support of the regime's economic policies.

Thus with Communist encouragement, the VdgB gradually encroached on areas of coop responsibility such as supplying credit to farmers and marketing the "free peaks" (although it left the more unpopular job of collecting mandatory deliveries to the coops). Several attempts to unite the two organizations were sidetracked in 1945-47, apparently out of fear that the larger coops would end up swallowing the VdgB rather than vice versa. In the end, however, with Stalinization in full swing, the farmers' cooperatives were assimilated into the Peasants' Mutual Aid organization in 1950.[32]

The consumers' coops, on the other hand, for all the problems with "reformist influences" in their early months, proved to be more reliable instruments of the new regime. Indeed, the KPD had to warn repeatedly against the overzealous assumption that these coops, like those in the Soviet Union, were institutions of socialism: "In a capitalist environment, they can be no more than self-help organizations of consumers." (The struggle against the German bourgeoisie had, after all, as yet barely begun!) Nevertheless, the consumers' cooperatives had their overseers too: first in the Central Administration for Trade and Supply, which coordinated the functions of their provincial associations in zonal and inter-zonal trade, but more importantly in the trade unions. "Advocacy of consumer interests" was only one of the many responsibilities deemed to be implicit in the FDGB's mandate as economic representative of the proletariat. This mandate entitled it to a decisive voice in developing and guiding not only consumers' organizations, but a whole range of important economic and social institutions of the new order.[33]

THE TRADE UNIONS CONFEDERATION

The FDGB was the keystone in the system of new "organs of the people." The trade unions were crucial to KPD plans for securing both political power and economic control. Politically, they were the model "transmission belts" to the masses: the most important workers' organizations with the allegiance of a large part of the laboring population, including many people with no formal political ties. As a time-honored symbol of workers' solidarity and power, moreover, they lent an aura of legitimacy to the new regime through their participation in it. Finally, the trade unions were the backbone of the SPD's support among the workers, and control of them was thus the key to political unification of the working class on KPD terms.[34]

Economically, expansion of trade-union power was an obvious way to restrict the independent power of private entrepreneurs in the name of industrial democracy. Once under KPD control the unions would become, as well, valuable extensions of the new regime's own apparatus for central planning and direction of the economy. Through their base organizations in each factory, they would be in a position to provide economic authorities with both a reliable source of information on industrial capacities (which capitalist managers tended for a number of reasons to conceal), and a mechanism for implementing central policies throughout every capillary of the economy. Above all, of course, the FDGB was the main instrument through which the working class itself would be mobilized to strengthen the new state being constructed on its behalf, through a steady increase in production.[35]

The Struggle for Political Control

The Communist campaign for political control within the FDGB organization was primarily a test of strength with the SPD. For this reason it had to be conducted with some discretion, so as to preserve the KPD-SPD alliance vis-à-vis the bourgeois parties and keep the latter from exercising any real power in trade union councils. While continuing to seek collaboration with Social Democrats in the FDGB's Berlin Preparatory Committee, the KPD simultaneously pursued its campaign to discredit the old ADGB leadership and to present its own trade union policies as the only correct ones. Within a few weeks after the Potsdam Conference, Bernhard Göring began speaking out in the Preparatory Committee against KPD propaganda, aimed at factories and other workplaces, which blamed the pre-1933 trade union leadership for the success of fascism or which sought to popularize KPD positions on sensitive questions of trade union policy before the FDGB leaders themselves had reached an agreement on them. Despite Göring's remonstrances, Paul Walter of the Preparatory Committee went public on 28 September with the KPD's controversial position on unionization of white-collar workers. Walter's interview with the SMA organ *Tägliche Rundschau* precipitated a "vehement debate" at the next day's Preparatory Committee session.[36]

The Communists' near-monopoly of communications media and the common knowledge that the KPD enjoyed the full confidence of the Soviet authorities made it easy for their leaders to give the impression, particularly in the provinces, that they spoke for the FDGB as a whole. Even those who knew better would scarcely have dared to challenge Communist representations publicly. The KPD's ability, in effect, to set FDGB policy unilaterally was demonstrated most dramatically by Ulbricht in a keynote address delivered to the first zonal trade union conference in Halle on 29 August 1945. The conference was entirely a KPD affair, intended to bolster the party's efforts to merge into the FDGB system the patchwork of ADGB organizations left behind in Saxony-Anhalt by U.S. occupation authorities, and to elicit trade union support for the KPD's land reform program.[37] Ulbricht assumed the task of elucidating, for the assembled labor leaders of all parties, the new social and political responsibilities of the trade unions. "One reason why we refer to them as 'new free trade unions,' " he noted, "is to draw a line of separation with respect to the policies of the former ADGB

Executive Council and its capitulation on May 1, 1933."
The new unions were to be expressly organs of working-
class political power, charged with educating the workers
in a spirit of class consciousness and eradicating fascist
and bourgeois ideological influences among them. They
must reject the doctrine of political neutrality being touted
by some bourgeois and other malicious or misguided trade
unionists and give explicit support to the KPD-SPD United
Front, which alone represented the interests of a unified
working class. "Political neutrality," Ulbricht warned, "is
spoken of today only by those trade union functionaries
who represent some special interest and are indifferent or
hostile to the United Front."[38]

The SPD was surprised, but not unduly alarmed by the
content of Ulbricht's speech. The brunt of his attack had
after all fallen on bourgeois trade unionism, and he had
reaffirmed the ideological and political leadership of both
the socialist parties. Of more concern to Social Democratic leaders, though, was the way in which the KPD
position was being publicized through FDGB channels
without regard for or prior consultation with SPD opinion.
The seriousness of the problem became still clearer when
it was learned that Ulbricht's speech had suddenly appeared in a trial issue of an FDGB newspaper, *Betrieb und
Gewerkschaft*, which hitherto had only been in the planning stages. At the Preparatory Committee session of 24
September, Göring inquired about the origin of this issue,
and particularly about why "Comrade Ulbricht's article
was accepted at the last minute, without other staff members being given the opportunity to redirect their own
articles so as to relate to this reprint." KPD representatives replied that publication of the newspaper "was made
contingent on the appearance of Ulbricht's article in it"—
presumably by the SMA.[39]

Although Göring elicited an understanding that henceforth all instructional materials would be submitted to
the FDGB leaders before going to press, the intrusion of

KPD propaganda continued. By late August, Communists were in effective control of the Preparatory Committee's Editorial Commission, which consisted of Karl Fugger (KPD), Otto Brass (KPD in fact if not yet in name), and Ernst Lemmer (CDU). On 31 October Fugger admitted that, despite Göring's objections to yet another attack on the prewar union leaders being included in an FDGB instructional pamphlet, Fugger had "felt obliged to include the criticized wording," and had done so. In November, Göring noted that complaints were flowing in from "a very wide circle of readers" of the new FDGB organ *Die Freie Gewerkschaft* "who are dissatisfied; who indeed even speak of a one-sided, almost partisan political stance." He requested that the editors amend their tone so as to avoid such an impression, and furthermore that they desist from their continued practice of commenting on important policy issues before the FDGB leadership had agreed on a position.[40]

While the SPD was thus being outmaneuvered in Berlin, the KPD was also waging an offensive at the grass-roots level. Especially in major industrial enterprises and places where the old ADGB's influence remained strongest, Communist agitators organized shop meetings and discussion sessions where they appealed directly to the workers. They invariably reviewed the ADGB's "treason" in 1933 as a cause of fascism and war, and proceeded to call for a united, politically-engaged trade union movement under new leadership that would prevent a repetition of Germany's catastrophe. Communist agitation was directed particularly at the many women and young people who had joined the workforce during and after the war, and who thus had no memory of the Weimar unions and no loyalties to surviving ADGB leaders. It was largely the receptivity of younger workers to KPD arguments that enabled the Communists eventually to neutralize the resistance of "reformist" ADGB veterans everywhere—to pressure, for example, the many local ADGB groups in

Saxony-Anhalt into self-dissolution in the weeks following Ulbricht's Halle speech, and to win support for a "progressive" trade union program at the FDGB's provincial
founding conference in Halle on 15 September.[41]

The KPD's influence in the factories was enhanced by
the very nature, as well as the quality, of the party's organization. While the SPD had always been organized in
residential neighborhoods like a typical Western political
party, the basic unit of the KPD since 1923 had been the
factory cell. From the beginning of the party's reorganization in 1945, the KPD Central Committee gave special
priority to rebuilding these factory groups, while the SPD
continued to rely on the trade unions as its foothold in
the workplace. Consequently, while Communist workers
were in constant active cooperation with one another to
promote KPD interests in the factories, Social Democrats
were often not even aware of each other as such—particularly since factories had experienced such a tremendous
turnover of personnel since 1933.[42]

The SPD's failure to recognize the fluidity of the political situation after 1945 and to secure its power base in
the factories with party organizations of its own proved
to be a major blunder, and one that the Communists exploited to the fullest in their struggle for control of the
unions. The KPD became the champion of "internal democracy" in factory trade union councils: the transfer of
decision-making processes out of the hands of (mostly
Social Democratic) functionaries and into mass meetings
of the general membership. There the solid bloc of KPD
activists could take a leading role in discussion and debate, making the most of the tactical advantage their unity
gave them. The Communists also enjoyed an advantage
in union elections, since they knew their own party's
candidates and could agree in advance to support or oppose
other candidates based on their performance in the mass
meetings. Overt politicking, on the other hand, which
would have benefited the SPD, was forbidden by an agree-

ment between the two socialist parties. Party affiliations were not even to be mentioned in union elections. The KPD's oft-repeated official stance was that workers should vote for the "best and most active" union members, regardless of party—and of course that the "capitulationists" of 1933 should be barred from office.[43]

By late August 1945, the KPD's organizational superiority and its success in gaining Communist "parity" in top union offices had already strengthened its position to a point where it felt ready to risk elections. On 29 August, the Preparatory Committee accepted a Communist proposal that voting be held for a Berlin Delegates' Conference to convene on 23 September, which would install an elected Berlin FDGB Executive Council and formulate FDGB policies. From the start, however, the non-Communist representatives began to have misgivings. Jakob Kaiser, whose constituency was mainly in the Western zones, warned that the present Berlin leadership had been constituted to represent trade union interests throughout the entire Reich. Its composition could therefore not be subject to alteration by a vote of the Berlin unions alone. Further, Kaiser called attention to several matters that might endanger the fairness of elections; for example: "What controls will there be to assure that only trade union members cast ballots?"[44]

It was on the issue of fair elections that SPD apprehensions focused. Göring and Schlimme pointed out in the Committee session of 31 August that KPD attacks on SPD trade union leaders and policies were not exactly consistent with the sort of nonpartisan elections the Communists were publicly promoting. On 6 September Schlimme suggested postponing the elections and Kaiser supported him, but they were overruled. Shortly afterward the Committee's secretary Karl Germer, already concerned about the KPD's potential for undue influence through its factory cells, became convinced that the Communists planned to pack the election assemblies with hastily-recruited "trade unionists" of their own party.[45] Germer contacted Social Democratic chairmen and vice-chairmen in the various industrial unions about these premonitions, and had them persuade their respective executive boards to pass resolutions stating that their organizations were still too unformed to hold elections. Germer then presented these resolutions personally to the KPD's Roman Chwalek.[46]

Meanwhile, both Germer and Schlimme (and probably other non-Communists as well) had also been in touch with the Western powers. Anglo-American authorities had been monitoring FDGB developments closely and with mounting suspicion, particularly since Ulbricht's Halle speech. On 5 September, a Colonel Bamford advised Schlimme to relay the British view that official creation of a new trade union organization for the Reich, possibly to include the present FDGB leadership, would have to await further developments. Bamford therefore urged emphatically that the planned Delegates' Conference be canceled. Ulbricht had a similar interview at about the same time with British officers who told him that they saw no need for the FDGB to be expanded beyond the level of city district organizations at present. Although somewhat taken aback by this British stance (Ulbricht later claimed virtually to have hurled it back in the officers' faces), Communists in the Preparatory Committee maintained that the FDGB was legitimized by SMA Order No. 2 and that it should inform the Western Allies accordingly, restating its intention to proceed with elections. A letter to this effect was sent 7 September, including an outline of planned electoral procedures. U.S. and British authorities responded by refusing to accede to elections until the Allied Kommandatura of Berlin was supplied with detailed information on the FDGB's statutes, voting regulations, membership figures, etc., to satisfy them of its democratic character—information which, as they undoubtedly knew, the FDGB could not possibly provide in its present state of organization. On 21 September, the Preparatory Committee was forced to postpone elections indefinitely.[47]

The sabotage of the Berlin FDGB elections with the complicity of some Social Democrats no doubt reinforced KPD apprehensions, which began to be apparent at about this time, that its hold over the SPD might be slipping. Since the KPD's rejection of immediate party unification the previous June, the SPD had evolved an independent political strategy that now stressed unification of the Reich, through unification of the SPD throughout the Reich, as a *prerequisite* for socialist unity. While bipartisan cooperation had proven invaluable to the KPD in the land reform, the Communist effort to undermine SPD support in the trade unions was now obviously building new suspicions and resentments against the KPD among some Social Democrats. Moreover, SPD membership was growing fast and its organization was improving. (After the aborted trade union elections, for one thing, the SPD finally began creating its own factory groups.) The specter arose of a united Social Democratic Party grown beyond the restraints of the Soviet Zone's Bloc system, asserting national political leadership on a platform contrary to Communist objectives.[48]

The KPD's inevitable renewed attempt to gain control of the trade unions thus became part of a wider campaign, beginning in September 1945, to consummate a KPD-SPD merger in the Soviet Zone while the KPD still held the political advantage. This campaign grew steadily more intense in the course of that fall and winter, as a series of developments seemed to suggest a "resurgence of reaction" and a weakening of the Communist position: (1) the increasing influence in SPD circles of Kurt Schumacher, based in the British Zone; (2) Social Democratic successes in factory council elections; (3) the humiliating defeat of the Austrian Communist Party, which garnered only 5.4 percent of the vote in free elections in November 1945; and (4) the KPD's own poor showing of 3.5 percent in U.S. Zone municipal elections in January 1946. Both KPD and SMA reacted with particular alarm when the SPD declined to join the Communists on 9 November in commemorating Germany's abortive 1918 revolution, and instead held its own rally on 11 November at which Otto Grotewohl questioned Soviet policy regarding reparations and annexation of German territory. In reference to unifying the socialist parties, Grotewohl went on to declare that such union could only come as an expression of the will of the party membership, and never through "central authorities" or as a result of "external pressure."[49]

The SPD was apparently coming to see its German constituents, rather than the SMA, as the source of its mandate, and to set itself up as an independent spokesman for German interests. In response to this threat, the Soviets abandoned the posture of benevolent neutrality they had hitherto assumed in intra-socialist affairs and threw their own weight solidly behind the KPD push for party unification. Grotewohl's freedom of speech was temporarily curtailed, and top SPD leaders were summoned repeatedly to Karlshorst for discussions. Meanwhile, the KPD began laying plans for a second and better-organized attempt at electing a new FDGB leadership.[50]

On 14 November, Roman Chwalek announced to the Preparatory Committee that the FDGB District Committee of Brandenburg had decided (at KPD initiative) to hold a meeting of union representatives from all over the Soviet Zone. The meeting would convene on 21 November in Potsdam—just beyond the reach of the Western powers in Berlin—to discuss preparations for a zonal FDGB Delegates' Conference and other important trade union questions. Over the objections of Jakob Kaiser, who remained ever wary of moves toward consolidating the FDGB in the Soviet Zone alone, the Berlin Committee decided to send Chwalek and Schlimme as its representatives. Shortly afterward, General Bokov invited top KPD and SPD leaders to SMA headquarters to inform them of the Soviet desire that the Delegates' Conference proceed without delay or "difficulties," and that the two socialist parties cooperate to that end.[51]

At the same time, the KPD leadership was coordinating a new political offensive. In a strategy session on 19 November, Ulbricht informed his fellow Central Committee members bluntly:

> We have failed to consolidate our positions in the factories and trade unions adequately, or to secure them as yet with a strong enough base. . . . We are of the opinion that there must be a decisive turnabout in our party's factory and trade union work.

Before the planned FDGB meeting in Brandenburg, he went on, the party must clarify its own policies and objectives regarding the trade unions. Then it would be in a position to provide proper guidance to its factory cadre on how to shape the decisions of workers' councils and trade union groups. KPD provincial leaders must assemble key Communist functionaries in industry, unions, and administrations to explain party aims to them and enlist their support. Communists must find out from the economic authorities which factories would be important in the 1946 production plan and draw up lists targeting these shops for special party recruitment efforts. Mass shop meetings should be convened to critique trade union policies, and new union representatives elected wherever voting had not been held in the last two months. Party leaders at all levels should assign their best functionaries to trade union work and make every effort to get them elected to influential posts. Above all, the "United Front" must be strengthened: enemies of socialist unity must be rooted out, and close KPD-SPD cooperation sought in addressing the tasks that lay ahead.[52]

The Brandenburg meeting was to set the stage. On 21 November, the FDGB representatives assembled as scheduled and formally resolved to hold elections for a General Delegates' Conference. They also appointed an Organization Committee led by Brandenburg FDGB chairman Franz Moericke to handle political and organizational preparations, and a smaller subcommittee of four Brandenburg and Berlin representatives to draft election rules and a platform for the new zonal FDGB.[53]

The resulting draft of "Principles and Tasks of the Confederation of Free German Trade Unions," released on 5 December, was in the Communist view a "victory over the advocates of reformism." It took a strong stand for unity, "internal democracy" (including election of more new, young leadership cadre), heavy trade union involvement in implementing the regime's economic policies, and education of workers to "solidarity and class consciousness." "The schooling of union members is all the more important," it noted, "because fascist propaganda was able to build upon the influence of bourgeois economic doctrines among the working class." Kaiser naturally objected to such wording, and indicated that it would further endanger hopes of extending the FDGB to the Western zones. As he himself remarked, however, his objections were academic, since the platform draft had already been published in the FDGB organ by the time he saw it. Kaiser and Lemmer had in any case been reduced by now to virtual impotence, made all the more complete because other commitments—occasioned no doubt by the departure of Hermes and Schreiber—began to prevent them from even attending Preparatory Committee sessions. The battle for control of the FDGB was shaping up ever more clearly as a contest between the two socialist parties to decide which of them would speak for a united working class.[54]

The KPD was determined to fight the battle on its own terrain. Having failed to consolidate its hegemony over the provisional FDGB national leadership organ—the Berlin Preparatory Committee—it had once again resorted to its familiar tactic of shifting the focus of the struggle to the provinces, where all the advantages of its unique political position could be brought to bear most effectively.[55]

Following publication of the new FDGB platform draft, the KPD launched an intense campaign to build grass-roots support for its trade union policies and for "political unity of the working class." Communists organized thousands of factory meetings, trade union assemblies, public rallies and convocations of every kind all over the zone, at which they pressed for ratification of resolutions prepared by them in advance. FDGB "schooling" sessions were stepped up and were used as a forum to present (often exclusively) KPD propaganda. Indoctrination efforts were aimed particularly at politically nonaligned workers, who still made up the majority of local union officials, and at the young and female workers who had entered the work-force since the old ADGB's demise. To them, the Communists presented their argument in its simplest and most persuasive form: a divided working class (under SPD leadership) had led to fascism; a united working class (under KPD leadership) would bring democracy, peace, and progress.[56]

The Soviets too were, in the words of a leading GDR account, "energetically supporting the development of the trade unions." About the end of 1945, Moscow sent one of its own leading trade unionists, one Natan Gussinski, to advise German Communists on strategy and help them "defend against anti-trade-union schemes on the part of the imperialist occupation powers."[57]

At the same time, both the Soviets and the KPD were working to neutralize any independent political initiative on the part of the SPD. After autumn 1945, SPD members were being encouraged ever more frequently and emphatically to attend the KPD's own cadre indoctrination sessions, at which "the increasing rapprochement of the two parties was promoted."[58] Local KPD cells, particularly in factories or remote rural areas where Communists predominated, elicited bipartisan resolutions calling for immediate KPD-SPD unification. Reports began to pour into SPD headquarters from every corner of the Soviet

Zone, complaining of a wide variety of KPD and SMA efforts to disrupt Social Democratic activities and corrupt or intimidate—sometimes physically—SPD members. Finally, despite deepening resentment against these tactics, the SPD Central Committee knuckled under. Abandoned to its own devices by the Schumacher faction in the West and in danger of being isolated or rent asunder by the polarization being fomented in the East, the Soviet Zone SPD leadership met with its KPD counterparts on 21-22 December 1945 and agreed in principle to party unification. Details were left to be worked out by a study commission.[59]

For the Communists, however, the battle was still far from won. They regarded the coming FDGB elections as the real test of their power to achieve a united party on KPD terms, with a working class mandate to legitimize it in the face of any potential challenge from a nonconforming wing of the SPD. The KPD therefore turned the trade union elections into a referendum on the unity question, adopting as its slogan, "Vote only for the advocates of unity!"—advocates, that is, of the 21 December agreement. In answer to fears that working class unification in only one zone might lead to permanent division of the Reich, KPD spokesmen replied that the achievement of socialist unity at once wherever possible must be regarded as a prerequisite for a united Reich. If the momentum for party unification were to be lost in waiting for even the most backward areas of Germany to come around, a reactionary resurgence might well thwart working class unity permanently and subject all Germany once again to the power of the great capitalists. Only a single great workers' party could guarantee the future. One speaker at the FDGB Delegates' Conference put it thus:

> We desire the unity of the working class nationwide with all our hearts. But should it not be possible to achieve this in the foreseeable future, we must move

ahead to unite with one another in the Soviet Zone, and the concentrated force of the working class must sweep across the Elbe like an avalanche. . . .[60]

Ulbricht was more succinct: "The reestablishment . . . of Germany's political unity is bound up inseparably with the establishment of the unity of the German working class."[61]

In order to "forge still more firmly the unity in the trade unions," a KPD-SPD pact of 10 December provided that the two parties would agree in advance on candidates and publish common lists showing only the names, and not the party affiliations, of these candidates. As elections got underway in earnest about the beginning of the new year, however, the atmosphere of distrust thickened with mutual allegations of having violated this agreement. The *Deutsche Volkszeitung* published repeated articles charging "enemies of unity" in the SPD with secretly publicizing party membership of candidates or exhorting workers *not* to vote for certain officially sanctioned candidates. The editors attributed these machinations to "foreign"— i.e. Western—influences. Meanwhile the FDGB in Berlin was also receiving letters of complaint from Social Democrats, of which Karl Germer has recently reprinted two examples: one accusing Communists of quietly arranging the nomination of only KPD candidates in the Pankow Metalworkers' Union, and another claiming that lists of nominees sent by a Leipzig union to the state capital in Dresden had subsequently been altered. Leaders of both parties made official pronouncements against such violations, and on 17 January Göring, Chwalek, and Walter signed a "Resolution of the Electoral Examining Commission" stating that wherever written propaganda for the candidates of a particular party had been circulated, the election was to be declared invalid. But the abuses went on regardless.[62]

Nor were these the worst allegations to come out of

this campaign. Wolfgang Leonhard later recounted his "astonished" reaction when, in the crucial Berlin elections in mid-January, he and other KPD functionaries received orders telling them when and where they were to vote: "Some of us—myself included—were even reenrolled quickly in different unions, so as to be able to cast our ballots there." According to Leonhard, Ulbricht telephoned last-minute instructions to KPD offices all over the city that Communists were to ignore the pact with the SPD and vote only for KPD candidates. The result was a clear majority for the KPD. Then, as a magnanimous gesture of working-class solidarity, the Communists offered the SPD "parity" in the Berlin FDGB leadership nonetheless.[63]

While no documentation has emerged either to support or refute Leonhard's account of Ulbricht's treachery (or to indicate the extent to which similar tactics might have been used in the provinces), the fact remains that the KPD, although still numerically the weaker party, gained a decisive majority in both the Berlin and the zonal elections. Of the 833 delegates elected from the provinces to attend the General Delegates' Conference of 9-11 February, 539 were Communists, 252 Social Democrats, 2 Christian Democrats, 1 a Liberal Democrat, and 27 were of undetermined affiliation.[64] In the zonal conference as in that for Berlin, the KPD subsequently accorded the other parties additional seats so as to give an appearance of greater balance, and "not to let so much as an impression arise that a minority might be aspiring to act as a majority." The new FDGB Executive Committee elected at the Conference consisted of nineteen Communists, eighteen Social Democrats, four Christian Democrats and four independent members. Ulbricht was to be the first of three joint chairmen. That the SPD was far from mollified by this "democratic" KPD gesture, however, was shown particularly by one telling incident recorded in the Conference protocol. Dr. Otto Suhr (SPD) made an address criticizing the new FDGB statutes for being too vague about how the economy was to be democratized and, more significantly, for failing to provide a democratic electoral procedure. A reply by the KPD's Hans Jendretsky that the elections just concluded had been a model of democratic procedure drew the following contradiction from Suhr (parentheses indicate interjections from the floor):

> I cannot agree with this judgment on the electoral procedure, and I believe that a great number of other colleagues will share my opinion: if an electoral procedure is that good, one doesn't have to correct the results of it afterward. (Quite right!—Ulbricht: You have been cooperating on the statutes for four months; in those four months you should have had time to put that in writing!—Applause.) I do not know whom Comrade Ulbricht means by "you." If you mean me, you are mistaken; I saw the statutes for the first time yesterday (hear, hear!).[65]

The General Delegates' Conference provided a forum for each of the old trade union factions to plead its own case one last time. In answer to Jendretsky's renewed attack on the Weimar SPD and ADGB leaderships, Bernhard Göring repeated his perennial contention that "in the future we must finally stop speaking about the sins of the past." (Through the lively applause that followed, Jendretsky shouted back an accusation of "General absolution!") Rather more pathetic—and prophetic—was Jakob Kaiser's warning about the dangers of reintroducing factional politics into the trade union movement. Hinting at the threat of Germany's being torn apart by the ideological differences of its occupiers, Kaiser admonished:

> Berlin is the city in which the powers of East and West meet. Berlin is the place in which the struggle goes on for the reshaping not only of Germany, but of Europe. . . . Friends, I am of the opinion that all depends on a

synthesis here: on the harmonization of unity and diversity; on the proper reconciliation of collective power and free development of independent personal volition. . . . Let us seek, comrades, a *German* expression.

Such rhetoric was tolerable precisely because it was now superfluous. This was Kaiser's swan song. The bourgeois faction was clearly reduced to a subordinate role by the FDGB Conference; Kaiser himself, despite his demonstrated popularity with the Berlin union electorate, was conceded only an honorary position as "advisory member" of the new Executive Committee. Eventually he fled to the West.[66]

As for the SPD, its loss of control over the trade unions deprived it of any remaining basis for an independent political existence in the Soviet Zone. A united socialist party under Communist hegemony was now a foregone conclusion. Grotewohl himself presented the FDGB Conference on its final day with a resolution, passed the same morning by the SPD Central Committee, convoking a party convention to decide the unification issue. The FDGB delegates in turn passed their own resolution addressed to the leaderships of both socialist parties, calling for their union before May Day. From the conclusion of the FDGB Conference until mid-April, the trade unions were mobilized in an all-out campaign to achieve this goal. Beginning as early as February, Communists even managed to arrange the unification of some factory party groups and other lower-level organizations ahead of time, thus bringing added pressure to bear on the SPD Central Committee to follow suit quickly or be isolated. Elsewhere, agitators were able to call forth a mounting tide of pro-unity resolutions from local party and trade union groups. East German historians have been unanimous in crediting the FDGB with a major role in bringing about the creation of the Socialist Unity Party on 21-22 April 1946.[67]

In the months following, the FDGB entered a period of

organizational and political consolidation. Industrial union and shop council elections were held in spring and summer 1946 as part of the effort to construct a unified, centralized workers' organization. At the same time, the new SED began a long struggle to subordinate the FDGB completely to its own leadership, over the opposition of the many old ADGB veterans still entrenched in influential positions who resisted party "meddling" in trade union affairs. Again, it was only with the advent of the Cold War in 1947-48 that Soviet and German Communists finally suppressed such opposition completely and transformed the FDGB, like all other institutions, into an outright tool of the regime.[68]

For all the Communists' manifest advantages, there remains the question: how was the KPD, in the space of less than a year, able in effect to swallow up the much older and larger Social Democratic movement in the Soviet Zone? Admittedly the presence of a Soviet Military Administration as ultimate arbiter was crucial. The SMA's influence, however, was far more subtle than is generally supposed. The overt and covert forms of pressure it exerted on the KPD's behalf could not by themselves have produced a viable Socialist Unity Party such as the one that emerged.

At least as important as the SMA's direct influence was the quiet way in which it allowed German Communists to assume, more or less as Soviet agents, de facto responsibility for running the society. Other than the SMA itself, there was in the first months no central administrative authority for the Soviet Zone as a whole. As the only centralized German political organization in existence, and enjoying as it did the complete confidence of the occupying power, the KPD stepped more or less "naturally" into the breach. "Thus a unified economic policy for the entire zone was only achieved," commented Fritz Selbmann, "by means of the Central Committee of the KPD . . . issuing appropriate guidelines to the provinces, either directly or through the district offices of the party."[69] Likewise in political matters, questions of democratization, trade union affairs, and in every other area, the KPD gained recognition as the unofficial spokesman of Soviet policy. The KPD was thus able to establish in fact its claim of being (for better or worse) the primary force, the "motor," behind the physical and moral regeneration of German society. It was the party that got things done.

The Communist Party could not have assumed this leading role had it not been for its own efficient and disciplined apparatus. Some more immediate political advantages which the KPD achieved through its superior organization, aided by the use of Soviet-controlled communications facilities, have already been discussed. Not surprisingly the German Communists, like their Bolshevik mentors, tended to regard this tactical superiority as proof of a superior ideology as well. What *is* surprising, though, is that the Social Democrats, or a majority of them, seem to have accepted this view—that they acquiesced so meekly to being cast in the role of Mensheviks bound for the dustbin of history. True, there were plenty of concrete reasons for the SPD's relative impotence: its own comparatively lax organization, isolation of its leadership, factional and regional rivalries, lack of internal communications channels or independent external news sources, and a politically heterogeneous membership,[70] to name a few. But the willingness of Social Democrats to *acknowledge* the leadership of the KPD and to allow their party, with its large mass constituency, finally to be absorbed intact into a Communist-dominated union, was the result not just of political defeat but of moral default. In this sense it was reminiscent of that psychic paralysis which rendered democratic leaders so helpless against political extremists in the twilight of the Weimar Republic.

The SPD was overwhelmed by a Communist mystique which tangible Communist successes merely intensified. It was the victim of a long process of polarization in which the "right" and "left" poles of the political spectrum had come to be defined respectively as fascism and communism. Since fascism was by common agreement the antithesis of democracy, the conclusion was hard to avoid that communism was democracy's most radical expression. This logic was particularly compelling in the context of Marxist dialectical thought. It seemed moreover to have been borne out by the events of the last three decades. Social Democrats remained burdened, in their own eyes as well as those of the Communists, with the failure of the German revolution and the Weimar Republic; and this "sickly conscience" (as Karl Germer has described it) encumbered them in every aspect of their political dialogue with communism. The KPD on the other hand, though its own Weimar record was far from clean, was invulnerable: its ideology was that of the socialist Soviet Union, the conqueror of fascism and the model for democracy in half of Europe. The very presence of Soviet troops on German soil was a daily reminder that Communists had succeeded as revolutionaries where Social Democrats had failed.

The purely psychological leverage of Communists over Social Democrats was thus immense. While it was greatly mitigated in the Western zones by the moral authority of the Anglo-American powers and of senior SPD leaders like Schumacher, in the Soviet Zone it was relentless, and Communists exploited it to the full. With Soviet support, the KPD portrayed itself as the only consistently Marxist, anti-fascist German party; its every success—no matter how obtained—became further proof that it possessed the mandate of history. Soviet and German Communists worked to persuade individual Social Democrats of the correct ideological conclusions to be drawn from recent historical developments. They intervened in the SPD's internal debates by publicly lauding "progressive" figures and damning by implication their less compliant colleagues, thus playing on the psychological need of many

Social Democrats to be certified as good Marxists after all. Quoting from Siegfried Thomas's official history:

> What Lenin said in 1920 about the correct tactics toward the Social Democratic-reformist parties was still determinative, to a great extent, for the KPD's policy of united action after 1945: "The Communists' proper tactics should consist in *utilising* these vacillations, not ignoring them; utilising them calls for concessions to elements that are turning towards the proletariat—whenever and in the measure that they turn towards the proletariat—in addition to fighting those who turn towards the bourgeoisie."

By these tactics, supplemented where necessary by cruder forms of pressure, the SPD was progressively divided, demoralized, and finally devoured. With it passed the only real potential for political opposition in the Soviet Zone.[71]

The Struggle for Economic and Social Power

The FDGB and the Workers. Parallel with its successful campaign for political power within the trade union movement, the KPD was also working to extend the economic and social influence of the FDGB as an agency of Communist reconstruction policies. This purpose was pursued partly by a series of campaigns and programs intended to demonstrate the progressive new leadership role the unions were now to play in society. "Spontaneous" initiatives for emergency repairs in the cities in spring 1945 were the first manifestation, followed closely by the "Harvest Aid" campaign and the FDGB's championing of land reform. As cold weather approached, the trade unions vigorously supported actions to provide warm quarters, fuel, and clothing for the needy, such as the KPD's Winter Emergency Program and the People's Solidarity movement in Saxony with its highly-publicized "Save the Children" campaign. Such praiseworthy efforts by the unions had tactical as well as humanitarian purposes: they gave the FDGB a good public image, they lent trade union power and prestige to KPD initiatives, and they helped accustom the union rank and file and the society as a whole to united action under KPD leadership. Finally, and by no means least, they provided a high moral justification for FDGB demands on the workers to make ever greater sacrifices to increase production.[72]

The achievement of higher production was to be a prime function of the FDGB. The material basis for socialism and for a strong workers' state had to be created; moreover, the enormous burden of reparations to the USSR had to be borne and somehow surmounted. This, the Communists frankly declared, could only be achieved by the sweat of the workers themselves. The FDGB's other main responsibility was to help the new regime gain centralized control over the economy, by wresting away the power of private entrepreneurs under the pretext of carrying on the workers' old struggle for codetermination in the factories.

Both tasks required a reeducation of the workers; a raising of their consciousness to grasp the new context of the class struggle and to recognize the KPD-led regime as the embodiment of their class interests. The trade unions' status as a traditional workers' organization made them the logical vehicle for this education process and, through the centrally-controlled FDGB structure, natural intermediaries between the regime and the workers. The Communists were not insensitive to the contradictions implicit in the new role of the unions; indeed, Lenin himself had noted them in 1922:

> On the one hand, the [trade unions'] principal method of operation is persuasion, education; on the other hand, as partners in state power, they cannot avoid participating in coercive measures. On the one hand their chief task is to defend the interests of the laboring masses; on the other hand, as partners in state power and build-

ers of the whole economic system in its entirety, they cannot forego the use of pressure.

Under the conditions of the continuing struggle to overcome capitalism and build socialism, the success of the proletarian regime simply had to be the first priority. As in the Soviet Union, so now in Germany, the proletariat had to be united behind its Communist vanguard to attain this end, even at a temporary sacrifice of workers' narrower interests.[73]

A crucial aspect of the Communist campaign for control of the economy thus became the effort to extend and deepen the FDGB's hold on the working class. In this effort the KPD and FDGB had their work cut out. The workers had their own perception of their interests which conflicted with that of the more "class-conscious" KPD elite. Their struggle to revive production and establish workers' control in their factories, while colored by vague ideas of socialism, was aimed primarily at immediate improvement of their own material conditions. Where politics played a concrete role, the issues were elementary: to drive out the bosses and Nazi bullies and to seize direct control of the means of earning a livelihood. Workers therefore resisted the interference of the regime; its attempts to purge managers whom they chose to retain, to appoint trustees to run their factories, and to suppress the "compensation" or barter system which was often their only source of needed goods. They were generally not interested in sacrificing themselves for the good of society, as the Nazis too had called upon them to do for years, and still less in expiating their sins by repaying Germany's fearful debt to the Soviet Union. They were interested in potatoes and coal to feed and warm their families.

The regime thus found itself faced with an apparent paradox. On the one hand the workers behaved, where their tangible interests were at stake, like models of revolutionary zeal. At the great Zeiss optical instruments factory in Jena, for instance, where U.S. occupiers had hitherto enforced a political and economic standstill, the entry of Soviet troops was greeted with a flurry of reconstruction efforts:

> In the normalization of economic life the workforce's achievements were . . . exemplary. With greatest élan, Zeiss workers dug free the instruments of production, rescued entire installations from the rubble and restored them to working order, so as to secure the factory for peacetime production.

On the other hand, Communists were forced to recognize the existence of widespread "ideological confusion," manifested as apathy or even overt opposition to the regime's economic policies:

> The attitude toward overtime and shift work was negative. No incentive existed to earn more money, since this couldn't be used to make any direct improvement in the low living standard. "Hoarding trips" in search of food and fuel were the order of the day, and had an unhealthy effect on factory morale.[74]

Soviet troops had to be called in at Zeiss to suppress passive resistance against production for reparations. Shop stewards there went to great lengths to protect "the most heavily incriminated corporate leaders and their closest confidants" from Communist purges. At AEG and Siemens plants in Berlin, Communist FDGB representatives met with vehement worker opposition against their attempts to incite a split with the parent companies. At Siemens this opposition spilled over into a critique of KPD and Soviet economic policy in general, led by lower-level FDGB functionaries. How, they demanded, was a single component factory of an economic complex to function as an independent unit? How would it secure credit, or raw materials from the West? What was the point of transferring factories to public ownership with no attempt to institute socialism? The result would merely be state capitalism—in other words, the Soviet system, which had done little to improve the lot of workers in Russia. How indeed, was the Soviet system better than the Western one, since both led to war? And how was Soviet imperialism better than Anglo-American imperialism? The benefits of the Soviet system were none too evident in Germany: the land reform had not noticeably increased the food supply in the East, while conditions in the West were not as bad as the Soviet Zone newspapers claimed.[75]

Confronted with such appalling attitudes, Communists concluded that the workers had no appreciation for the exigencies of creating a democratic economy—for the hard work and radical restructuring that were needed. Rather, workers seemed to think in terms either of the old economic system, or of an ideal socialist order which they expected to achieve immediately. The need for a strong guiding hand in the form of class-conscious trade unions was painfully clear. Communists attributed the workers' faulty consciousness largely to the confusion wrought by fascism, and to the dilution of the prewar workforce with large numbers of nonproletarians forced into the factories during the war and fascists purged from high places after the war. Conservative technicians were another problem, since the regime had reluctantly concluded that it could not afford to fire many politically obnoxious experts whose skills were indispensable, although their ideological influence was pernicious. Some of the greatest difficulties, however, arose from old proletarians whose ideas of workers' democracy differed from those of the KPD. It was mainly this group that provided the leadership for the spontaneous factory committees—the chief vehicle of expression for the workers' own interpretation of their interests, and hence the chief obstacle to the FDGB.[76]

As with the Antifa Committees, KPD planners had originally projected an important role for workers' committees, although they had always intended the trade unions to be the party's main "transmission belt" to the masses. The KPD's February 1945 program saw a resurgent shop councils movement, similar to that which had followed World War I, as the economic backbone of the Antifa or "People's Committees"; the "controlling organs of the movement" upon which economic authorities would depend to implement their policies in both public and private enterprises. The Communists' pessimistic reassessment of the workers' revolutionary consciousness toward the end of the war, however, and their consequent greater emphasis on revolution from above as documented in the new guidelines of 5 April 1945, affected their position regarding the shop councils as well as the People's Committees. These later guidelines stated only that the factory committees of the workers were to be subordinate to the economic sections of the new administrations: "They are charged with increasing production and securing labor discipline, conducting anti-fascist reeducation of the work force, and concluding agreements on working conditions in accordance with the general instructions of the municipal administration. . . ." As soon as possible, local trade union groups were to be founded.[77]

The vigor of the workers' committees after the war was thus something of an embarrassment to the KPD. On the one hand, the party welcomed the committees' spontaneous anti-fascism and their push for codetermination, and sought to make the most of them to weaken private entrepreneurs. Workers generally expected a full restoration of their Weimar rights of participation in factory management, and with Communist encouragement often demanded a good deal more. On the other hand, Communist leaders feared the independent ideological and economic influence of the committees, which in their view threatened to seduce workers away from the KPD's rigorous program and into a short-sighted, egoistic syndicalism. By promoting the interests of factory workers as a separate group, the committees risked creating frictions within the alliance of social groups upon which Communists based their strategy for working class leadership of society. By perpetuating a barter system, they obstructed development of an orderly economy and central planning. Finally, as truly popular organs they were a potential rallying point for anti-Soviet resentments, particularly over reparations and dismantling.[78]

For a brief time as the FDGB was being established, the KPD seems to have considered abolishing the workers' committees outright as it had the Antifa committees. In early July 1945 the *Deutsche Volkszeitung* announced:

> As soon as a factory trade union leadership has been constituted, it takes the place of the preexisting shop councils or the anti-fascist factory committee. Since there is still no legal basis for the activity of shop councils, the only organs of the workforce in the factory are the trade unions' factory leadership bodies.[79]

The workers' committees were not so easily disposed of, however. They were in de facto control of many factories, and unlike the Antifas they enjoyed a strong basis of popular support in precisely the social group which the KPD could least afford to alienate. Moreover, their emphasis on immediate improvements in workers' conditions found considerable resonance in "reformist" SPD circles. An overt Communist attack on the committees could thus have backfired politically against the KPD. Instead, the Communist leadership had to resign itself to a slower process of easing out spontaneous workers' committees in favor of elected shop councils which, it hoped, could be coopted into the FDGB system.

During the summer of 1945 the KPD and FDGB sought to define the proper role of these shop councils. They were to be the representative organs of the entire workforce in each factory and hence the FDGB's link to the broad mass of workers, including nonunion members. Within their respective shops they were responsible for propagating anti-fascist ideology, promoting the transition to peace-time production, and protecting the rights of workers vis-à-vis management. As the instruments of workers' co-determination, they would negotiate on equal terms with management over the details of pay, working conditions, and factory regulations, and would help to enforce the norms agreed upon. The overall framework for such negotiations, however—the establishment of standard pay scales and conditions of labor for an entire industry—was left to the trade unions. In general, the FDGB was to be the workers' representative to the society at large.[80]

The KPD's ultimate aim was to reverse the *direction* of the councils' representative function, so that rather than reflecting existing worker attitudes, they would instead transmit the regime's policies downward to the workers and shape worker attitudes to conform with these. This aim became increasingly clear after the Potsdam conference, as the Communist transformation program got underway in earnest. The KPD launched an attack on the economic power of large corporations, which included an intensified drive for workers' codetermination. Shop councils were to be established in all enterprises where they did not yet exist and to assume a powerful role as adversaries of the great capitalists—all, however, "under the leadership of a *single* force, the united Confederation of Free German Trade Unions" (original italics). FDGB propaganda warned that the councils could only fulfill their function as instruments of working-class power if they acted as "organs of the trade unions," rather than waging isolated struggles for petty reforms as in Weimar times. Trade union functionaries, in turn, were reminded that the source of their power was in the factories. They must therefore take an active role in shop council affairs, sitting in as advisors in worker-management negotiations, providing ideological guidance for anti-fascist reeducation, and even nominating candidates to serve on the councils. According to Ulbricht, "All important questions are to be discussed with the factory union leadership."[81]

Above all, the FDGB was to prepare workers and their councils for new responsibilities as the ultimate executors of a planned economy:

> In the final analysis, all economic plans will be realized in the factory; the tempo at which a plan is fulfilled or surpassed will depend on the shop council. . . . A comprehensive schooling of council members is necessary, in order to provide them with the knowledge they will need to direct and execute economic tasks.[82]

The shop councils would share responsibility with union leaders for persuading the workers to use their powers of codetermination to promote higher production, not least of all as a means to a higher living standard for themselves. To set an example, the FDGB leadership called on the various industrial unions in August 1945 to begin setting up "model factories." In a four-week campaign, union representatives were to convene FDGB functionaries in a few selected shops and agree with them on a production plan. The cooperation of the shop council was to be secured, the plan submitted to an assembly of workers for "discussion and acceptance," and the details of implementation worked out with management. Finally, "the creation of such a model must then be exhaustively publicized through special circulars, meetings, and the press, as an example showing the way for others."[83]

On 10 October, Thuringia passed a new Shop Councils Act in an attempt to fix the councils' prescribed new role in law. Included was a list of "Responsibilities and Rights of Shop Councils" drawn up by the FDGB.[84] The Thuringian law, too, became a model of sorts, as the FDGB pushed for similar legislation in every province of the Soviet Zone. A few weeks later, the FDGB also arranged for general shop council elections in conjunction with the trade unions' own elections for their zonal Delegates' Conference. According to an FDGB pamphlet, "The voting usually proceeded in such a way that the factory trade union group made a series of nominations to the workers, the workers added some names, and from these nominations the workers elected the shop council by direct secret ballot." Union functionaries also took charge of counting the ballots. In the course of these elections, the last of the spontaneous workers' committees were eliminated. Needless to say, the FDGB was well represented in the shop councils that succeeded them.[85]

By the beginning of the first annual economic plan in 1946, the shop councils seemed to be in harness and ready to pull their share of the load. It was a large share indeed. Councils were first consulted for information on plant capacities and resources, and for recommendations as to what goods they could best produce. In cooperation with a factory "production committee" of workers, technicians, and supervisors, they were then to coordinate worker efforts to reach each factory's assigned production target. It was their task to inspire workers with enthusiasm and a sense of joint responsibility for plan fulfillment through open discussions of goals and problems. In the face of an Allied Control Council ruling establishing a standard eight-hour day, the regime prevailed on shop councils to support voluntary overtime work and to specify in public pronouncements that this extra time was being donated to the community. "The additional labor," noted Ulbricht, "thus acquires a political character." The SMA went still further and began organizing Soviet-style production competitions, led by the FDGB and the councils of the respective factories or mines. Besides boosting production, the shop councils were called upon to help enforce the regime's wage and price policies, especially by watching their factory owner's books to be sure that the entrepreneurs were not inflating prices by overestimating costs. The councils were also exhorted to join in FDGB and administration efforts "to see to it that the goods produced by the workers . . . reach the hands of consumers rather than becoming, as presently happens, objects of black-marketeering."[86]

The confidence placed in the councils was only apparent, however; in fact they never really became satisfactory instruments of the regime. They were rooted in the factories and they continued, despite all, to express the attitudes of the workers who composed them—attitudes that remained grossly at variance with the KPD's idea of class consciousness. Behind a smoke screen of official optimism, Communists lamented the average worker's intractability:

> He is not used to managing things as we would like him to do. But we speak to this worker about economic planning; we tell him: "You must organize this and that in the factories! Try to arrange it thus and so!" The worker responds: "Why me? We have an employer over us; I'm certainly not the one in the shop to recommend anything or give people advice. . . ."[87]

This from workers who on their own a few months earlier had been rebuilding factories from ruins, barehanded! Moreover, far from helping to suppress the black market, shop councils continued to feed it through extensive "compensation" trading. Instead of battling capitalist entrepreneurs, many councils were cooperating with them for mutual profit. In sum, the workers and their councils remained endlessly resourceful about their own immediate interests, but indifferent toward the grand schemes of a self-styled workers' government put in power by a foreign occupier.[88]

Therefore, while the Communists continued trying to wrest economic power from private capitalists in the name of the workers and with maximum involvement of workers in the struggle, they also persisted in trying to limit the autonomous expression of worker power through the shop councils. Efforts to supervise the councils through the trade unions continued and were intensified in spring 1946 after the consolidation of Communist control over the FDGB, and in response to a new Shop Councils Act promulgated by the Allied Control Council in April. On the one hand, the FDGB expressed disappointment at the relatively modest powers the new law granted to the councils as opposed to management. It urged workers to interpret the law as broadly as possible, using the councils' prescribed right to negotiate new contracts with management as a weapon with which to extract maximum concessions on codetermination. Eventually the FDGB and SED mounted a major offensive to force such contracts on all factory managements during the summer of 1946. Every form of pressure was used, including some strikes and in rare instances even direct Soviet intervention, to win "full codetermination" for the councils. On the other hand, however, the FDGB maintained that the new law clearly made shop councils mere auxiliaries of the unions, since it specified that they were to perform their duties "in cooperation with the recognized trade unions." From this vague language, the FDGB concluded that "the shop councilman of today is practically a functionary of the trade union, even if he is elected by all the workers."[89]

"Codetermination" thus became in effect a catchword for greater centralized control by the regime. Nor were workers to go beyond codetermination and seek to run an enterprise on their own. For this responsibility the regime considered them neither ideologically nor technically qualified, a view which it saw as borne out in the sometimes disastrous results of workers' attempts to meddle in complicated affairs of industrial management. The FDGB carefully circumscribed the workers' proper purview:

Neither the shop council in a factory, nor the trade unions in the scope of a larger economic unit, are to assume the functions of economic management. That is what the plant managers and administrative organs are there for.[90]

Rather, the workers' organizations were to act as a check on the managers, helping to determine the "general direction of the economy" and to "secure fulfillment of specific tasks" in accordance with KPD policy. At best, they were vouchsafed a decisive role in selecting new managers. Where shop councils had already succeeded in establishing direct workers' control, the regime began imposing its own authority after mid-1946. In a speech some two years later, Communist economic expert Fritz Selbmann expressed his party's views on the subject with remarkable candor:

> We had a few experimental attempts in Saxony in 1945 and 1946 to socialize on the basis of the old utopian socialists of the early 19th century. I am thinking of the founding of production cooperatives through the takeover as workers' property of businesses owned by Nazi criminals. . . . Don't think it would not have been possible to let a wave of such socialization experiments sweep over the land. Simply to "socialize" the factories . . . in this way would not have been difficult. But because it is wrong and misleading and because we knew that it does not promote development or bring us forward, because we knew how stupid these experiments are and that they work out to the detriment of the experiments themselves, we therefore liquidated such attempts quickly and quietly.[91]

The problem with the shop councils was that they represented an approach to proletarian revolution that Leninism had long since repudiated. At issue was the old question of mass spontaneity versus the leading role of the Party. Insofar as the shop councils were consciously socialist, their idea of socialism was a simple one: control of the means of production by the workers. By seizing power for themselves in the factories, they felt they had realized this condition—and a good many Social Democrats tended to agree! The Communists saw the matter as far more complex, however. From both the Russian and German revolutionary experiences they had acquired the conviction that capitalism was a clever and resilient enemy whose defeat required not only the force of the working class, but also the political skill and determination that only a schooled Marxist elite could provide. Left to themselves, the workers would not destroy the roots of capitalist power, nor would they build a strong state of their own. Rather, they would dissipate their energies in token reforms and meaningless gestures, and eventually they would succumb. The KPD, as a Leninist party, saw itself called to save the workers from their own ignorance: to thwart their impulse to dabble prematurely with (and thus discredit) the forms of socialism; and to lead them instead through the arduous process of creating the social, economic, and ideological foundations upon which true socialism must stand.[92]

The German workers' resistance to this unwanted tutelage was unorganized and inarticulate—under the circumstances it could hardly have been anything else—but it was nonetheless obstinate, as reflected in FDGB records prior to 1948. Shop council elections organized by the unions in July 1946 were a disappointment: while the number of councils increased,[93] the workers remained apathetic to the FDGB's political message ("Down with the big capitalists, up with production!"). Indeed, the relative weakness of the unions in the factories, on which this apathy was partly blamed, was aggravated by the FDGB's policy of electing its own best cadre to shop council posts: "The factory trade union groups thereby often became appendages of the shop councils. . . ." Union officials called for greater speed in creating local FDGB departments for shop council affairs, in order to head off "unhealthy tendencies toward the development of a separate

shop councils movement, independent of the trade unions."
FDGB reports and correspondence complained continually of the councils' general failure to participate in drawing up factory production plans, or even to find out what these plans contained. Therefore no factory work programs were being drafted, no worker supervision of price calculations was taking place, and no mass discussions of production goals were being held in most factories. Shop councils were only rarely supporting the Communists' drive to secure new contracts guaranteeing codetermination, even when sample contract formats were supplied by the FDGB. On the other hand, as noted in one report from Mecklenburg in early 1947, "Compensation trading expanded to such an extent that the use of force became necessary; even shop councilmen were jailed."[94]

As the SED regime extended its control over the economy, the "shop-egoism" of the councils became an ever greater obstacle to its policies. Gradually the trade unions whittled away council powers and prerogatives. Finally long-range central planning began to be both feasible and necessary, and the disruptive influence of the councils could no longer be tolerated. In late 1948, as a comprehensive planning system was being installed, the shop councils were abolished and their functions turned over completely to the FDGB. Like the old farmers' cooperatives, they were institutions of the old order and proved unadaptable to the demands of the new.[95]

The FDGB Role in Civil Administration. The guiding hand of the FDGB made itself felt not only among the workers, but throughout the economy and the society. As the representative organs of the working class, the unions had a responsibility, for both ideological and practical reasons, to participate in administering the new regime. They would thereby influence the class character of government institutions, demonstrate the leadership of the proletariat, and accustom workers to handling the instruments of power. They would also be in a position to fulfill their "transmission belt" function more effectively, conveying economic data upward to the decision-makers and economic policies downward to the factories and workplaces.

The KPD's 1944 Action Program had called for new "popular organs" to be created alongside traditional administrative bodies in order "to monitor and secure the implementation of laws passed and measures taken, and to draw the mass of the people into active participation in public life." In the first period of occupation, trade union groups cooperated with the Anti-Fascist Bloc parties in various local arrangements to advise and support the new administrations. By late 1945, such informal arrangements were already being superseded in many cities by formal advisory councils composed mainly of representatives of the parties and trade unions, but including as well other "mass organizations" such as the VdgB, Free German Youth (FDJ), and Women's Committees. During 1946 the SED made such councils mandatory for all levels of government. It was the particular province of the FDGB to advise the administrations on matters of social insurance, worker protection, and personnel policy; questions in which the unions were given a substantial voice. In Saxony, for instance, trade unions could boast by early 1946 that they were consulted by the state administration in all hiring decisions, and that no social legislation could be passed without their prior approval.[96]

In addition, the FDGB achieved significant influence through its role as a prime source of reliable cadre to staff civil service positions left vacant by anti-Nazi purges. In spring and summer of 1945, Soviet commanders appointed many trade union veterans as mayors, rural district presidents, and other top officials. As the new regime then began to take shape after the Potsdam agreement, the FDGB was called upon to recommend workers to serve as teachers, judges, police officials, etc., and also to nominate working-class candidates for admission to universities and technical schools. Part of the FDGB's task was to prepare workers for such responsibilities by teaching them necessary job skills and educating them to view all state institutions "correctly" as instruments of class power. Political qualifications were paramount. According to Ulbricht, the unions must help insure that administrative organs were staffed "with men who stand for the unification of the working class and the unification of antifascist, democratic forces."[97]

Naturally the FDGB's most important contribution was in the economic organs. As official historians Griep and Steinbrecher have observed,

> The trade unions had the most comprehensive view of the production process, and could thus effectively support the efforts of state and economic organs to restart production and initiate economic reconstruction. It was particularly crucial that the mass of the working class be drawn into a sense of shared responsibility. . . .

The FDGB was supposed to act as a link between workers and administrators, guaranteeing the former their rightful voice in economic planning and the latter the sympathy and support of the labor force. In practice, of course, it gained the regime added leverage over both: on the one hand as a political check on unreliable bourgeois economic experts in the administrations, and on the other as an instrument for implementing Communist economic policies in the field. The FDGB called upon its lower-level directorates to supply needed information on the economic structure and potentials of their respective districts for use by planning authorities. FDGB representatives then collaborated in the actual planning process through joint "work committees" set up with economic officials at all levels of government, and through their individual positions in various administrative bodies. They also helped found and run local and provincial agencies to control prices and combat the black market. Finally, as discussed above, the unions strove to mobilize the workers as agents of the regime in the factories, who would use their new powers of codetermination to translate policy into action, plan into production.[98]

The overall goal was to create a new mechanism of economic coordination to supplant that of capitalism—the powerful cartels and employers' associations. This was all the more important since the capitalists themselves could not for the moment be dispensed with. Rather, they too had to be coordinated into the system in some innocuous form that put their skills at the service of the regime. Here again, the FDGB was to prove a valuable instrument of Communist control.

THE CHAMBERS OF INDUSTRY AND COMMERCE AND THE CHAMBERS OF HANDICRAFTS

Communist policy toward associations of entrepreneurs at first seemed somewhat ambiguous. While the SMA quickly abolished the existing employers' associations and Economic Chambers as fascist institutions, the KPD and the new administrations began calling at the same time for a maximum of independent initiative by private entrepreneurs to restart the economy. President Rudolf Paul of Thuringia told a convention of businessmen on 28 July that free enterprise "should take over one hundred percent. That is also the standpoint of the Soviet Military Administration." Given the general propensity to interpret democratization as more or less a restoration of Weimar institutions—an interpretation that proved correct in the Western zones—it is hardly surprising that the entrepreneurs felt free to reestablish their familiar employers' associations as they had known them under the Republic. That they often did so in good faith was indicated by the fact that several such associations applied for official recognition. Indeed, one section of the Thuringian state

administration was itself sufficiently confused about Soviet policy that it actively encouraged the foundation of
employers' associations throughout July and August 1945,
regarding them as the logical counterparts to the new
trade unions in contract negotiations. The LDP and CDU
tended to share this view. The Communists, however,
saw the employers' associations as attempts by capitalists
to reconstruct *their* machinery of economic dominion,
generally in deliberate defiance of Soviet prohibitions. After
a persistent struggle, they succeeded in stamping them
out by the middle of 1946.[99]

The old Chambers of Commerce, on the other hand,
were to be restored. Unlike the employers' associations,
which had arisen in the late nineteenth century as organs
to concentrate the economic and political power of industrialists vis-à-vis organized labor nationwide, these
Chambers were older and relatively apolitical organizations of local businessmen. Their traditional concern had
been to promote and regulate local trade and manufacturing, in cooperation with government and often in a
semi-official capacity. They therefore had some potential
as tools for coordinating the entrepreneurs into the economic development program of the new regime.

To replace the centrally-directed Economic Chambers
instated by the Nazis, then, the KPD called for new "independent" Chambers of Industry and Commerce (Indus-
trie- und Handelskammern, or IHK), which it quickly put
to work in the effort for economic revival. In summer and
fall 1945, the new Chambers sponsored industrial exhi-
bitions all over the Soviet Zone to demonstrate methods
by which local manufacturers could resume peacetime
production using salvaged war materiel and other scrap.
These fairs also served to establish new business contacts
or reestablish old ones. Additionally, the IHK helped the
administrations to mitigate the worst disruptions of war
and dismantling, as indicated by the following directive
issued in Saxony-Anhalt:

The provincial administration shall determine, on the recommendation of the Chamber of Industry and Commerce, which firms shall have to render certain material assistance to dismantled plants for the purpose of restoring them to production. This will involve primarily delivery of machines and materials. If necessary, the Chamber of Industry and Commerce can direct that production be resumed temporarily in underutilized space at other plants.[100]

Yet the IHK were a difficult tool to manage, particularly at the beginning. In western Mecklenburg (first occupied by Anglo-American troops), Chambers of Commerce took it upon themselves to appoint trustees for abandoned industries in order to preclude similar action by public authorities. The Chamber in Schwerin, which for a while controlled a larger staff than the provincial Economic Department, allegedly made no effort to aid in reconstruction and even engaged in "open sabotage." By the end of summer 1945, the IHK were still strictly organizations of local capitalists who could be relied on to cooperate with the regime only when it was manifestly in their interest to do so. This basis for cooperation was bound to become inadequate once the Communists began seriously to implement their own economic policies.[101]

After Potsdam, the Communists therefore undertook a thorough reorganization of the Chambers of Industry and Commerce. The most important aspect of this reorganization had already been set forth in KPD policy guidelines issued the previous June: in future, IHK boards of directors were to be composed equally of representatives of business, the FDGB, and the administrations. The president of each provincial Chamber was appointed by the provincial administration and was, like most of his counterparts at the county level, a full-time civil servant. By late 1946 the SED could claim, "All presidents of Chambers of Industry and Commerce are men who have come out of the labor movement." The expenses of the Chambers, however, were borne by the entrepreneurs through a special fee assessed on all of them.[102]

The responsibilities of the new IHK included helping the administrations to draw up and implement the 1946 economic plan. They were called upon to supply information and advice needed for setting production schedules, distributing raw materials, and fixing prices; and were expected to provide technical or even financial help to individual businesses in their districts. They had authority to examine the books and inspect the products of their member firms and to issue regulations governing the production process. Smaller firms were often coordinated into the economic plan through production and distribution contracts with the IHK. The Chambers also served as a forum for labor-management negotiations, with the labor departments of the administrations acting as the final arbiters in case of a deadlock. Finally, like all Soviet Zone economic organs, the IHK had political responsibilities as well: "educating those involved in the economy to think and act democratically." This was a tall order for organizations made up largely of men who until recently had been executing the policies of the Third Reich. Moreover, the Chambers themselves were put in charge of systematically purging their own ranks by setting up denazification committees to rid business and industry of political undesirables, under the supervision of the provincial administrations.[103]

It was nonetheless impossible to transform the Chambers of Industry and Commerce overnight into a mere "extended arm of the provincial governments" (to borrow the FDGB's sanguine description). An economic official of Saxony, where the IHK system was best developed, reported in early 1946 that the Chambers there had hitherto been unable to play a large part in the production process because until their reorganization they had still been composed of "95 percent Nazis." Although KPD,

SPD and trade union members were taking control of the top offices and working to bring the IHK as a whole into line with administration policies, there were not enough reliable people to infiltrate the entire system. Thus in February 1947 the central FDGB leadership was still admonishing that the committees of the IHK for various trades

> should be staffed with appropriate experts and with representatives of the FDGB. This is not yet the case, however. In Saxony wherever state-level committees and subcommittees have so far been created they consist entirely of industrialists, and hence of employers.

Another FDGB circular later that year warned,

> It must be avoided that, due to the scarcity of [FDGB] functionaries, the entrepreneurs bring their shop councilmen along to the trade committee conferences.[104]

Not only was the new three-way parity system imperfectly implemented, but in general the transition to new organizational forms was slow, uneven, and confused. In Magdeburg and Dessau the IHK remained joined to artisans' organizations in structures resembling the old Economic Chambers. In Berlin, the Allied Kommandatura delayed introduction of the Soviet Zone reforms. Other isolated IHK remained independent of their provincial Chambers. These and other anomalies, and the "class confrontations" that accompanied them, continued to plague the IHK and to prevent their becoming completely responsive to the policies of the SED regime until 1948, when the general crackdown brought another and more radical reorganization.[105]

The artisans' organizations developed along similar lines. Small craftsmen were still vitally important to the economy, especially in the early postwar period when larger and more complex industries were crippled by war damage and dismantling. Farmers depended on the village smithy to patch up their dilapidated equipment and keep it working. After the land reform, the need to set up thousands of new independent farmsteads created an insatiable demand for carpenters, blacksmiths, and wheelwrights. In cities, artisans were needed to repair buildings and to mend or replace all kinds of tools, machinery, and manufactured goods. Part of the FDGB's "Immediate Program" for Thuringia, for instance, was to convert the cottage industries of the Thuringian Forest "from hollow glass to flat glass" and "from toys to household articles." In 1946, Mecklenburg had roughly 70,000 artisans employed as opposed to 20,000 factory workers, while even industrial Berlin had about an equal number of both.[106]

Politically, the artisans played an important part in the KPD's scheme of class alliances. Marxist theory categorized them along with small farmers and shopkeepers as part of the petty bourgeoisie. This class, while lacking the consciousness and the will to wage a consistent struggle of its own against the great capitalists, was considered nonetheless to be democratically inclined and could be expected to follow the proletariat once the latter had established its social leadership. Thus, while the KPD hoped at best to neutralize the small and middle entrepreneurs politically, it courted the active support of the artisans. Pointing to the vast numbers of independent craftsmen who had been ruined in Hitler's war economy, Communist spokesmen reassured artisans that their businesses would be helped rather than hurt by KPD economic reforms. Far from seeking to expropriate them, the KPD promised to secure their continued existence as an integral part of the national economy—provided, of course, that they were not active fascists.[107]

The problem was that so many were indeed fascists: in Saxony-Anhalt, for example, 27 percent of artisans had been Nazi party members, and the figure touched 90 percent in some trades. The powerful master craftsmen were particularly implicated. As much as any socio-economic group, the artisans required a new organization for their economic control and political reeducation. The abolition of the Nazi artisans' associations and reinstatement of the old guild system in the first months proved an inadequate measure, even when the guilds were bound together in provincial associations under handpicked chairmen. Attempts to grant the FDGB "parity" in them also had little effect. Finally, the guilds were abandoned altogether. On 27 May, 1946, SMA Order No. 161 recognized the reconstructed Chambers of Handicrafts as the artisans' sole economic representatives and specified an organizational form for them like that of the Chambers of Industry and Commerce, with trade union and government representatives to counterbalance the political influence of the master craftsmen. All independent artisans were to be members.[108]

Like the IHK, the Chambers of Handicrafts were to act both as advisors and "extended arms" of the provincial planning authorities, and as a source of expert technical assistance to their constituents. Their voice in the distribution of raw materials gave them, of course, a tremendous economic weapon with which to compel the cooperation of individual producers. When an individual shop was incapable (for whatever reason) of surviving independently, the Chamber was responsible for incorporating it into an artisans' cooperative. The regime promoted these coops—and indeed forced them on many— as one more means by which to assimilate small craftsmen into the economic planning system, citing the need to rationalize artisan production and direct it to meeting present priorities. "The artisans," one official writer warned, "can only take advantage of their chance for a part in the export business and in large contracts if they overcome their often still active individualistic—not to say idiosyncratic—spirit.[109]

The role of the trade unions in these organizations was, according to the FDGB, to steer the further development of the handicrafts in such a way that they can fulfill their exceptionally important assignment in supplying the needs of the people. There must be no matter of importance to the whole economy which is resolved by artisans without the cooperation of the trade unions.[110]

Guided by the FDGB, the artisans' Chambers and their subordinate coops were to serve as an instrument for establishing unified control over handicraft industries without recourse to "an overly-bureaucratic direction of each separate little shop," of which the administrations would in any case not yet have been capable. The FDGB of course also bore major responsibility for political reorientation of the artisans themselves through ideological schooling and a purge of the worst fascists among them.[111]

Here as elsewhere, however, there were limits to what the FDGB could accomplish in a short time. Artisans of all political persuasions resented trade union interference in and efforts to politicize their organizations, and they cooperated to minimize the influence of FDGB appointees. A group of FDGB functionaries visiting Halle in autumn 1946 noted, "We observe here and there that the artisans are gathering in special meetings without trade union representatives, to form a sort of faction." Trade unionists, for their part, lacked understanding or interest for the artisans' problems and often skipped meetings of their own accord—the extra duty was, after all, unpaid. Nor was the FDGB's position enhanced by the habit some of its functionaries had of describing artisans as all a pack of reactionaries anyway, who were bound to be expropriated sooner or later. FDGB efforts to recruit members among the artisans themselves met with slight success, and none outside of the larger shops and cooperatives. Thus, despite some ten thousand trade unionists assigned to oversee artisans' organizations, the FDGB could only extend its influence in these gradually, partly by training

reliable young journeymen to replace older master craftsmen in positions of power. In an article advocating more
advanced technical training for young artisans, the
Deutsche Volkszeitung noted:

> The selection of master craftsmen must be made with
> great care, both in regard to technical qualifications and
> from the viewpoint of political attitude. We must guar-
> antee ourselves a new generation of competent, pro-
> gressive, and democratically-minded artisans.[112]

THE BEGINNINGS OF ECONOMIC PLANNING

Shaky as its new institutions of social and economic control were in the first months, the Communist regime still
lost no time, after the interregnum of summer 1945, in
introducing the first measures for central economic planning. It justified these measures publicly as necessary to
eliminate waste and duplication and to restore an orderly
national economy. One official wrote:

> The development of each individual's initiative, with-
> out central direction, was a matter of primary urgency
> in the months after the collapse. . . . The restoration of
> normal economic conditions of production, however,
> requires systematic planning and direction of produc-
> tion.[113]

Such practical considerations led to temporary economic
controls in the Western zones as well. Yet the Soviet Zone
measures were not intended to be temporary (despite KPD
statements to the contrary), nor were they motivated purely
by practical considerations. The KPD's own internal policy guidelines of 1944-45 called for "direction and control
of the economy by the organs of the democratic state in
close cooperation with the shop councils and trade unions"
as an integral part of democratization. Politically the
Communists saw no other alternative: to restore eco-

nomic order on the basis of the capitalist market mechanism meant restoring power to the capitalists themselves, and hence ultimately to the fascists. While there
could be no question of a full-scale socialist economy for
the time being, the new machinery of working class economic control nevertheless had to begin functioning immediately if it was ever to function at all.[114]

As in the Soviet-occupied countries of Eastern Europe,
so in East Germany efforts at economic planning began
with short-range, partial plans designed to secure reliable
production of key goods. During summer 1945 the provincial administrations were already setting up offices to
organize food production and rationing and, along with
the FDGB, to promote and coordinate industrial recovery.
Some directed production occurred in the form of Soviet
levies on particular factories. KPD/FDGB emergency programs also led to short-range production goals being established "spontaneously" in a few plants, as in the 1945
harvest campaign. Meanwhile, Soviet and German authorities were building up the German Central Administrations which would eventually function, under SMA
supervision, as economic coordinating agencies for the
entire zone. By 1 October the regime felt ready to introduce a series of production plans for the last quarter of
1945, still based on Soviet directives, stipulating the quantities of certain critical products such as coal, energy, glass,
and building materials to be delivered by each specified
producer.[115]

Even as these preliminary plans were being implemented, the regime was already gearing up for a far more
comprehensive undertaking. SMA Order No. 103 of 19
October 1945 called upon the German administrations to
present for Soviet approval by the beginning of December
a draft plan for the year 1946, broken down by quarters
and covering all sectors of the economy. Working independently of each other but with extensive SMA supervision, the five provincial administrations began by es-

timating their requirements in the way of consumer goods, capital investment, and necessary repairs for the coming year. At the same time they drew up lists of all industrial enterprises in their jurisdictions, and sent out questionnaires to these calling on them to provide information on their potential output in 1946 and on the raw materials they would need to achieve it. On the basis of these statistics, and with the help of the FDGB and its client organizations, each province then drafted its own industrial plan. Similar projections were drawn up for the fuel and transport industries and for agriculture. Finally the Central Administrations compiled the provincial plans, also with FDGB help, into an overall Soviet Zone plan for submission to SMA headquarters. The Soviet authorities, for their part, reviewed the documents in draft form, compared them with data collected through SMA channels, made corrections or ordered revisions as they saw fit, and eventually issued production directives to implement the finished plans.[116]

The 1946 plan remained limited in scope. The new economic officials were not yet experienced enough, nor was the economy itself functioning smoothly enough, to permit coordination of all aspects of production. Efforts had to be concentrated on improving and rationalizing the most vital areas of production and on overcoming the worst economic bottlenecks. Perhaps the most urgent priority was the allocation and, where possible, the acquisition of scarce raw materials, parts, and equipment. As industry began to recover, leftover stocks of these necessities were depleted to the point where some factories even had to shut down operations again. The textile industry was helped by shipments of cotton and flax from the USSR, and some imports were possible from other East European countries. The real problem, though, was the continued dependence of the Soviet Zone's predominantly light, finished-products industries on the basic industries and coal of West Germany. "Thus," according to East German economist Horst Barthel, "in the territory of the GDR immediately after the war it was not even possible, for example, to produce a complete bicycle without deliveries from the Western zones."[117]

For a combination of economic and political reasons, such deliveries were not always forthcoming. The resulting difficulties fueled mounting apprehensions about a de facto partition of Germany occurring through the divergent policies of the occupation regimes, despite the Potsdam commitment to treat Germany as an economic unit. Precisely because of West Germany's vastly greater economic weight, however, the Communists firmly resisted all pressures for closer interzonal cooperation that might in any way lead to a compromise of their transformation program. The FDGB proclaimed that

> ... the creation of economic unity must not be allowed to bring only an easing of trade from zone to zone. . . . The slogan of economic unity also means unity in banishing the monopolists from their positions of power and in securing the genuine participation of the trade unions in the responsibilities of economic management. . . .[118]

Ulbricht himself addressed the question of a joint food policy:

> We say yes, indeed, we agree about achieving a unified supply system; but that will only be possible when all regions of Germany have carried out the land reform and are operating according to a unified, democratic agricultural plan.[119]

Until the Western powers were prepared to institute these basic measures of economic democratization, Soviet Zone planners would have to work to minimize their reliance on imports from the West.[120]

At the same time, however, the Communists were at this point still trying to avoid deepening the East-West rift through unnecessary ideological confrontations. They rejected calls from left Social Democrats for a completely planned economy, not only because Germany was economically and politically unready for this step, but also on the grounds that to attempt it would needlessly aggravate the problem of maintaining economic unity. KPD/SED spokesmen repeatedly insisted that their present objective was democratization, not socialization, and that capitalism per se was not under attack.

Yet these protestations could scarcely obscure a basic difference in policy, the effects of which grew ever more pronounced as events on both sides acquired a momentum of their own. For the Communists, democratization was a form of social revolution in which the capitalist elite and its economic institutions had to be eliminated, and replaced by a system of proletarian control exercised through the organs of the state. Once state planning had become the mechanism for regulating the economy, the natural way to rationalize the economy further would be by a greater extension of state controls and a corresponding restriction of private enterprise. Economic as well as ideological motives thus impelled the Soviet Zone's style of democratization in a direction that was ultimately indistinguishable from communization in Western eyes.[121]

In the West, democratization was approached more as a restoration than as a revolution. Indeed, the Western powers were trying to prevent a revolution of the left while simultaneously undoing what they saw as a Nazi revolution of the right. Far from dismantling any aspect of the free enterprise system, their aim was rather to purge it of unwholesome influences and set it on its proper competitive basis again. Since they had no alternative system or elite to install, the Western Allies had to depend on some presumably anti-Nazi and anti-monopolist segment of the existing capitalist elite to restore a healthy economy in their zones. In fact, Anglo-American authorities soon found themselves depending on a great many people whose anti-fascist credentials were questionable at best, and their early enthusiasm for trust-busting was gradually dampened by fears of economic chaos and Communism. From the Communist perspective, then, it began to appear that the West was unwilling to follow through with a genuine democratization, even to preserve Germany's unity. In their view this was all the more reason to secure a sound basis for "working-class power" in the Soviet Zone.

FIVE

The Expropriation of Major Industries

From the beginning the Communists had made clear their view that democratization of Germany must include destruction of the influence of "monopoly capitalists." In the first months of occupation, however, they were deliberately vague about how they defined this group and about the specific changes they intended to make in the prevailing industrial structure. The phrasing of the initial call for expropriation of the "Nazi bosses and war criminals" in the KPD's founding declaration, the concentration of Communist attacks on the most notorious industrial trusts and magnates of the Third Reich, and the party's repeated pledges to preserve the capitalist system, all served to nourish the impression that Soviet and Western occupiers were pursuing common aims: a breakup of the great cartels and a purge of pro-fascist economic leaders. The Potsdam accords appeared to ratify this relatively limited and unrevolutionary approach to economic democratization.

In fact, it was precisely the radical nature of the transformation planned by the Communists which led them to soft-pedal this aspect of their program for a while. The reform of industry, like the land reform, was to be directed against an entire class. Its goal was the removal of all remaining economic power from the hands of the upper bourgeoisie by placing all significant industries directly and permanently under the control of the regime. The industrial managers, however, were not so easily swept aside as the great landowners. For one, their expertise was needed to help rebuild factories and restore production. They constituted, moreover, a more numerous and powerful social group than the landed gentry, and retained some political influence through the CDU and LDP. The liberal strains of their political tradition made them less susceptible than the Junkers to blanket characterization as "reactionary" or "parasitic," as did their obvious contribution to economic reconstruction. Nor would their expropriation directly benefit any large segment of the population as the land reform had done; the only obvious beneficiary would be the new regime. Far more than the land reform, then, an immediate expropriation of major industries would have aroused suspicions of a Communist intent to "bolshevize" the Soviet Zone. To guard against such an impression and to disarm potential opposition both internally and in the West, this most crucial step in the KPD program required careful economic and ideological preparation.

The Communists therefore postponed a sweeping industrial expropriation until other key aspects of the new order had been secured: a functioning national economy; control of agriculture and neutralization of the peasantry; and a KPD-dominated system of political parties, civil administrations, and mass "organs of the people." The delay also gave Soviet authorities time to evolve a reparations policy and thus to clarify the question of which enterprises were to be removed from German control altogether. Meanwhile, the KPD worked to undermine the position of the entrepreneurs by whittling away their power in the factories and by persuading the German public of the connection between Nazism and "monopoly capital." Expropriation, when it finally came, had to appear as a spontaneous act of popular anti-fascism, consistent with the stated aims of the "anti-fascist, democratic republic."[1]

WEAKENING THE ENTREPRENEURS

At first, the Communists seem to have hoped that the expropriation of capitalist elites might occur in large part as a concomitant of denazification efforts in all four zones.

They were encouraged in this hope by several Western laws and directives, notably Military Government Law No. 52 and Joint Chiefs of Staff Directive No. 1067, which called for confiscation of properties held by persons arrested as Nazis or war criminals. Indeed, in the southwestern part of the Soviet Zone seizures of Nazi properties continued for months to be carried out under laws originally imposed by the temporary American occupation regime, since the SMA had not yet issued any comparable legislation. The KPD called repeatedly and stridently for the harshest possible judgments against leaders of the Third Reich, including economic leaders, by Allied and German courts. If Communists expected thereby to prod the Western powers into widespread nationalizations, however, they were soon disappointed. Such expropriations of individual magnates like Krupp, Flick, and Röchling as did occur in the West were empty gestures from the Communist point of view, since "the administration of the confiscated enterprises . . . remained in fact in the hands of the old managers, and leading representatives of monopoly capital stood at the head of the trusteeship bodies that were created."[2]

In the Soviet Zone, the socialist parties' emphasis on economic democratization and revolutionary justice, coupled with the lack of any central directive regarding expropriation, led to a spate of uncoordinated confiscations by local authorities in the first weeks which soon threatened to become an embarrassment to the new regime. While such actions were carefully supervised by the KPD in Berlin and other major cities, activists elsewhere evolved a wide variety of policies and political criteria for expropriation. In some places Nazis and war criminals still exercised property rights over their houses and businesses, even when they had fled West; in others, accused Nazi party members might be stripped of all possessions, their businesses forced to close, and managers and stockholders of large corporations driven out as "monopoly capitalists." A Brandenburg provincial ordinance of 25 August reported a wave of complaints that local authorities had been seizing allegedly "abandoned" enterprises and disposing of machines, inventory, etc., to their own advantage. Such actions amounted, the ordinance declared, to sabotage of SMA Order No. 9 on the reconstruction of industry. Factories taken over directly by workers or Antifa groups presented yet another problem. Throughout the summer and into the fall of 1945, provincial administrators battled with overzealous local officials to gain central control of expropriations policy. Their main concerns were to speed restoration of economic order, to preserve some semblance of correct legal procedure (particularly with an eye to appearances in the West), and to create a uniform and coherent policy consistent with Communist strategy for weakening the capitalists as a class.[3]

The Communists were careful to point out that the seizures which they authorized were *not* equivalent to legal expropriation, since no decision had yet been made to transfer actual title to the properties concerned. Some outright expropriations did in fact occur during the first months, but these were mostly due to specific Soviet actions such as dismantling or to the land reform (which affected lands held by corporations as well as by individuals). In general, the Soviet Zone regime preferred to avoid any appearance that it was taking unilateral and irreversible steps affecting Germany's future economic structure. It therefore postponed de jure nationalizations, and concentrated instead on gaining de facto control of industry under the pretext of enforcing the economic democratization and decentralization measures mandated by the Potsdam agreement.

Beginning in August 1945, the provincial administrations issued a series of laws for the political "cleansing" of industry, designed to coordinate the heretofore spontaneous anti-Nazi purges and guide them into approved channels. The object was to weaken the capitalist economic elite as much as possible by removing "factory owners and managers, directors and company officers who had abandoned their enterprises, were active fascists or were sabotaging reconstruction," while minimizing unnecessary damage to the economy caused by workers purging "little" Nazis among their own ranks. As a rule, nominal Nazi party members with no history of political activism were to be given a chance to redeem themselves; but this rule did not apply to important capitalists. The real test was economic power, as Walter Ulbricht explained:

> With company managers or stockholders we do not differentiate between active Nazis and others. Members of the Hitler party and its affiliated organizations who were company directors or held management positions must be removed in all cases. For the position of a manager is so important that one can lend no credence to any claim of "I was only a nominal Nazi."[4]

The economic purge presented on the whole greater difficulties than the purge of civil administration. Guilt was harder to prove, especially in cases involving persons with no formal connections to the Nazi party, since their fascist or criminal activity was often not documented and colleagues tended to cover for them—as indeed their workers frequently did, too. Seriously incriminated managers were occasionally able to evade detection by finding new jobs elsewhere in the economy. Sometimes sufficient evidence was found to purge only part of a company's management. In such an event, according to Josef Smolka of the Saxon state administration, "We left the rest in place, but not as company managers; rather, in all these cases we installed a trustee." Yet even when the entire management of an important enterprise had kept its hands clean, Smolka and his collaborators still found an entree:

There are a number of companies in which we have not been able to get at the entrepreneurs by any device. They were neither Nazi party members, nor can we prove that they have been reactionary. Here we have chosen a different tack. They might have, for example, a half million in debts with us or with some other banking institution. Then we tell them, "We'll give you another half million to go with it, and you in turn will provide some security, perhaps some stock or land"; and in this way we use the money to gain a decisive influence over production.

In other ways, too, the banks seized by the Soviets proved a useful tool in gaining control of industry:

Recently a lot of people have contacted us claiming to be stockholders in this or that company. We asked them, "Where do you have your stock certificates?" They never had them, since those that were kept in the banks are in our possession, and we wouldn't think of turning them over or issuing any duplicates. What we will do with the stock—well, that isn't clear yet. For the time being, everything in the banks is subject to seizure.[5]

To oversee the purge process and to administer the fast-growing system of quasi-public enterprises, provincial authorities created an assortment of new committees, corporations, and bureaus such as the Thuringian Administrative Corporation and Saxony's Office of Factory Reorganization. Aided by the FDGB, these agencies helped target enterprises for seizure, took custody of their assets, and appointed politically reliable trustees to run them. Not surprisingly, elimination of the entrepreneurs did not proceed without resistance. Some owners and managers enlisted the help of their employees in preventing appointment of a trustee or, failing that, tried to continue exercising authority indirectly through their erstwhile subordinates who remained on the scene. A few even arranged to have themselves confirmed in their positions by the Russian officers assigned to watch over their factories. The battle extended into the provincial administrations as well, with "reactionary" economic officials occasionally coming under Communist attack for attempting to obstruct or nullify workers' purges of management, usually with the ostensible aim of maintaining economic order.[6]

The KPD put itself in the position of referee between the radical ideologues and the bureaucrats; a sort of fulcrum balancing its dual interests of revolution and control. While it was itself the prime mover behind the administrations' efforts to hold spontaneous anti-fascism within prescribed bounds, it also remained ever wary of excessive "legalism"—let alone the occasional deliberate sabotage—which could dampen revolutionary ardor. Above all, the Communists sought to generate a mood of class struggle among the workers. To this end they gave wide publicity to the crimes of capitalists, both as individuals and as a class, to the efforts of entrepreneurs and their "clandestine agents" in the administrations to prevent justifiable sequestrations, and to the continued triumphs of class-conscious proletarians in overcoming this opposition. The campaign for workers' codetermination orchestrated by the FDGB, as discussed in the previous chapter, was another and a concurrent attempt to recruit the laboring masses into the struggle against the great capitalists. Restriction of the employers' power over the workers themselves was an important goal of this campaign but not the primary one, according to the GDR's Stefan Doernberg: "Basically, the issue was the creation of workers' control as the most important prerequisite for the eventual destruction of the power of the imperialist upper bourgeoisie through nationalization of the enterprises of war criminals and those responsible for the war."[7]

After September 1945, the KPD devoted particular attention to an attack on the great cartels and "monopolist enterprises" like AEG, Siemens, and I. G. Farben. These were, to begin with, the archenemies whom Lenin had early identified as the authors of imperialism and war, and whose continued existence as independent economic power-centers threatened KPD plans for a centralized national economy. Moreover, they were proving particularly resistant to Communist control. The main problem was that they had their headquarters in (or had moved them to) the West, beyond the reach of Soviet Zone authorities. There, senior managers who survived the more narrowly political Anglo-American denazification programs were able to start reestablishing communications with and authority over the individual units of their corporate empires. These efforts received a tremendous boost when the Western Allies took over their sectors of Berlin, removing the trustees whom the city's Magistrat had put in charge of "monopolist" enterprises there. From the forward bases now provided them, the corporations began dispatching their representatives into East Berlin and the Soviet Zone by late summer, to reassert their control of factories whose original managements had mostly fled or been purged.[8]

The disruption caused by these agents was due less to the legal claims they pressed than to the economic power and personal loyalties their corporations still commanded. They could generally count on at least some immediate support from faithful executives, white-collar employees and skilled technicians, and often from a number of workers as well. Others could be won over by a combination of threats and promises: if reinstated, the corporation might invest money to help rebuild or expand the plant; if not, it would withhold vital patents, plans, etc., and of course could not pay worker pensions. Then too, how viable would a single, specialized plant be outside of the economic organism to which it belonged?

The force of these arguments was compounded, ironically, by the fact that they complemented a current line of thinking among Social Democrats and some Communists, who regarded the great cartels as highly-advanced economic structures which (like the Junker estates) should be nationalized intact, not broken up. However correct this position may have seemed from a purely theoretical standpoint, the KPD leadership condemned it as a disastrous tactical blunder that played directly into the hands of the monopolists. Its effect was not only a further "ideological confusion" of the workers in the factories, but a noticeable tendency on the part of the SPD and KPD economic officials to concentrate on purging and seizing smaller enterprises rather than attacking the powerful trusts.[9]

The KPD response was a massive "break away from the trusts" campaign, aimed at persuading workers to declare their plants independent of the Western-based corporations. From late September 1945 until the beginning of the next year, Communist journals were full of articles detailing the fascist activities and war crimes of various industrial giants and the successful struggles of their workers to end all ties with them. In Saxony, the FDGB instructed its functionaries to use a planned day of commemoration for concentration camp victims as an occasion to dig out information on the use of slave labor by major industries, adding: "Reports on this should be sent to the press, the Bloc of Anti-Fascist, Democratic Parties, and the state trade union committee." Newspapers reported that corporate agents were exploiting their positions to remove plans, equipment, and skilled personnel to the West. KPD and FDGB spokesmen appeared at rallies in factories and elsewhere to denounce these agents and call upon the workers to throw them out. Their attempts to restore the old monopolies were, Communists declared, a violation of the Potsdam accords. Allied courts were even now trying the worst industrialists for their crimes and could be expected to move against the cartels soon; but the workers must not wait for the occupation powers to take all the initiatives—they should strike the first blow themselves, now![10]

In answer to the economic arguments in favor of cartels, the KPD assured workers that the German administrations would assume the economic coordinating functions once performed by corporate management: "Plants which represent an integrated labor process and need to gear their production to one another will in future . . . be managed by the state and provincial administrations or, where plants in different provinces are involved, by the Central Administration for Industry." The regime was also capable of bringing its own forms of economic pressure to bear. "The old cartel managements," announced the *Deutsche Volkszeitung*, "are excluded from integration into the production plan"—meaning presumably that they would be cut off from production orders and from the raw materials needed for production. On the other hand, workers were given to understand that breaking away from the parent corporations would speed the economic recovery of their factories. At AEG in Berlin-Treptow, where resistance was particularly stubborn, Communists told SPD shop council leaders point-blank that their factory would "immediately receive work for several years" as soon as it abandoned the cartel, but not before. Economic authorities were advised to put less pressure on small entrepreneurs and more on the big combines. The principal speaker at a KPD economic conference observed,

> We consider it wrong when economic organs occasionally try to direct all the activities of small and middle-sized companies. We also consider it politically and economically mistaken when economic organs focus their main attention in a negative sense on the small entrepreneurs and producers. . . . Let us direct our special attention to the big ones, to the war profiteers, to the industrial barons, to the lords of AEG, Siemens, Telefunken. . . .[11]

Referring to seizures of raw materials from manufacturers by various administrative authorities, Ulbricht remarked:

> Take what you need from the really big ones, from the war profiteers; but leave the little ones in peace. The district administrations should take an interest in these small businessmen, small industrialists, etc., and pursue along with them the struggle against the great war criminals.[12]

THE MOVE TOWARD FORMAL EXPROPRIATION

By the end of 1945, purges, property seizures, and the anti-monopoly movement had succeeded in placing almost all large industries in the Soviet Zone under the control of the provincial administrations. Yet well before that time the machinery was already in motion for full legal expropriation, despite continued KPD protests that such a move was not on the agenda. The *Thüringer Volkszeitung* reported on 15 September that the Thuringian state administration had decided to nationalize all mineral resources and film theaters. Other provinces followed suit in succeeding weeks. Then on 29 October, the State of Saxony announced the outright expropriation of all assets within its borders belonging to Friedrich Flick, a notorious steel magnate, amid a torrent of propaganda about the misdeeds of Flick in particular and monopolists in general. In the expropriation decree, the Saxon administration justified its action as follows:

> The principal guilt for Hitler's criminal policy of war is borne by German monopoly capital. . . . The only means of preventing German monopoly capital from plunging the world into the disaster of another war is . . . by removing the power of the German monopoly capitalists.[13]

The following day the SMA published its Order No. 124, inaugurating its own massive sequestration program which would eventually lead to a sweeping expropriation of major industries throughout the Soviet Zone.[14]

The Communists' hand may have been forced a bit in moving so quickly to expropriations. In contrast to the KPD, the SPD had been calling openly for nationalization of key industries ever since its founding declaration, and apparently enjoyed widespread support among workers for its position. The Communists may have feared being outflanked on this critical issue in the political maneuvering going on between the two parties during fall of 1945. Further evidence that KPD leaders did not favor expropriations at that time has emerged in a recently-published letter sent by Wilhelm Pieck and the KPD Central Committee to the Mecklenburg party leadership on 17 October. In it, Pieck noted that several provinces had been passing resolutions to nationalize mines and commented, "We had expressly indicated earlier that there should be no talk about a nationalization of mining." Aside from all this, the seizures of industrial properties being conducted by the provincial administrations were encountering difficulties due to the corruption or conservatism of economic officials, varying and contradictory policies, etc., that begged for some sort of central resolution. The promulgation of SMA Order No. 124 might thus be seen, in part at least, as an attempt by Communist authorities to regain control of the expropriation movement and reduce it to a unified, coherent program under the aegis of the Soviet Military Administration—whose authority, moreover, unlike that of the German administrations, was above all legal challenge.[15]

But there were other and deeper reasons for the SMA's move. The Soviets were becoming increasingly uneasy about developments in the West, or rather the lack of them: failure to pursue a radical purge of the old industrial elite, continuation of cartels, suppression of Communist political and trade union activities, removal of Soviet Zone appointees in West Berlin, and so forth. They were also

impatient with the Western powers' "policy of postponement" toward any agreement in detail on how the Potsdam accords were to be implemented. They suspected
their allies of trying to ride out the first wave of anti-
fascist revolutionary zeal while giving the German
bourgeoisie time to regroup and reestablish a conservative, pro-Western regime. SMA Order No. 124 was a gesture to indicate the Soviets' very real intention of going
ahead with a separate transformation of their own zone
if the West did not quickly come to terms on a program
to restructure all Germany along lines acceptable to Moscow. It was intended, too, as a precedent for future Western or four-power legislation, both in concept and in implementation. The Communists were prepared to mollify
bourgeois sensibilities by observing legal forms; they would
not, however, become bogged down in endless legal proceedings. Like the "anti-fascist, democratic republic" itself, the expropriation of the great capitalists was to be
bourgeois-democratic in appearance but revolutionary in
content.[16]

Finally, on an immediate practical level, Order No. 124
was aimed at securing Soviet control of factories that might
be required for reparations, either as objects of dismantling or, more commonly after the first months, as sources
of current production. The order itself stated its intention
as being "to prevent theft and other misuse" of certain
categories of property (that is, according to Doernberg,
their "sabotage" by the monopolists), and to insure their
rational use "for the needs of the local populace and the
occupation troops." Included were properties belonging to
the following:

(a) the German state and its central and local agencies;

(b) the functionaries of the National Socialist Party,
its leading members and influential followers:

(c) the German military authorities and organizations;

(d) the societies, clubs and associations prohibited and dissolved by the Soviet Military Command;

(e) the governments and nationals (physical and legal persons) of the countries which participated in the war on the side of Germany;

(f) persons designated by the Soviet Military Command through special lists or in other ways. . . .

A supplementary directive, SMA Order No. 126, specifically added the National Socialist Party itself to the above list. In addition, Order No. 124 called for "ownerless" property—that which had been abandoned or remained unclaimed—to be taken into provisional Soviet custody.[17]

For the time being, the Soviets and their KPD colleagues continued pointedly to avoid any reference to expropriation. Ulbricht warned, "We must not allow . . . a propaganda line to be pursued in our zone which makes it easier for hostile elements to make inflammatory remarks in the West against 'Bolshevism' and the 'Bolshevist' economic policies in the Soviet-occupied area." The SMA's measures were, the Communists maintained, strictly a sequestration with no effect on legal ownership status.[18]

Nevertheless, this "sequestration" was to be carried out with revolutionary suddenness. Order No. 124 required all persons holding property covered in its provisions to inform local authorities accordingly within fifteen days. The authorities then had another five days to review the information received, seize the properties concerned, and dispatch an inclusive list of these properties to the appropriate Soviet commander. These deadlines proved to be unrealistic, to say the least. In Chemnitz, a KPD stronghold in Saxony, officials had not received a single property declaration by 15 November. They were promptly pounced upon by Soviet General Supranov, who assembled local party leaders and accused them of taking an "apathetic" stance toward the SMA's order. He recommended that they form their own sequester committee to supplement that of the city administration. Before they could do so, however, the city's KPD mayor threw together a provisional list of fifty-eight enterprises, compiled after an "urgent call" to the local trade unions, and fired it off to SMA headquarters. On 13-14 November, Marshal Zhukov met with provincial presidents and leaders of the Central administrations to resolve similar difficulties encountered throughout the zone. Shortly afterward, Thuringia abandoned its preexisting state mechanism for property seizures in favor of a new system based on Soviet recommendations. Something comparable happened in Mecklenburg, where authorities had up to now virtually ignored the new Soviet order: "Only on November 13 did the President of the state administration first call upon the anti-fascist parties to support the [Soviet] action. . . ." Eventually, centralized and more or less uniform sequestration procedures were established in all five provinces.[19]

The system was similar to that used in the land reform. In each city or rural district a special commission was set up, composed of representatives of each of the Bloc parties, the FDGB, and the German administrations. These commissions were charged with examining the case of every enterprise seized and assigning each to one of three lists: "List A" for enterprises recommended for confiscation, "List B" for enterprises to be returned to their owners for lack of sufficient evidence against them, and "List C" for enterprises classified as "ownerless" and therefore subject to continued provisional management by the SMA pending final disposition. Properties regarding which the commissions could not reach a unanimous decision were also placed on "List C." Evidence considered by the sequester commissions included documents and statements supplied by trade unions and shop councils, and testimony taken from workers employed by the business in question. The findings of local commissions were carefully reviewed at the county level and difficult cases were passed on to a Presidial Commission of the provincial administration for a final decision.[20]

The status of properties owned by the Nazi party and the state was easily determined under the provisions of Orders 124 and 126. Despite their prominence in the Soviet decrees, however, these classes of property represented only a relatively insignificant fraction of what was sequestered. The greatest part came from the category of "functionaries of the National Socialist Party, its leading members and influential followers"—a category subject to a wide range of interpretation. According to the official interpretation put on it by the Saxon state administration, it included anyone who had held an important position in the fascist state, economy, or bureaucracy or had "supported or defended the reign of terror of the Hitler regime through actions, words, writings, or pictures." While some Social Democrats complained that the law was "elastic and therefore hardly enforceable," the KPD and Soviets soon demonstrated their intention of using this elasticity to maximum advantage. The state sequester commission in Saxony, for instance, enjoyed the unflagging support of SMA Major Grigorian, who helped produce incriminating evidence against entrepreneurs and lectured commission members repeatedly about the tactics of adversaries (such as using the CDU or LDP for a platform) and the need to enlighten the workers regarding the crimes of their employers. In Mecklenburg, where sequestrations still lagged in early 1946, warnings from Berlin were followed by a personal visit from Ulbricht and a purge and reorganization of the state sequestration system. Under such pressures, sequester commissions adopted a "better-safe-than-sorry" policy of attaching, pending further review, all properties even suspected of falling under the Soviet legislation.[21]

Entrepreneurs, meanwhile, fought back with all the means at their disposal. Some burned company books to hide their guilt. Others tried to bribe commission officials or to transfer property titles to unincriminated friends or foreigners. Most commonly, employers sought character references from their workers:

> People were constantly showing us these "testimonies of innocence" in the commission sessions and in hearings, thinking we would be taken in by them. It was above all the older SPD comrades who had fallen victim to the cries and complaints of their contemporaries. They wrote out these "Persil certificates" [so named after a popular laundry soap] in their good-heartedness and thoughtlessness . . . and left us with the work. But often it was members of certain shop councils, too, who were subject to such vacillations.[22]

Particularly troublesome were those employers, especially owners of smaller factories in small towns, who had a close relationship with their workers and had perhaps won their gratitude as well by concessions or favors. A typical case involved a textiles manufacturer who occasionally slipped his workers a few nylon stockings from the factory's production to barter on the black market. Workers in this factory and in many others like it were all for expropriation of the "Nazis and war criminals" whom the KPD so vehemently condemned, but were equally sure that *their* employer did not belong in this category. Such loyalties were not all that was holding the workers back, though: often they were simply afraid that sequestration would mean closing or dismantling of their plants and loss of their jobs. The FDGB warned its functionaries not to neglect this issue in their efforts to rally worker support against the entrepreneurs:

> It is most especially important to show that . . . the *danger of unemployment* in no way threatens workers in the factories concerned, but that on the contrary, the prospect exists . . . that these factories will be rebuilt

on the largest possible scale and their production will
increase, especially since they will have a far better
guarantee of receiving raw materials, machines and
workers under the new conditions than at present.[23]

By early 1946, the nationalization of major industries
had already been achieved in fact, if not in name. Although Order No. 124 was framed as a measure of the
occupation authorities with German officials merely handling the paper work, control of the entire operation was
gradually turned over to the Germans. SMA Order No. 97
of 29 March formally placed the sequestered properties,
with some specified exceptions, at the disposal of the German administrations, and established a German Central
Commission for Attachment and Sequestration to coordinate the management of these properties throughout the
Soviet Zone. The same day, preparations began for a formal transfer of ownership: a conference of functionaries
of the Saxon state administration, including representatives of all four parties, drafted a "Decree on the Expropriation of the Property of War Profiteers and Active Fascists." Within a month, Saxony was ready with more
detailed guidelines on the categories of persons to be expropriated. Briefly, these were: (1) Nazi criminals—all those
who had committed crimes against humanity or had gained
wealth or advantage from fascism; (2) active Nazis—members of the SS, SD, Gestapo, and the higher levels of the
Nazi Party or its affiliated organizations; and (3) war profiteers—those who had produced war materiel for Germany, had plundered conquered lands, or had procured or
mishandled foreign laborers. As Stefan Doernberg has can-
didly noted,

Basically, then, practically all large enterprises, and of
course all enterprises of the cartels, fell within these
designations. The entire imperialist upper bourgeoisie
had participated in one form or another—according to

the wording of these guidelines—in the preparation and execution of the predatory fascist war.[24]

THE SAXON REFERENDUM AND THE COMPLETION OF EXPROPRIATION

The KPD's one remaining concern was to make the actual decision for expropriation appear to be a revolutionary and democratic act of the German people, rather than an administrative act by a Communist-dominated regime. To this end, the Communists hit on the idea of submitting the issue to a referendum. As the Province of Saxony-Anhalt had been used to spearhead the KPD land reform program, so the State of Saxony was chosen to be the proving ground for industrial expropriation. It could boast not only 48 percent of Soviet Zone industry and a strong labor tradition, but also the most powerful and coherent Communist Party in the zone. According to GDR historian Otto Schröder, it was Saxony's KPD chief Hermann Matern who first suggested a referendum at a conference of party secretaries on 14 February. After some public discussion of the idea in following weeks, the Saxon administration passed a law on 4 April providing for the holding of plebiscites. On 21 May, the SMA published Order No. 154/181, transferring possession (but not yet ownership) of the sequestered enterprises to the German administrations, subject to the same exceptions made in SMA Order No. 97. Four days later, Saxon authorities granted a petition submitted unanimously by all three parties and the FDGB for a referendum on the proposed expropriation law, to be held 30 June 1946.[25]

Meanwhile, the Communist prpaganda machine was gearing up for its greatest campaign to date. The ostensible issue of the referendum—whether or not the "List A" enterprises would be permanently expropriated—had of course been decided long ago. The real purpose of the vote was to demonstrate broad mass support for the nationalization of industry in particular and for Communist policy in general. Through it, the new SED and its model for the democratization of all Germany were to be legitimized. Further, the Saxon referendum was conceived as a carefully-controlled exercise in class struggle which would raise the political consciousness of the masses, the "subjective factor" identified by Doernberg as "still the weakest point" in the Soviet Zone system. The choice before the voters, as framed by SED propaganda, was between restoring power to the capitalist "Nazis and war criminals" or transferring it into "the hands of the people" as represented by a worker-led state. The line between "progressive" and "reactionary" was thus neatly drawn: a stand against fascism implied a commitment to the Communist program.[26]

Still, the SED reiterated the old KPD assurances that its economic policies were not anti-capitalist, but merely anti-fascist and anti-monopolist. Expounding the correct party line for a meeting of the SED Executive Council on 14-15 May, Walter Ulbricht warned that the primary tactic of opponents would be to represent the referendum as an attack on all private property. A special effort would have to be made to refute this idea. In a pamphlet, Ulbricht went on to state flatly, "This is not a question of social transformation." The SED took the position that the property transfer proposed in the Saxon referendum differed from nationalizations taking place elsewhere in Europe because of the unique situation in Germany, where monopoly capital and the fascist state were inextricably intertwined. While in foreign countries expropriations occurred because of a political preference for state control, in Germany they represented measures to punish crime and prevent its recurrence. Moreover, expropriation would make sure that the real criminals, and not the people as a whole, would bear the cost of Nazi crimes. Germany would pay its reparations debt out of the confiscated holdings of the great capitalists, rather than letting them exploit the reparations crisis to make still more profits as they had done after World War I.[27]

A vote for expropriation, then, was a vote for peace, reconstruction, and democracy—this was the theme that the SED and its client organizations like the FDGB, VdgB, and FDJ constantly repeated in the weeks preceding the referendum. Only by eliminating the war criminals and monopolists could the German people guarantee against future catastrophe. Only by such a gesture, too, could they hope to convince other peoples that they had the strength and will to reform and could be trusted to govern themselves again. In this connection, Communists reminded the public that in turning over the sequestered enterprises to the German administrations rather than keeping them for reparations, the SMA had expressed the intention that they be used for the good of the people. The Soviet commandant of Saxony, General Dubrovski, remarked in a newspaper interview about the referendum that the SMA "would thereby have an opportunity to see for itself the extent to which the German people are prepared to resolve important problems independently in a democratic spirit." Finally, scorning such subtlety, the SED announced plainly in its declaration for the referendum: "Every 'yes' vote is a vote to shorten the period of occupation."[28]

The main propaganda offensive began on 1 May, and developed in three phases. The first was a flurry of mass meetings and demonstrations for expropriation: five thousand of them in Saxony over one ten-day period, with five hundred of these in factories. Topics of meetings included the character of fascism, the role of monopolists and bankers in war, the nature of democracy, the historical necessity of the referendum, and (notably) its effect on the struggle for German unity. Fears about the future status of private property were answered with assurances that the political attitude of an entrepreneur and his activities under the Nazi state, not the size of his enterprise, would determine the question of his expropriation. Communists further stressed that the expropriation of the "war criminals," like the land reform, was an extraordinary measure that would not be repeated. In future, no confiscations would be possible except by due process of law.[29]

Phase two of the campaign began on 25 May, with the Saxon administration's formal approval of the Bloc parties' request for a referendum, and involved, according to an FDGB circular, "A wave of ideology with appropriate pictorial, oral and written materials (posters, leaflets, newspapers and . . . local gatherings)." Newsreels and radio announcements also supported this phase. This barrage was supplemented, finally, with "direct personal work on each individual family, but especially on the women" to corral the last holdouts. The FDGB advised,

> Every local resident must be worked on personally by our members and functionaries. During the referendum we will, accordingly, organize a "hauling service," so as to get every last voter who we think will vote for the referendum to the ballot box.[30]

To coordinate the last two phases, the Bloc parties and the mass organs—FDGB, FDJ, Women's Committee, Cultural League—set up a central state project committee. This committee supplied party and trade union groups at the county and local levels with posters, handbills, and other propaganda materials, most of them directed at specific segments of the population. Women, for example, were exhorted to think of their bombed-out homes, their hungry children, and the many widows and orphans left by the war, and then to end such horrors forever by voting "yes" on the referendum.[31] Peasants, too, were reminded of their sufferings in the war, and of the fact that the expropriation of the "monopolists" was part of the same struggle that had freed them from the yoke of the Junkers and given many of them the land and tools to make a livelihood. Particular attention was paid to the petty bourgeoisie: "The majority of artisans and small businessmen regard the referendum with suspicion," the SED informed its functionaries, "because they fear they will be the next to be expropriated." To win their support, propagandists recalled for them how artisan shops had been closed or placed under the control of large industries by the Nazis. Removal of the great capitalists would eliminate the danger of this recurring and allow artisans to flourish unhindered. It would also end the threat of war, permitting the small trader to develop contacts abroad. As a final dramatic gesture to win over this crucial bloc of votes, a few days before the referendum the regime returned the majority of sequestered small and middle-sized businesses—1,900 of them in all—to their original owners. In festive ceremonies arranged for the occasion throughout Saxony, Communist officials announced that here was proof positive of the referendum's character as a measure directed strictly against war criminals, not against private property.[32]

Even more important was the effort to overcome remaining resistance to expropriation among Saxony's large proletariat. Here the FDGB's role was decisive. Trade union members represented a large portion of the electorate—more than half of all voters in Dresden and Chemnitz—and were looked upon as the backbone of the movement for the referendum. From the time of their victory at the FDGB General Delegates' Conference in February 1946, the Communists had made "liquidation of the cartels" a top trade-union priority. By the end of May it appeared to be virtually the only priority, at least in Saxony:

> The carrying out of agitation for the referendum . . . is at present the most important task of the Free Trade Unions. All other tasks, such as elections for the leadership of the industrial unions, must be brought into harmony with this campaign and implemented in conjunction with it.[33]

The FDGB and SED devoted their main attention to dispelling the "conciliationist" sentiments toward the great capitalists still common among workers, particularly in "List A" enterprises. The SED directed that factory propaganda commissions be organized to make up and display pro-referendum posters, banners, slogans, and announcements, and to persuade workers through personal contacts to support the referendum. Special attention was to be paid to women, youth, and white-collar workers. On 13 June, FDGB headquarters in Saxony sent out an "Information Sheet" calling for assemblies of shop councilmen to be convened in individual factories in order to sound them out on the referendum. Any attitude such as "I'm for the referendum, but *my* factory mustn't be expropriated" was to be condemned as "An impossible position for union-affiliated councilmen," and was to be considered seriously in choosing FDGB nominees for upcoming shop council elections. Trade union and SED functionaries labored on continuously, even after sequestration, to dig out as much damning information as possible about factory owners and to publicize it locally through posters, leaflets and newspaper articles. According to SED instructions, a summary of this information was to be presented to the assembled workers of the factory concerned prior to the referendum, along with a proposed resolution for expropriation. The summary should document, as appropriate: (1) the entrepreneur's role in war industries; (2) his part in and profit from the occupation of foreign countries; (3) his procurement and treatment of foreign laborers; (4) his collaboration with the Gestapo, threats of imprisonment for recalcitrant workers, etc.; (5) his spoken or written support for the war; and (6) his chauvinistic remarks and behavior and his position (if an officer or official) in the Nazi system. "The entrepreneur must be illuminated from all sides, and in the course of this we will find quite a lot of facts which identify him as a Nazi criminal or war profiteer."[34]

A correspondent for the *New York Times* in Saxony to cover the referendum reported being struck by the fact that, in contrast to the deluge of propaganda calling on citizens to vote "yes" for expropriation, not a single appeal for a "no" vote appeared. Public opposition to the referendum, while not technically forbidden, was practically impossible because the regime equated it with support for fascism. Opposition was therefore driven underground and expressed itself mainly in nocturnal smearing of slogans on walls and defacing of SED propaganda. Persons caught in these acts were arrested, tried by summary courts, and quickly punished as "saboteurs." Some rural clerics also spoke out against expropriation, but their influence was far outweighed by numerous expressions of support elicited from church leaders, including the Roman Catholic bishop of Meissen and the Saxon leadership of the Evangelical Lutheran Church.[35]

The only serious attempt at resistance was from within the two bourgeois parties. Even here, dissent was voiced cautiously and behind closed doors by people who remembered the fate of Hermes, Schreiber, and Koch. Ulbricht took care to warn the CDU and LDP that they were on trial:

> The execution of the referendum is a test for all three anti-fascist, democratic parties. Here they will demonstrate to what extent they are really democratic parties . . . or to what extent certain reactionary people are still to be found in one party or another. . . .[36]

Officially both bourgeois parties supported the referendum, and the SED did its best to make this support appear wholehearted, insisting that the CDU and LDP participate actively in all aspects of the propaganda campaign. Both also emphasized in their public statements, however, that expropriation must be restricted to genuine Nazi leaders and war criminals. Moreover, it must not alter the basic economic structure of Germany. This reservation reflected continued serious misgivings within these parties, particularly in the CDU, that a widespread expropriation was in fact the business of a parliament to be elected by the entire nation. Any such major step taken unilaterally by the provisional administrative authorities of one zone would, they feared, risk "loosening the framework of the Reich."[37]

These misgivings were aired at a meeting of party leaders of the Anti-Fascist Bloc in Berlin on 16 May. Responding to a request by CDU chairman Jakob Kaiser that the SED insure against "premature decisions" being taken in Saxony that could prejudice questions of significance to the entire German people, Pieck rejected the suggestion summarily, replying that the call for a referendum arose from among the people themselves. At the next meeting of the Bloc on 29 May, the CDU presented a formal draft of guidelines aimed at preventing any measures "which amount to a change in the economic and social structure in Saxony." This effort was sidetracked: a committee was set up that eventually produced some recommendations for Saxon officials on the proper interpretation of terms like "active Nazi" and "war criminal." Nor were the bourgeois parties in Saxony able to make any headway in their attempts to arrange for closer examination of appeals for reclassification of "List A" industries, even on grounds of "irreproachable personal conduct on the part of owners of firms." Unable to budge the SED and fearing to oppose it openly, the CDU and LDP finally went along with the referendum and hoped for the best.[38]

For former Nazis, too, the referendum was to be the ultimate test of "democratic" loyalties. The Communists, true to their policy of identifying the economic and political elite of Hitler's regime as the real criminals, worked to enlist the erstwhile rank and file of the Nazi party against these. While persons branded as "active Nazis" were disqualified from voting in the referendum, the overwhelming majority of former Nazis were not only permitted but urged to vote, and were mustered out for mass demonstrations in support of expropriation. SED propagandist Anton Ackermann boasted that former Nazi party members and their families represented "a good half of all eligible voters in the State of Saxony." Many "nominal" Nazis were among those whose small businesses were released from sequester on the eve of the plebiscite. Ulbricht expressed the view that these people should have their property returned to them since they had been, as they could now see, mere dupes of the great capitalists. The point was made even more explicit in the SED's appeal for the referendum:

> Every former nominal member of the Nazi party now has the opportunity to take part, with the full rights of a citizen, in the democratic reconstruction of Germany. Your "yes" will earn you this trust. Therefore—vote "yes!"[39]

In response, no doubt, to Western objections at Potsdam against restrictions on press coverage of elections in Eastern Europe,[40] the Soviet Zone regime gave foreign journalists full opportunity to observe the voting procedures in Saxony on 30 June. They reported no irregularities: votes cast by secret ballot were counted by electoral commissions composed of members of all three parties and the FDGB. The success of the referendum thus represented all the more of a propaganda victory for the Communists, repaying their efforts of the past few weeks. Out of 3,676,441 eligible voters, 3,459,658 went to the polls. Of these, 2,683,401 or 77.7 percent favored expropriation, 571,600 or 16.5 percent were against it, and 204,657 or 5.8 percent cast invalid ballots.[41]

In analyzing the voting returns, Doernberg has concluded that workers supported the referendum most enthusiastically but that artisans, businessmen, professional people, and intellectuals also supported it in considerable numbers. These results confirmed in the SED's view the soundness of its tactical line in the referendum, and indeed in the whole process of "anti-fascist, democratic transformation." According to Wilhelm Koenen, SED chairman of Saxony,

> Only by consistently giving democratic justification for the referendum, refuting slogans about socialism and presenting the expropriation of the war criminals as a political and anti-fascist task to secure peace, were we able to make the referendum such a great success. The bourgeois concept of property would have caused many voters to react defensively to a definition of the probelm in social terms. These bourgeois, anti-fascist voters were prepared, however, to help bring about a political decision against war criminals and activists as a punitive measure, because of the monstrous crimes they had committed in the name of the German people.[42]

Communists also pointed to the success of the land reform in winning support from the peasants, and particularly to the significance of the KPD-SPD merger, which "unified the working class" and allowed political opposition to be confined to the bourgeois parties where it could be stifled with relative ease. But the price paid for this façade of unity in the Soviet Zone was soon evident, particularly in the appearance of a reorganized SPD in West Berlin as the most trenchant critic of SED policies. Its new party organ *Der Sozialdemokrat* editorialized,

> On the issue itself, we agree completely with the aims set forth in the proposed law submitted to the referendum. The demagogy connected with this referendum is another matter. . . . We reject a referendum which certain organizations are able to introduce without a popular initiative. We consider a referendum bad when its object has not been discussed, and tasteless when it is carried out against an opponent who is prostrate.
>
> This Saxon referendum therefore represents for us

> merely a part of the new policy of the SED, which has proclaimed the "assault on the middle classes" as its next task, and which wants to win this assault by strictly banning any mention of socialism and by promising something to everyone. . . .[43]

The opposition which could no longer gain expression in the East was crystallizing in the West, thus promoting a further hardening of ideological differences along geographic lines.

Following the referendum in Saxony, 1,861 "List A" enterprises were expropriated out of a total of 4,700 originally sequestered. The state administration took over 1,002 large and middle-sized enterprises and resold 380 smaller ones to deserving refugees, "victims of fascism," and other worthy recipients. The rest were distributed among local administrative authorities and official institutions: cities took over bakeries, construction firms, printing houses, and the like; department stores and food-processing facilities went to the farmers' and consumers' cooperatives; and the VdgB received a few dairies. Despite the persistent contention of East German writers that fascist or criminal activity was the only criterion used in deciding expropriation, the fact remains that the "List B" enterprises returned to their owners were all small or unprofitable ones for which the regime had no use. Communists have argued that the owners and managers of the major enterprises were in fact the people who had contributed most to fascism, while Western commentators have alleged that the definition of "fascist" was extended to cover anyone whose property the SED coveted. A remark made by Josef Smolka of Saxony at a KPD economic conference back in early January of 1946 speaks for itself:

> We will probably . . . return a considerable portion of the smaller plants which are of minor significance for the economy to the entrepreneurs, if they were not war criminals or active fascists. Which plants these will be

depends first upon their economic importance, and secondly upon the persons who previously owned them.[44]

No referendum was held in the other provinces of the Soviet Zone. Although there was some opposition to following the Saxon example, particularly from the bourgeois parties in Thuringia, the SED managed to push through expropriation laws everywhere in the zone by mid-August 1946. These purportedly based themselves on the will of the people as expressed in the Saxon referendum and in a flood of petitions and resolutions evoked by Communist agitators. Similar legislation passed by the Berlin Magistrat on two occasions in 1947 was thwarted, however, by the intervention of the Western powers. After the formal division of the city into two administrative units in 1948, these expropriation measures were finally carried out in East Berlin alone.[45]

The "List A" industries taken over by the state and provincial administrations evolved into the system of People's Enterprises (Volkseigene Betriebe, or VEB) which has since formed the backbone of the East German economy. A large number of "List C" enterprises also joined this system in 1948, having remained temporarily under Soviet control while the sequester commissions tried to establish their property status (most were stockholder-owned corporations). In addition, 213 "war industries"—the enterprises withheld from German control under SMA Orders No. 97 and No. 154/181—were transferred to direct Soviet ownership by SMA Order No. 167 of 5 June 1946. Those that were not dismantled continued producing for reparations as Soviet Stock Corporations until they, too, were eventually turned over to the East German government during the late 1940s and early 1950s. The old banks were not formally confiscated until 1948, but they were in effect already liquidated in late 1946 when the new banks and savings institutions chartered by the provincial administrations took over their properties. Their expropriation, when it came, was made retroactive to 8 May 1945. Soviet Zone authorities also carried out some other, relatively minor expropriations independently of the sequestration process, for example under Allied Control Council Directive No. 38 of 12 October 1946 which dealt with punishment of "war criminals, Nazis, and militarists."[46]

As with the land reform, the bourgeois parties tried for many months beginning in fall 1946 to arrange for a review of some industrial expropriations which they claimed had been carried out unjustly. In Saxony, the LDP submitted a list of 211 such cases, the CDU a list of 89. The ensuing discussions in the Anti-Fascist Bloc were met with a wave of supposedly spontaneous strikes and protest resolutions from factory workers throughout the state. After a meeting with workers' delegates on 24 January 1947, representatives of the state administration, the Bloc parties and the FDGB finally agreed not to return any enterprise to its original owner without first consulting with the workers of that enterprise. The issue was thus essentially closed in Saxony. Somewhat later, the bourgeois parties in Thuringia actually persuaded the state administration there to reverse a large number of expropriations, but were once again confronted with the threat of strikes. This time the "reactionaries" were taught a lesson: "Under pressure from the protests of the working class," Communist authorities undertook a reexamination of the entire sequestration procedure and discovered that many properties classified as "List B" in Thuringia had actually belonged on "List A." The number of expropriated enterprises in the state shot up from 359 in 1946 to 1,155 in 1948.[47]

The courts were no more help. To avoid legal tangles and circumvent an unreliable judiciary, Communists had seen to it that the Saxon law on plebiscites contained no provisions making them liable to judicial review as Weimar legislation had done. Attempts to appeal expropriation on the basis of Control Council rulings or preexisting German laws were doomed to failure by the one overriding fact that the Soviet Military Administration was sovereign in its own zone. Having the power to change or interpret law to suit the needs of the working class, the Communists would not be hamstrung by laws evolved by capitalists to enforce their own class rule.[48]

The bourgeois parties had yet to grasp fully that despite appearances, the "anti-fascist, democratic transformation" was not conceived as a legal process, but rather as a revolutionary process to be carried out wherever possible by legal means. The means were a matter of tactics and, in true Leninist fashion, might be changed to suit the circumstances, but the revolutionary ends were fixed. When SMA Order No. 64 formally concluded the sequestration program on 17 April 1948, it noted that 40 percent of the productive capacity of the Soviet Zone had been nationalized. The Soviet Stock Corporations accounted for about another 20 percent. "It is hereby established," the order went on, "that the property of the people is inviolable. Sale or transfer to private persons or organizations of industrial enterprises which have become the property of the people is accordingly forbidden."[49]

SIX

Conclusion

With the nationalization of all important industries in the Soviet Zone, the first and most virulent stage of the "antifascist, democratic transformation" came to a close. The foundation had been laid for a Germany which the Communists felt could be relied upon to remain peaceful and friendly to the USSR. The old ruling classes were gone: the landed aristocracy had disappeared altogether; while the bourgeois entrepreneurs and managers, although still present in large numbers, had been stripped of real power by the codetermination movement, price and wage controls, central planning, taxation, and the elimination of their most influential stratum. The "commanding heights" of society and economy were now in the hands of a united proletarian party dominated by Moscow-trained Communists.

A period of about three years followed in which the East German social and economic structure remained essentially as it stood by summer 1946, and emphasis shifted to consolidating the gains already made. The SED worked to secure its hold over the political system and the labor movement, to perfect a mechanism of economic planning based on the new People's Enterprises, and to establish the small peasants as the dominant class in the countryside under the political tutelage of the proletariat. Meanwhile, the Communists worked to secure their own dominance within the SED.[1]

But for a few further refinements, then, the Soviet Zone of summer 1946 was already the "democratic people's republic" of prewar Communist theory.[2] In a 1947 article entitled "New-Style Democracy," Soviet economist Eugen Varga summarized the typical characteristics of this new social construct, better known in its postwar incarnation as the People's Democracy: "By 'new-style democracy' we mean the existence in a country of conditions in which the remnants of feudalism—the large land holdings of the rural gentry—have been eliminated; in which the system of private ownership of the means of production continues, but the great enterprises of industry, transport and credit belong to the state and the apparatus of state power no longer serves the monopolist bourgeoisie, but rather the laboring masses of city and country."[3] The regimes of all the Soviet-occupied states of postwar Europe were shaped on this model and all followed the same plan of development, despite variations of timing and tactics. Thus the land reform and the expropriation of industries carried out in 1945-46 in East Germany as measures against "fascists, militarists, and war criminals" had been going on since 1944 in Eastern Europe as part of Communist-led nationalist movements to expel German minorities and punish native collaborators. The effect was the same: destruction of the old elites and concentration of their economic power in government hands. In all cases these measures were introduced under the banner of national regeneration, *not* of socialism. In all cases, too, native Communists relying on Red Army support forged an alliance of left and center parties as the basis for parliamentary-style provisional governments, while securing for themselves key positions of political power.

The result was a social system that in theory was neither capitalist nor socialist, but something new and unique. Since the basis for socialism was supposedly already established in the nationalization of the principal means of production and the political hegemony of a Communist-led working class, the transition to socialism could, it was claimed, occur peacefully within the framework of the existing political order. Socialist economic forms would merely be strengthened progressively until they supplanted the remaining vestiges of capitalism. The German expression of this theory of gradual transition was the "German path to socialism" thesis introduced by the KPD's Anton Ackermann during the final push for KPD-SPD unification. Ackermann and his colleagues argued that Germany had several advantages which Russia had not enjoyed at the time of her revolution, including a vastly larger proletariat, a highly developed economy and cultural establishment, and the lack of a Menshevik opposition (now that there was to be a single working-class party). With such favorable preconditions for the development of socialism, Germany could be expected to follow a different and easier evolution than the Soviet Union.[4]

Wolfgang Leonhard, who had access to the innermost councils of the KPD at the time, has concluded that the "German path" thesis was intended purely as a tactic to quiet Social Democratic fears about the KPD's Moscow ties, and thus to ease the transition to a unified proletarian party.[5] This judgment has been widely accepted in the West, particularly by those who have tended to regard the whole People's Democracy idea as a Communist stratagem to fool bourgeois adversaries. In many respects the logic of their argument has been persuasive, particularly in view of subsequent Soviet behavior in Eastern Europe. Certainly Communists at the time were aware of apprehensions both there and in the West about a "Bolshevization" of Eastern Europe, and were hopeful that their talk of preserving bourgeois political forms and a capitalist economy would disarm potential opposition to their program. Just as certainly their *ultimate* goal remained the realization of socialism on the Soviet model—they never denied this, even when they chose not to emphasize it.

Yet there is evidence to suggest that the Communists genuinely held the People's Democracy to be an accurate reflection of the present stage of the international class

struggle in 1945, corresponding to the bourgeois-democratic phase of the Russian Revolution in 1905-1917. Lenin's writings of that period, especially his "Two Tactics
of Social Democracy in the Democratic Revolution," were
intensively studied within party circles during the mid-
1940s, and have since been cited frequently by Communist sources as the inspiration for postwar policies. As
Isaac Deutscher has pointed out,

> . . . the concept of a people's democracy, as distinct
> from the Soviet system and the proletarian dictatorship,
> was for a time taken very seriously by the leaders of
> the Communist parties; and it was earnestly discussed
> by leading Russian political theorists *pro foro intero*.
> Stalin himself, it will be remembered, had been brought
> up on the notion of a system that was to have been
> neither fully capitalist nor socialist. This had been the
> idea behind the formula of the democratic dictatorship
> of the proletariat and the peasantry, to which he had
> stuck until 1917, and which he had put forward again
> in 1925-7, in the debate over the Chinese revolution.
> Towards the end of the war and some time later that
> idea was apparently back in his mind.[6]

Communist theorists appear to have updated Lenin as
follows: the victorious struggle against fascism had dealt
a deathblow to the feudal aristocracy and the most reactionary segment of the bourgeoisie, and had heightened
the class consciousness of the masses. It did *not*, however,
herald the advent of socialism, but rather the temporary
ascendancy of petty-bourgeois democracy. The goal of proletarian parties in all countries must therefore be to ally
themselves with the most progressive petty-bourgeois elements, in order to push the bourgeois democratic revolution as far as it could go in the present historical phase.
Where possible, as in Eastern Europe, Communists were
to make themselves the dominant force even within the
bourgeois republic. The task of the USSR as the inter-

national representative of the proletariat was analogous: to strengthen its own position in the world while seeking cooperation with progressive forces among the bourgeois powers.

Such a theoretical line took into account the concrete needs of the Soviet Union. As the leader of a badly exhausted and overextended nation, Stalin sought a postwar *modus vivendi* with his wartime allies that would keep his hard-won security gains from unraveling. His eagerness to agree on spheres of influence during the wartime conferences and his later efforts to rein in Communist activities in areas of Western interest such as Greece were evidence of this ambition. Anglo-American acquiescence was critical to his goal of forging a chain of friendly buffer states along his country's western frontier.[7]

Equally important, however, were structural changes within these states to prevent the resurgence of fascist or anti-Soviet forces. While more of a nationalist than a revolutionary, Stalin was still a Marxist and doubtless genuinely equated democratization with progress toward socialism. Especially after the experience of Hitler, though, he must have been deeply pessimistic about the ability of the wheel of history to roll forward of its own accord, at any rate in the foreseeable future. So much greater was the need, then, to create social systems that would at least not roll *backward* toward fascism as Germany and its allies had done.

The times called for compromise, and the People's Democracy was a formula for compromise. It included the minimum of social restructuring and Communist control which the USSR needed to guarantee an anti-fascist and pro-Soviet regime. At the same time it offered several concessions calculated to satisfy the (in the Communist view) more formalistic Western definition of democracy: (1) a multi-party state; (2) freedom of expression (subject, as under Western occupation regimes, to such limitations as necessary to suppress fascism); (3) free trade unions, independent of formal government or party control; and (4) retention of small-scale capitalism, purified of the dangerous monopolist concentrations abhorrent to Communist and petty bourgeois alike. Even Western-style elections were conceivable once fascist influences were under control, as the Saxon plebiscite was no doubt intended to show.

The real test of the People's Democracy model, of course, would be Germany, the archenemy now occupied jointly by the USSR and the West. Yet if Germany was therefore politically the most sensitive of all occupied areas, it also seemed to offer the greatest potential for cooperation, in that the occupying powers were all agreed on the need for basic reforms there. The main economic points of the Communist program—land reform and the elimination of private industrial concentrations—had already been endorsed in principle by the Western powers themselves.

By the time of the Potsdam conference the differences among the Big Three were becoming manifest. Yet the Anglo-American shift to a position opposing dismemberment of Germany—a shift that in itself must have deepened Soviet suspicions about Western intentions—seemed to offer Moscow at the same time added leverage with which to compel Western acceptance of the Soviet democratization scheme. The Soviets, having no strong preference for either unity or dismemberment, evolved a policy clearly aimed at setting precedents in their own zone which the West would have to follow if it wished to keep Germany intact. "What now set in," according to Doernberg, "was figuratively speaking a race between revolutionary democracy led by the working class, and imperialist reaction, for the fastest possible establishment of a strong, organized front." As the land reform, industrial sequestrations, the introducion of economic planning, and the union of the two socialist parties followed one another in rapid succession, Ulbricht and other Communist leaders proclaimed repeatedly that it was up to the Western powers to extend these democratic measures to their own zones, or to bear themselves the blame for partitioning Germany.[8]

The Communists, of course, miscalculated; and the policy of unilateral *faits accomplis*, when it became mutual, contributed to the deepening Cold War that finally divided Germany. A British Foreign Office report of June 1946 concluded that the Communist actions would bring a "complete communisation of the Eastern Zone" and "the creation of an economic structure so different from the rest of Germany as to render future amalgamation of the Eastern and Western zones administratively and economically impossible." This analysis strengthened the growing perception in London that the Soviets intended to exploit the Potsdam provisions on German unity to their exclusive advantage, and that Britain must therefore abandon its own adherence to the unity ideal and (in the words of the British ambassador to Moscow) "push ahead with the same vigour in organising our zone."[9]

The Americans, meanwhile, had long been suspicious that similar transformation measures elsewhere in Eastern Europe were aimed at installing Communist regimes behind a pseudo-democratic façade. The unilateral actions taken in the Soviet Zone were interpreted in this light and probably made U.S. authorities even less sympathetic than they otherwise might have been toward initiatives for economic reform in their own zone. When a 1946 referendum in Hesse produced a 71 percent majority in favor of a proposed article of the state constitution calling for socialization of industry, General Lucius Clay suspended the article's operation. Occupation authorities subsequently resisted delegating extensive economic powers to the German administrations for fear of further socialization attempts. A mild land redistribution forestalled the more radical restructuring sought by socialists.[10]

The question still remains, though: did the People's

Democracy model in fact represent a reasonable basis for compromise upon which a united, democratic, and neutral Germany, acceptable to both East and West, could have been built? Communist historians, as well as some Western revisionists, maintain that it did, and that the opportunity was lost through Western perfidy. Their arguments usually include the following two points:

(1) The Western powers were insincere, or at best halfhearted, in their commitment to democratization. They feared above all a true revolution that would threaten their hegemony abroad and their socioeconomic systems at home. Therefore, having contented themselves with a superficial purge of nominal Nazis, they concentrated their main energies on combating the threat of communism which they saw lurking in every effort to break down the old power structure in Germany. In so doing they removed any possible basis for compromise with the Soviet Union and created a new threat of neo-fascist West German revanchism which (especially after West Germany was rearmed and pumped up with economic aid) could only be answered by a tightening of controls and a crackdown on dissent in the East.

(2) The Communists alone offered a truly democratic solution for Germany. The Communists in the Soviet Zone sought and obtained genuine mass support for their transformation program. The Soviets provided overall guidance, but the program was implemented by Germans and was aimed at identifying the democratic elements in Germany itself and encouraging them to assert their power. By contrast, the Western powers suppressed all popular initiatives and looked to conservative Weimar politicians and the Nazi-ridden civil service for the instruments with which to reestablish capitalist rule.

There is no disputing that Western (particularly American) occupation policies were in fact negative, defensive, and often inimical to genuine democratic development. The Anglo-Americans regarded liberal democracy—not without reason—as a feeble growth in Germany, threatened by powerful radicalisms of both right and left. They therefore tended to see any spontaneous political activity as potentially fascist or communist in character. They also lacked their own clear conception of how, exactly, Germany was to be reconstructed as a democratic society. Such questions were expected to be resolved by inter-Allied agreements at a later date. This "policy of postponement," as it has been called, toward formulating a positive reconstruction program meant that Western efforts were perforce mainly negative: removal and punishment of Nazis and suppression of political activity.

Yet the lack of a positive program and of an alternative elite such as the KPD to help implement it, hampered the Western powers in their ability to reform the preexisting socioeconomic system. By eliminating the entire ruling elite of the old society, the Soviet Zone swept away at a stroke the main perpetrators and beneficiaries of fascism. The Anglo-Americans were unprepared to take such a radical course for a number of reasons: respect for law and private property, concern for the welfare of innocent individuals, and not least of all fear of social disruption that could foster communism. They therefore fell back on an unwieldy process of quasi-judicial denazification hearings which proved to be neither effective nor equitable. Many important Nazis and fascist sympathizers ultimately evaded prosecution while nominal Nazis were tried and punished. The economy and civil service remained full of reactionary (if apparently "apolitical") administrators rather than being staffed with technically less qualified but politically more reliable cadre as in the East.[11]

While the Western occupiers acknowledged the pernicious influence of Germany's military-industrial complex and backward agricultural system, the Americans in particular tended to see Nazism primarily as a moral evil arising out of some deep-seated perversion in the German psyche. Mass media in the U.S. Zone bombarded the German public with evidence of Nazi atrocities and with insistent reminders that they were all collectively responsible for these horrors. But no possibility of atonement or rehabilitation was offered: with all political initiatives regarded as suspect, the average citizen's safest course was still, as under the Nazis, passive obedience. The effect of the American preoccupation with collective guilt was thus to deepen alienation and cynicism among the German people and to encourage a sense of community between Nazis and non-Nazis, who were all tarred with the same brush.[12]

These failings of Western denazification serve to highlight the best features of the Communist program. The Communists looked to a reactionary socioeconomic system rather than to human wickedness as the source of the evil, and sought the active support of the German people in changing the system and rebuilding society. Isolating a relatively small group of active Nazis and economic leaders as the real criminals, they thereby enlisted the political energies of genuine anti-fascists on behalf of reconstruction, and offered a path of rehabilitation to the mass of lesser Nazis and to Germans in general. The spectacular recovery of the Soviet Zone in the first months of occupation showed the value of this positive approach.[13]

The problem with the Communist concept of democratization, however, was the narrowness of its focus. In concentrating on socioeconomic restructuring as a panacea—admittedly a valid strategy from a Marxist, materialist point of view—the Communists completely missed the significance of democracy in human terms. The "anti-fascist, democratic transformation" was, quite simply, a strategy for control. Its premises were neat: true democracy required the hegemony of the proletariat within society; the proletariat, however (particularly under the prevailing conditions of ideological confusion) must be guided by its Communist vanguard.

To insure proper development of the class struggle, then,

the Communists had to have all institutions "in our own hands," to use Ulbricht's phrase: the labor movement through a tightly-controlled FDGB riding herd over the workers' councils; the peasants through a centralized VdgB; the businessmen, artisans, shopkeepers, etc., through their own centralized organizations under FDGB surveillance; and finally the political system itself through a bloc of all licensed parties. The KPD's "compromises" were made in advance, in a vacuum, as part of an abstract political calculation that left no room for negotiation. KPD collaboration with other groups became ever more forthrightly an effort to secure their acquiescence in the KPD program by whatever means necessary. Popular anti-fascism, once mobilized, was directed into prescribed channels in which the correct "democratic" solution to every problem was worked out beforehand and any opposition automatically labeled "fascist."

It was this insistence on control, more than any of the radical measures introduced by the Soviet Zone regime per se, which violated the Western concept of democracy and lay at the heart of East-West misunderstanding on Germany's democratization.[14] The Anglo-American focus on guilt, however misdirected, reflected the important perception that the violence and inhumanity of fascism had a moral dimension, not just economic causes, and that some sort of spiritual regeneration was needed to build a peaceful and humane German society. By the standards of their own societies Western leaders could envision a "democratic" German government only as one that would represent the majority of Germans. The virtues that would make such a government a responsible member of the world community would therefore have to come from within the German people themselves, through an arduous process of learning tolerance for diversity—the very opposite of the passion for control. These virtues might be promoted by removing and punishing criminal leaders, advancing liberal-minded new leaders, and building democratic institutions; they could not, however, be imposed from without.

The Western powers viewed the Communist effort to democratize Germany by acquiring control over its political and economic system as nothing more than a thinly-disguised "Bolshevization," the exchange of one ideological tyranny for another. To the Soviets, on the other hand, the Western failure to destroy the old German elites utterly was a betrayal of the anti-fascist cause. "The so-called non-interference of the Western occupation powers in the process of Germany's democratization," writes former SMA political advisor Sergei Tjulpanov in retrospect, ". . . meant essentially the prevention of democratization, since *this process could not develop spontaneously.*"[15]

The relative merits of these divergent viewpoints can still be debated, and indeed still are. Certainly there were serious errors made on both sides. Over thirty years' experience with the two German states seems to justify the conclusion, however, that to the degree democracy has indeed become established in Germany, it has been and could only be the creation of the German people themselves.

Notes

CHAPTER ONE: THE COMMUNIST STRATEGY FOR GERMANY, 1935-1945

1. Arnold Sywottek, *Deutsche Volksdemokratie. Studien zur politischen Konzeption der KPD, 1935-1946,* "Studien zur modernen Geschichte" (Düsseldorf: Bertelsmann Universitätsverlag, 1971), pp. 27-28.

2. Ibid., pp. 35-39, 44-45; Wilhelm Pieck, *Advancing to Socialism. Report, Reply to the Discussion, and Resolution on the First Point of the Agenda: The Activities of the Executive Committee of the Communist International,* "Seventh World Congress of the Communist International" (Moscow-Leningrad: Cooperative Publishing Society of Foreign Workers in the U.S.S.R., 1935), p. 40.

3. Wilhelm Pieck, *Der neue Weg zum gemeinsamen Kampf für den Sturz der Hitlerdiktatur* (Berlin: Dietz Verlag, 1954), pp. 65-68, 163-64. The "Brussels" Conference was actually held at Rublevo, near Moscow. The name was a ruse to mislead Nazi intelligence.

4. Sywottek, *Dt. Volksdem.,* pp. 31-32, 48-49, 58-59.

5. Lewis Edinger, *German Exile Politics: The Social Democratic Executive Committee in the Nazi Era* (Berkeley and Los Angeles: University of California Press, 1956), pp. 42-117 passim.

6. Ibid., p. 133. Sywottek, *Dt. Volksdem.,* pp. 61-62.

7. Sywottek, *Dt. Volksdem.,* pp. 34, 48-49, 52-53, 60-62; Edinger, *German Exile Politics,* pp. 145-78 passim; Pieck, *Der neue Weg,* pp. 122-23.

8. "Resolution der Berner Konferenz der KPD," in *Zur Geschichte der Kommunistischen Partei Deutschlands* (Kiel: Rotfrontverlag und Literaturvertrieb, n.d.), pp. 393-95; Sywottek, *Dt. Volksdem.,* pp. 66-85 passim. The "Bern" Conference was held at Draveil, south of Paris.

9. Sywottek, *Dt. Volksdem.,* pp. 93-96.

10. Peter Kleist, *Zwischen Hitler und Stalin, 1939-1945* (Bonn: Athenäum-Verlag, 1950), pp. 242-43.

11. Jesco von Puttkamer, *Irrtum und Schuld* (Neuwied-Berlin: Michael Verlag, 1948), pp. 41-42.

12. Ibid., pp. 36-37, 43; Bodo Scheurig, *Free Germany,* trans. Herbert Arnold (Middletown, Conn.: Wesleyan University Press, 1969), pp. 34-36, 42-44; Heinrich von Einsiedel, *I Joined the Russians* (New Haven: Yale University Press, 1953), p. 61; Sywottek, *Dt. Volksdem.,* pp. 115-16.

13. Einsiedel, *I Joined,* pp. 66-67; Sywottek, *Dt. Volksdem.,* pp. 132-34; Scheurig, *Free Germany,* pp. 46-49.

14. Puttkamer, *Irrtum,* pp. 53, 55, 76; Sywottek, *Dt. Volksdem.,* pp. 127-30; Scheurig, *Free Germany,* pp. 102, 114-18.

15. Sywottek, *Dt. Volksdem.,* pp. 134-38, 142-44; Scheurig, *Free Germany,* pp. 163-65. Puttkamer attributes to a leading KPD emigré the following reply to a query about the future of the senior NKFD officers: "Do you seriously think, Herr von Frankenburg, that people of your class can still play a part in the new Germany? The first concern is to see that the Communist Party gains ground in Germany. And we Communists cannot burden ourselves with you and your class comrades. Even if our policy should require cooperation with the bourgeois parties in the beginning, that can never be more than a temporary solution" (*Irrtum,* pp. 83-84).

16. Alexander Fischer, *Sowjetische Deutschlandpolitik im Zweiten Weltkrieg, 1941-1945* (Stuttgart: Deutsche Verlags-Anstalt, 1975), pp. 60-75 passim; Adam B. Ulam, *Expansion and Coexistence: The History of Soviet Foreign Policy 1917-67* (New York and Washington: Praeger Publishers, 1973), pp. 351-56; Scheurig, *Free Germany,* pp. 78-79, 139-41.

17. Horst Laschitza, *Kämpferische Demokratie gegen Faschismus* (Berlin: Deutscher Militärverlag, 1969), p. 90. Dimitrov's key role here and in later decisions on KPD strategy, despite formal dissolution of the Comintern in May 1943, points up the continued coordination of Soviet policy toward Germany with that toward other East European countries in this period. Cf. Dietrich Staritz, *Sozialismus in einem halben Land. Zur Programmatik und Politik der KPD/SED in der Phase der antifaschistisch-demokratischen Unwälzung in der DDR* (Berlin: Verlag Klaus Wagenbach, 1976), pp. 142-46.

18. Laschitza, *Kämpf. Dem.*, pp. 106-7. Cf. Fischer, *Sow. Deutschlandpolitik*, pp. 86-88.

19. V. I. Lenin, *Two Tactics of Social Democracy in the Democratic Revolution*, in V. I. Lenin, *Selected Works*, Vol. 3: *The Revolution of 1905-07* (New York: International Publishers, n.d.), p. 102. Original italics.

20. Ibid., pp. 73-102 passim; Laschitza, *Kämpf. Dem.*, pp. 104-6.

21. Laschitza, *Kämpf. Dem.*, pp. 82-92.

22. Peter Kirste, "Wirtschaftspolitik und antiimperialistische Umwälzung. Zur Erarbeitung wesentlicher Grundsätze der wirtschaftspolitischen Konzeption der KPD für die antifaschistisch-demokratische Umwälzung (February 1944-April 1945)," *Jahrbuch für Geschichte* 14 (1976):240; "Aktionsprogramm des Blockes der kämpferischen Demokratie," in Laschitza, *Kämpf. Dem.*, pp. 194, 200-201.

23. Kirste, "Wirtschaftspolitik," pp. 242-44; Laschitza, *Kämpf. Dem.*, pp. 94-95; "Aktionsprogramm," p. 195; Fischer, *Sow. Deutschlandpolitik*, pp. 90-94.

24. "Aktionsprogramm," pp. 196, 201-2.

25. Laschitza, *Kämpf. Dem.*, p. 196; "Aktionsprogramm," pp. 201-2; Edwin Hoernle, "Das Agrarprogramm des Blocks der Kämpferischen Demokratie," in Edwin Hoernle, *Zum Bündnis zwischen Arbeitern und Bauern* (Berlin: Dietz Verlag, 1972), p. 341.

26. Hoernle, "Agrarprogramm," pp. 333-34, 338; Sywottek, *Dt. Volksdem.*, pp. 176-77. The Action Program's promise of "free cooperatives" was obviously intended to call to mind something like the old Raiffeisen cooperatives abolished by Hitler, rather than any socialist institution.

27. Sywottek, *Dt. Volksdem.*, pp. 152-54; Laschitza, *Kämpf. Dem.*, pp. 92, 94, 116-17; Fischer, *Sow. Deutschlandpolitik*, pp. 86, 94-95; Hoernle, "Agrarprogramm," p. 338.

28. "Report of the Crimea Conference," in U.S. Department of State, *Foreign Relations of the United States. Diplomatic Papers. The Conferences at Malta and Yalta, 1945* (Washington: U.S. Government Printing Office, 1955), p. 970; Sywottek, *Dt. Volksdem.*, pp. 172-73; Fischer, *Sow. Deutschlandpolitik*, pp. 80-81; Ulam, *Exp. and Coex.*, p. 370.

29. U.S. Dept. of State, *Malta and Yalta*, pp. 613-16; "Protocol of the Proceedings of the Crimea Conference," ibid., p. 978.

30. Isaac Deutscher, *Stalin: A Political Biography*, 2d ed. (New York: Oxford University Press, 1967), pp. 539-40; Fischer, *Sow. Deutschlandpolitik*, p. 131; Ulam, *Exp. and Coex.*, p. 381; Ilya Ehrenburg, *Men, Years—Life*, Vol. 5: *The War 1941-45*, trans. Tatiana Shebunina and Yvonne Kapp (London: MacGibbon & Kee, 1964), pp. 176-77. Cf. Sywottek, *Dt. Volksdem.*, pp. 159-62.

31. Günter Benser, "Die Befreiung Europas vom Faschismus durch die Sowjetunion und der Beginn des Übergangs vom Kapitalismus zum Sozialismus auf dem Territorium der DDR," *ZfG* 23, no. 4 (1975):370; Sywottek, *Dt. Volksdem.*, pp. 172-73, 179-80.

32. Laschitza, *Kämpf. Dem.*, pp. 136, 138-39, 156; Edwin Hoernle, "Die Agrarpolitik des Blocks der kämpferischen Demokratie," in ibid., pp. 214, 218-19; "Richtlinien für die Arbeit der deutschen Antifaschisten in dem von der Roten Armee besetzten deutschen Gebiet," in ibid., pp. 251, 253.

33. "Richtlinien für die Arbeit," pp. 250-52; Paul Schwenk and Paul Wandel, "Richtlinien für die Tätigkeit der lokalen Volksausschüsse auf dem Gebiet der Wirtschaft," ibid., p. 231.

34. Günter Benser, "Die Anfänge der demokratischen Blockpolitik," *ZfG* 23 (1975):757; Laschitza, *Kämpf. Dem.*, pp. 114-15, 117. Cf. Sywottek, *Dt. Volksdem.*, pp. 191-92.

CHAPTER TWO: A NEW FOUNDATION, SPRING AND SUMMER 1945

1. Wolfgang Leonhard, *Die Revolution entlässt ihre Kinder* (Cologne and Berlin: Kiepenhauer & Witsch, 1955), pp. 348ff.; Rudolf Dörrier, *Pankow. Kleine Chronik eines Berliner Bezirks* (Berlin: Das neue Berlin [1949]), pp. 59-60, 64, 79; J. P. Nettl, *The Eastern Zone and Soviet Policy in Germany* (London: Oxford University Press, 1951), pp. 56-57; "Wohin mit den Flüchtlingen und Evakuierten?" *Deutsche Volkszeitung* (official KPD organ in Berlin, hereafter *DVZ*), 10 July, 1945, p. 1.

2. Siegfried Thomas, *Entscheidung in Berlin. Zur Entstehungsgeschichte der SED in der deutschen Hauptstadt, 1945/46* (Berlin: Akademie-Verlag, 1964), pp. 23-27, 32-33; Helfried Weh-

ner, "Dresden in den ersten Jahren des revolutionären Umwälz-
ungsprozesses und die Hilfe der Sowjetunion," in Helfried Wehner, ed., *Kampfgefährten, Weggenossen: Erinnerungen deutscher
und sowjetischer Genossen an die ersten Jahre der antifaschistisch-demokratischen Unwälzung in Dresden* (Berlin: Dietz Verlag, 1975), pp. 39-40; Alexander Solowjow, "Meine ersten Ein-
drücke als Politstellvertreter des Stadtkommandanten," in
Wehner, ed., *Kampfgefährten*, p. 107; Max Seydewitz, *Zerstörung und Wiederaufbau von Dresden* (Berlin: Kongress-Verlag,
1955), pp. 256, 264; Dörrier, *Pankow*, pp. 64-65.

3. Heinz Vosske, "Zur Tätigkeit der Initiativgruppe des ZK
der KPD von Anfang Mai bis Anfang Juni 1945 in Mecklen-
burg/Vorpommern," in Bernhard Weissel, ed., *Befreiung und
Neubeginn. Zur Stellung des 8. Mai 1945 in der deutschen Geschichte* (Berlin: Akademie-Verlag, 1968), p. 193; Laschitza,
Kämpf. Dem., pp. 140-41.

4. Karl Urban, "Die Herausbildung der Aktionseinheit der
Arbeiterklasse und der demokratischen Selbstverwaltungsor-
gane unter Führung der KPD in der Provinz Brandenburg (Ende
April bis Anfang Juni 1945)," *BzG* 5, no. 5/6 (1963):888, 890-91;
Vosske, "Zur Tätigkeit," pp. 194-95; Wehner, "Dresden," pp.
25-31; Laschitza, *Kämpf. Dem.*, pp. 142, 154.

5. Walter Ulbricht, "Die geeinte Arbeiterklasse führte das Volk
aus der Katastrophe," in Walter Ulbricht, *Zur Geschichte der
deutschen Arbeiterbewegung*, Vol. 2, first supplement (Berlin:
Dietz Verlag, 1966), p. 221; Laschitza, *Kämpf. Dem.* pp. 159-60.

6. "Ein Tag beim Block-Obmann," *DVZ*, 8 July 1945, p. 4.

7. Karl J. Germer, *Von Grotewohl bis Brandt: ein dokumentarischer Bericht über die SPD in den ersten Nachkriegsjahren*
(Landshut: Verlag Politisches Archiv, 1974), p. 15.

8. Karl Fugger, *Aktuelle Fragen der Gewerkschaftsbewegung*
(Berlin: Vorstand des Freien Deutschen Gewerkschaftsbundes,
[1946?]), p. 24; Letter by General Lucius Clay to the U.S. Secretary of War, dated 13 October 1945, in Jean Edward Smith,
ed., *The Papers of General Lucius D. Clay: Germany 1945-1949*,
Vol. 1 (Bloomington: Indiana University Press, 1974), p. 102;
"Clay to Hilldring" (letter dated 5 July 1945), in Smith, ed., *Clay*,
p. 47.

9. Seydewitz, *Dresden*, p. 268.

10. Karl-Heinz Gräfe and Helfried Wehner, "Zur Politik der

Sowjetischen Militäradministration in Sachsen," *ZfG* 23
(1975):899-900; Edgar Böttcher, *Der Kampf des Nationalkomitees "Freies Deutschland" rettet Leipzig am Ende des zweiten Weltkriegs vor der Zerstörung* (Leipzig: Museum für Geschichte der Stadt Leipzig, 1965), pp. 16-18; Gerd Rackow, Martin Heyne, and Oswald Kleinpeter, *Rostock 1945 bis zur Gegenwart* (Rostock: VEB Hinstorff Verlag, 1969), p. 34; Thomas, *Entscheidung*, pp. 20, 29-30.

11. Manfred Unger, "Herausbildung revolutionär-demokratischer Staatsorgane in Kreisen des Bezirks Leipzig, Mai-Oktober 1945," in Karl-Heinz Schöneburg et al., *Revolutionärer Prozess und Staatsentstehung* (Berlin: Akademie-Verlag, 1976), pp. 31-35; Hans Gottwald, "Die Entmachtung der Grossgrundbesitzer und Naziaktivisten und die Herausbildung neuer Produktionsverhältnisse in der Landwirtschaft während der ersten Etappe der demokratischen Bodenreform im Herbst 1945 auf dem Territorium des heutigen Bezirks Erfurt" (Ph.D. dissertation, Univ. of Halle-Wittenberg, 1974), p. 117; Ulrich Seemann, "Der Beginn des antifaschistisch-demokratischen Neuaufbaus in Rostock im Mai 1945," *Rostocker Beiträge* 1 (1968):168; "Zur Auflösung des Antinazikomittes," *Thüringer Volkszeitung* (a KPD organ, hereafter *TVZ*), 19 September 1945, p. 5.

12. Thomas, *Entscheidung*, p. 30.

13. Ibid., pp. 20, 31; Ute Schmidt and Tilman Fichter, *Der erzwungene Kapitalismus. Klassenkämpfe in den Westzonen 1945-48* (Berlin: Verlag Klaus Wagenbach, 1971), pp. 49-50.

14. Thomas, *Entscheidung*, pp. 30-31; Leonhard, *Rev. entlässt*, pp. 381-82; Walter Ulbricht, "Aus einem Brief an Genossen Dimitroff" (9 May 1945), in Ulbricht, *Gesch. . . . Arbeiterbew.* 2:419; Walter Ulbricht, "Aus einem Brief an Genossen Wilhelm Pieck" (17 May 1945) in Ulbricht, *Gesch. . . . Arbeiterbew.*, 2:1st supp., p. 204; Interview with Prof. Walter Bartel, Professor Emeritus of History at Humboldt University of Berlin and former personal consultant to Wilhelm Pieck, 26 May 1977.

15. Ulbricht, "Brief an Dimitroff," p. 419.

16. Leonhard, *Rev. entlässt*, pp. 356-58; Karl-Heinz Schöneburg, *Von den Anfängen unseres Staates* (Berlin: Staatsverlag der DDR, 1975), p. 35; Sywottek, *Dt. Volksdem.*, pp. 185, 198; Wolfgang Diepenthal, *Drei Volksdemokratien*, "Abhandlungen des Bundesinstituts für ostwissenschaftliche und internationale

Studien," Vol. 29 (Cologne: Verlag Wissenschaft und Politik, 1974), p. 146; Walter Ulbricht, "Protokoll einer Beratung mit Parteileitern der KPD der Provinz Brandenburg in Berlin" (27 June 1945), in Ulbricht, Gesch. . . . Arbeiterbew., 2:1st supp., p. 232.

17. Thomas, *Entscheidung*, pp. 32-34; Fischer, *Sow. Deutschlandpolitik*, p. 153; Horst Eisermann, "Die städtischen Mittelschichten in der revolutionären Umwälzung von 1945 bis 1949/50, die Entwicklung ihrer Struktur und ihrer Stellung in der Gesellschaft, insbesondere zur Arbeiterklasse, dargestellt am Beispiel des ehemaligen Landes Sachsen-Anhalt" (Ph.D. dissertation, Univ. of Leipzig, 1973), p. 27; Berlin-Lichtenberg, Örtliche Kommission zur Erforschung der Geschichte der deutschen Arbeiterbewegung, *Die Grosse Kraft: Erlebnisberichte vom Kampf um die Einheit der Arbeiterklasse, Berlin-Lichtenberg, Juni 1945-April 1946* (Berlin: SED Kreisleitung Lichtenberg, 1966), p. 19; Wehner, "Dresden," pp. 25-31, 57. In fairness to the KPD, it should be noted that the composition of the administrations did reflect in part the far greater number of Social Democrats and Communists who had proven their anti-fascist sympathies in the resistance movement, and the apolitical or anti-Communist attitudes of most middle-class citizens.

18. Thomas, *Entscheidung*, pp. 86-87; Rudolf Eberhard, *Ein Jahr Aufbauarbeit in Magdeburg. Rechenschaftsbericht der Stadtverwaltung über die im ersten Jahr nach dem Hitlerkreig geleistete Arbeit, erstattet in der 1. Beratenden Versammlung am 27. Juli 1946 von Oberbürgermeister Eberhard* (Magdeburg: n.p., [1946?]), pp. 14, 17; Schöneburg, *Anfängen*, p. 39; Dörrier, *Pankow*, pp. 63-64.

19. Anton Ackermann, "Wohin soll der Weg gehen?" *DVZ*, 14 June 1945, p. 1.

20. Walter Ulbricht, *Volksentscheid und Wirtschaftsaufbau* (Dresden: Sachsenverlag, Druckerei und Verlags-Gesellschaft m.b.H., [1946?]), p. 9; Anton Ackermann, "Gebot der Selbsterhaltung," *DVZ*, 16 June 1945, p. 1; "Was tun mit den kleinen Pgs?" *DVZ*, 29 June, 1945, p. 1; Stefan Doernberg, *Die Geburt Eines neuen Deutschland 1945-1949* (Berlin: Rütten & Loening, 1959), p. 95.

21. Doernberg, *Geburt*, pp. 280-281; Horst Lipski, *Der Kampf der deutschen Arbeiterklasse und aller demokratischen Kräfte*

unter der Führung der Partei um die Errichtung der antifaschist-isch-demokratischen Ordnung in Deutschland (1945-1949) (Berlin: Parteihochschule "Karl Marx" beim ZK der SED, 1960), p. 46. See Chapter Four below.

22. Benno Sarel, *La Classe ouvrière d'Allemagne orientale* (Paris: Les Éditions Ouvrières, 1958), p. 22; *Aus der Praxis der Betriebsräte: Tatsachen, Erfahrungen, Aufgaben in der sowjetischen Besatzungszone* (Berlin: Freier Deutscher Gewerkschaftsbund, 1946), pp. 6-7; Walter Ulbricht, "Aus der Diskussionsrede auf der Wirtschaftstagung des Magistrats von Gross-Berlin mit Gewerbetreibenden, Unternehmern, und Gewerkschaftsvertretern" (July 25, 1945), in Ulbricht, *Gesch. . . . Arbeiterbew.*, 2:1st supp., pp. 250-54.

23. Fred Oelsner, "Die wirtschaftlichen Aufgaben der Gewerkschaften und Betriebsräte," *DVZ*, 30 Sept. 1945, p. 3; Interview with Dr. Claus Montag of the Institute for International Relations (GDR), 12 March 1975.

24. Dörrier, *Pankow*, pp. 72, 79-80; Horst Barthel, "Probleme der wirtschaftlichen Entwicklung der Deutschen Demokratischen Republik in der Nachkriegsperiode (1945-1949/50)" (Dissertation for habilitation, Humboldt University of Berlin, 1968), pp. 132-33; Thomas, *Entscheidung*, p. 90; Office of Strategic Services (OSS), "Field Intelligence Study 8: Russian Economic Policies in Germany," dated 13 July 1945 (NARS, Record Group 260: General Correspondence of U.S. Group Control Council, OMGUS, 1944-45; hereafter NARS RG 260), p. 18.

25. Dörrier, *Pankow*, pp. 79-80; Fritz Selbmann, Anfänge der Wirtschaftsplanung in Sachsen," *BzG* 14, no. 1 (1972):76-77.

26. Eberhard, *Magdeburg*, pp. 21-22, 51; Dörrier, *Pankow*, pp. 54-55, 57, 77; OSS, "Russian Econ. Policies," p. 8; Erhard Forgbert, "Die Entstehung eines neuen, demokratischen Finanzwesens," in Johannes Schildhauer et al., ed., *Befreiung und Neubeginn* (Berlin: Staatsverlag der DDR, 1966), pp. 235-36.

27. Sarel, *Classe ouvrière*, pp. 22-23; Fritz Selbmann, *Demokratische Wirtschaft*, "Dokumente der neuen Zeit," Vol. 3 (Dresden: Dresdener Verlagsgesellschaft K.G., [1948]), p. 58; Dörrier, *Pankow*, p. 80.

28. Barthel, "Probleme der . . . Entwicklung," pp. 137-38; Dörrier, *Pankow*, p. 80; Thomas, *Entscheidung*, p. 90; Selbmann, "Anf. der Wirtschaftsplanung," p. 77.

29. Barthel, "Probleme der . . . Entwicklung," pp. 2, 8-10;
Staritz, *Sozialismus*, pp. 12-14.

30. Barthel, "Probleme der . . . Entwicklung," pp. 25, 33-39;
Staritz, *Sozialismus*, pp. 12-14.

31. OSS, "Russian Econ. Policies," pp. 13-17, 19-20; "Antwort
Walter Ulbrichts vom 11. Juli 1945 auf Fragen über die Ziele der
antifaschistisch-demokratischen Landwirtschaftspolitik," in Institut für Marxismus-Leninismus beim Zentralkomitee der SED
(hereafter IML), *Dokumente und Materialien zur Geschichte der
deutschen Arbeiterbewegung*, Series 3, Vol. 1: *Mai 1945-April
1946* (Berlin: Dietz Verlag, 1959), p. 57; "Der Landeinsatz der
Berliner," *DVZ*, 8 July, 1945, p. 1; "Rostock im Landeinsatz,"
ibid.; "Verlassene Höfe benötigen Arbeitskräfte," ibid.

32. Walter Ulbricht, *Zur Geschichte der neuesten Zeit*, Vol.
1, first semi-volume (Berlin: Dietz Verlag, 1955), p. 243; "Befehl
No. 1 des Chefs der Besatzung der Stadt Berlin betr. Banken-
schliessung, 28. April 1945 (Auszugsweise)," in Günther Kohlmey and Charles Dewey, *Bankensystem und Geldumlauf in der
Deutschen Demokratischen Republik 1945-1955* (Berlin: Verlag
Die Wirtschaft, 1956), p. 115; "Befehl O1 vom 23. Juli 1945;
Neuorganisierung der deutschen Finanz-und Kreditorgane," in
ibid., pp. 115-18; *Neuaufbau der deutschen Wirtschaft. Richtlinien der KPD zur Wirtschaftspolitik* (Berlin: Verlag neuer Weg,
[1946]), p. 25; Diepenthal, *Drei Volksdem.*, pp. 155-56.

33. D. Bach, "20 bis 25 Prozent," *DVZ*, 21 November 1945,
p. 1; "Abhebungsfreigabe für Kleinkonteninhaber," *DVZ*, 12
March 1946, p. 1; "Die Organisation der Finanz-und Kreditin-
stitute in Deutschland (Bekanntgegeben am 4. August 1945),"
in Kohlmey/Dewey, *Bankensystem*, pp. 118-19.

34. OSS, "Russian Econ. Policies," pp. 2-3; Philip M. Raup,
"Land Reform in Post-War Germany: The Soviet Zone Experiment" (Ph.D. dissertation, Univ. of Wisconsin, 1949), p. 322.
Raup, who was chief land specialist with the Office of Military
Government for Germany, U.S. (OMGUS) from 1945 to 1949,
asserts that Red Army requisitions, particularly of livestock,
"unquestionably" damaged postwar East German agriculture more
than the war itself. Lt. Gen. Lucius D. Clay, deputy military
governor of the U.S. Zone, reported to Assistant Secretary of
War John J. McCloy in October 1945 that "East of the Elbe . . .

the Russians have requisitioned about 70 to 80 percent of the livestock" (Smith, ed., *Clay*, p. 97).

35. Josef Deckers, *Die Transformation des Bankensystems in der sowjetischen Besatzungszone/DDR von 1945 bis 1952*, Osteuropa-Institut an der Freien Universität Berlin, "Wirtschaftswissenschaftliche Veröffentlichungen," Vol. 36 (Berlin: Duncker & Humbolt, 1974), pp. 24-27. Deckers argues convincingly that all other objectives given as reasons for this Soviet action could have been achieved by other means, such as the temporary limitations on bank account withdrawals imposed by the Western powers to restrict the money supply. "Since the cash balances of the old financial institutions were not taken over by the new banks that were later founded," he adds, "one can fairly well assume that they were indeed confiscated by the Soviets."

36. Wolfgang Schumann et al., *Carl Zeiss Jena: Einst und Jetzt* (Berlin: Rütten & Loening, 1962), p. 605; *Neuaufbau der deutschen Wirtschaft. Referat und Diskussion über die Richtlinien der KPD zur Wirtschaftspolitik* (Berlin: Verlag Neuer Weg, [1946]), p. 16; Barthel, "Probleme . . . der Entwicklung," p. 127.

37. Sarel, *Classe ouvrière*, pp. 23-24; Gert Leptin, *Die deutsche Wirtschaft nach 1945: Ein Ost-West Vergleich* (Opladen: Leske Verlag, 1970), pp. 49-51; Staritz, *Sozialismus*, pp. 15-21. Staritz offers here a good summary of available information about the extent and economic effect of reparations. Official statistics have never been released by the Soviets or East Germans. Barthel, "Probleme der . . . Entwicklung," p. 100; Leonhard, *Rev. entlässt*, p. 412; Sozialistische Einheitspartei Deutschlands (SED), Kreisleitung VEB Leuna-Werke "Walter Ulbricht," *Befreites Leuna (1945-1950)*, Part 2, "Geschichte der Fabriken und Werke," Vol. 8 (Berlin: Verlag Tribüne, 1959), pp. 140-45; Raup, "Land Reform," p. 322.

38. Sarel, *Classe ouvrière*, pp. 23-24; Horst Schützler, "Die Unterstützung der Sowjetunion für die demokratischen Kräfte Berlins in den ersten Nachkriegsmonaten," *ZfG* 13, no. 3 (1965):414; Andreas Loewe, *Andreas Loewe: Eine Familie und ihr Werk von 1872 bis heute* (Lüneburg: Nordland-Druck, 1968), p. 62. Also from numerous private conversations.

39. OSS, "Russian Econ. Policies," p. 13.

40. Fritz Selbmann, "Die UdSSR unterstützte den Wiederaufbau des Wirtschaftslebens," *Deutsche Aussenpolitik* 10, spe-

cial issue 1 (1965): *20 Jahre Danach: Deutschland 1945/1965,* p. 109.

41. Leonhard, *Rev. entlässt,* pp. 416, 462; Schmidt/Fichter, *erzwungene Kap.,* pp. 88-90; Gabriel Kolko, *The Politics of War: The World and United States Foreign Policy, 1943-45* (New York: Random House, 1968), p. 516; Selbmann, "UdSSR unterstützte," p. 111; Barthel, "Probleme der . . . Entwicklung," pp. 96-97; SED, Betriebsparteiorganisation Bewag, *Unsere Kraft: Betriebsgeschichte der Bewag,* Part 1: 1884-1945 (Berlin: n.p., [1974?]), pp. 81-82; Freier Deutscher Gewerkschaftsbund (hereafter FDGB), Landesausschuss Sachsen, "Rundschreiben Nr. 13," dated 23 November 1945 (Zentralarchiv des FDGB, FDGB Bundesvorstand: Folder No. A687).

42. Hence the summary annexation by the USSR of all of eastern Poland and part of Czechoslovakia, and its exaction of reparations from Rumania, Bulgaria, Finland, Austria, and Hungary. Cf. Deutscher, *Stalin,* pp. 536-37.

43. Ibid., pp. 537-38. Deutscher's conclusion (pp. 536-42) that Stalin was primarily a conservative leader pursuing the interests of the Russian state, but that he was forced to assume a more revolutionary stance by the pressures and expectations of domestic Communist elites, is reinforced in a recent study by William O. McCagg, Jr., entitled *Stalin Embattled 1943-1945* (Detroit: Wayne State University Press, 1978).

44. Milovan Djilas, *Conversations with Stalin,* trans. Michael B. Petrovich (New York: Harcourt, Brace & World, 1962), p. 114.

45. Cf. Ulam, *Exp. and Coex.,* p. 392.

46. Djilas, *Conv. with Stalin,* p. 114.

47. Cf. S. I. Tjulpanov. "Die Zusammenarbeit der SMAD und der SED im Kampf für Demokratie und Sozialismus," in E. Kalbe and S. I. Tjulpanov, ed., *Einheit—im Kampfe geboren* (Leipzig: Karl-Marx-Universität Leipzig, 1975), p. 95; S. I. Tjulpanov, "Die Rolle der Sowjetischen Militäradministration im demokratischen Deutschland," in Gertraud Teuschner et al., *50 Jahre Triumph des Marxismus-Leninismus* (Berlin: Dietz Verlag, 1967), p. 49. Colonel (later General) Tjulpanov was political advisor to the chief of the SMA, and thus the main coordinator of Soviet political activities in Germany in 1945-46.

48. Ulbricht, "Brief an Pieck," pp. 204-5; Sywottek, *Dt. Volks-*

dem., p. 196; Lutz Niethammer, *Entnazifizierung in Bayern* (Frankfurt a.M.: S. Fischer Verlag, 1972), pp. 112-14.

49. Ulbricht, "Brief an Pieck," pp. 204-5; Sywottek, *Dt. Volksdem.*, p. 199; Office of the Director of Intelligence, OMGUS, "Recent Evidences of Russian Interference in German Political Activity," dated 5 February 1946 (NARS RG 260), pp. 1, A-1.

50. "Protokoll einer Beratung mit Parteileitern der KPD der Provinz Brandenburg in Berlin" (27 June 1945), in Ulbricht, *Geschichte. . . . Arbeiterbew.*, 2:1st supp., pp. 232-33.

51. Kommunistische Partei Deutschlands, *Der Sieg des Faschismus in Deutschland und seine Lehren für unseren gegenwärtigen Kampf,* "Vortragsdisposition No. 1" (Berlin: Kommunistische Partei Deutschlands, [1945]), pp. 5-10; Franz Dahlem, "Die Organisationspolitik der Partei," in Kommunistische Partei Deutschlands, *Bericht über die Verhandlungen des 15. Parteitages der Kommunistischen Partei Deutschlands (19. und 20. April in Berlin)* (Berlin: Verlag Neuer Weg, 1946), pp. 64-66.

52. KPD, *Sieg des Faschismus,* passim; cf. Staritz, *Sozialismus*, pp. 60-61.

53. Walter Ulbricht, "Entwurf zu Anweisungen für die Anfangsmassnahmen zum Aufbau der Parteiorganisation" (18 February 1945), in Laschitza, *Kämpf. Dem.*, pp. 228-29; Thomas, *Entscheidung*, p. 41.

54. Jürgen Klein, *Vereint sind sie alles! Untersuchungen zur Entstehung von Einheitsgewerkschaften in Deutschland von der Weimarer Republik bis 1946/47,* "Schriften der Stiftung Europa-Kolleg Hamburg," Vol. 23 (Hamburg: Fundament-Verlag Dr. Sasse & Co., 1972), pp. 231-32; Frank Moraw, *Die Parole der "Einheit" und die Sozialdemokratie,* "Schriftenreihe des Forschungsinstituts der Friedrich-Ebert-Stiftung," Vol. 94 (Bonn-Bad Godesberg: Verlag Neue Gesellschaft, 1973), pp. 82-84; Germer, *Grotewohl-Brandt*, pp. 19-20, 24, 30-31.

55. Cf. Benser, "Die Anfänge," pp. 759-60.

56. Leonhard, *Rev. entlässt*, pp. 402-5; Laschitza, *Kämpf. Dem.*, pp. 125-26, 187-88.

57. "Statement by the Governments of the United Kingdom, the United States, the USSR, and the Provisional Government of the French Republic on Zones of Occupation in Germany (5 June 1945)," in Beate Ruhm von Oppen, ed., *Documents on Germany under Occupation, 1945-1954* (London: Oxford Uni-

versity Press, 1955), p. 35; "Declaration Regarding the Defeat of Germany and the Assumption of Supreme Authority with Respect to Germany by the Governments of the United Kingdom, the United States, the USSR and the Provisional Government of the French Republic (5 June 1945)," in ibid., pp. 29-35; "Soviet Military Administration Order No. 1: The Organization of the Military Administration for the Administration of the Soviet Zone (9 June 1945)," in ibid., p. 37; "Soviet Military Administration Order No. 2: Establishment of Anti-Fascist Parties and Free Trade Unions in the Soviet Zone (10 June 1945)," in ibid., pp. 37-38; "Aufruf der Kommunistischen Partei Deutschlands," *DVZ*, 13 June 1945, p. 1; Letter published by Karl Maron (KPD), first deputy mayor of Berlin, cited in Henry Krisch, *German Politics under Soviet Occupation* (New York and London: Columbia University Press, 1974), p. 57; Germer, *Grotewohl-Brandt*, p. 31.

58. Germer, *Grotewohl-Brandt*, pp. 31, 35; Leonhard, *Rev. entlässt*, pp. 402-5; Thomas, *Entscheidung*, pp. 46-47.

59. "Gründungsaufruf der Christlich-Demokratischen Union Deutschlands" (26 June 1945), in German Democratic Republic, Ministerium für auswärtige Angelegenheiten, and USSR, Ministerium für auswärtige Angelegenheiten, *Um ein antifaschistisch-demokratisches Deutschland: Dokumente aus den Jahren 1945-1949* (hereafter *Dokumente 1945-49*; Berlin: Staatsverlag der DDR, 1968), pp. 78-81; Peter Hermes, *Die Christlich-Demokratische Union und die Bodenreform in der Sowjetischen Besatzungszone Deutschlands im Jahre 1945* (Saarbrücken: Verlag der Saarbrücker Zeitung, 1963), pp. 20-22.

60. "Gründungsaufruf der Liberal-Demokratischen Partei Deutschlands" (5 July 1945), in *Dokumente 1945-49*, pp. 88-91; Diepenthal, *Drei Volksdem.*, pp. 96-97.

61. "Aufruf des Zentralausschusses der Sozialdemokratischen Partei Deutschlands zum Aufbau eines antifaschistisch-demokratischen Deutschlands" (15 June 1945), in *Dokumente 1945-49*, pp. 67-71.

62. Ibid.; Germer, *Grotewohl-Brandt*, pp. 39, 86-87; Moraw, *Parole*, pp. 87-88. The "eastward orientation" pursued by the Grotewohl faction was not only resisted by a significant minority in the Berlin SPD, but was bitterly opposed by SPD leaders in the West, such as Erich Ollenhauer and Kurt Schumacher,

with far more seniority in the party than any in the Central Committee. In both KPD and SPD the impulse for immediate merger throughout Germany tended to be strongest among the junior and middle-ranking functionaries who had cooperated with one another in resistance and Antifa groups during and just after the war. (See: Edinger, *German Exile Politics*, pp. 236-38, 240; Germer, *Grotewohl-Brandt*, pp. 38-39; Staritz, *Sozialismus*, p. 66.)

63. Freier Deutscher Gewerkschaftsbund, *Protokoll der ersten allgemeinen Delegiertenkonferenz des Freien Deutschen Gewerkschaftsbundes für das sowjetisch besetzte deutsche Gebiet, 9.-11. Februar 1946, Berlin* (Berlin: n.p., [1946]), pp. 127-28 (speech by Ulbricht); Sywottek, *Dt. Volksdem.*, pp. 206-7; Thomas, *Entscheidung*, pp. 58-60, 69.

64. "Aufruf der KPD"; Benser, "Die Befreiung," p. 365.

65. Cf. Nettl, *Eastern Zone*, pp. 77-78; Sywottek, *Dt. Volksdem.*, pp. 205-6.

66. Wilhelm Pieck, "Feste Einheit der demokratischen Kräfte," *DVZ*, 13 June 1945, p. 1; Thomas, *Entscheidung*, pp. 65-66.

67. Diepenthal, *Drei Volksdem.*, pp. 93, 104, 140-41; Sywottek, *Dt. Volksdem.*, p. 192; Tjulpanov, "Rolle der Sow. Militäradm.," p. 57; Leonard Krieger, "The Inter-Regnum in Germany: March-August 1945," *Political Science Quarterly* 64, no. 4 (1949):529-30.

68. Sergei I. Tjulpanov, "Die Rolle der SMAD bei der Demokratisierung Deutschlands," *ZfG* 15 (1967):248; Moraw, *Parole*, p. 95; Krieger, "Inter-Regnum," pp. 530-31.

69. Germer, *Grotewohl-Brandt*, pp. 29-30, 53.

70. Klein, *Vereint . . . alles!*, pp. 34-43.

71. Ibid., p. 233; Germer, *Grotewohl-Brandt*, pp. 29-30. Klein notes that some SPD trade unionists went so far as to address a letter to the "Allied Commission" on 16 May 1945, asking it to intervene to prevent a one-sided resolution of the trade union question to the KPD's advantage in the Soviet Zone. The letter went unanswered, since the Allied Control Commission for Germany had not yet been formed.

72. Erwin Lehmann, ed., *Aufbruch in unsere Zeit. Erinnerungen an die Tätigkeit der Gewerkschaften von 1945 bis zur Gründung der Deutschen Demokratischen Republik* (Berlin: Tribüne Verlag, 1976), pp. 12-14; Günter Griep and Charlotte

Steinbrecher, *Die Herausbildung des Freien Deutschen Gewerkschaftsbundes. Zur Geschichte der deutschen Gewerkschaftsbewegung von 1945 bis 1946,* "Beiträge zur Geschichte der deutschen Gewerkschaftsbewegung," Vol. 9 (Berlin: Tribüne Verlag [1967]), p. 28.

73. Klein, *Vereint . . . alles!*, pp. 233-34; Germer, *Grotewohl-Brandt*, p. 54.

74. Germer, *Grotewohl-Brandt*, p. 54.

75. Ibid., pp. 54-55; Klein, *Vereint . . . alles!*, pp. 233, 278 (n. 394); Lehmann, *Aufbruch*, p. 14.

76. Horst Bednareck, Albert Behrendt, and Dieter Lange, ed., *Gewerkschaftlicher Neubeginn. Dokumente zur Gründung des FDGB und zu seiner Entwicklung von Juni 1945 bis Februar 1946* (Berlin: Tribüne Verlag, 1975), pp. xvii, xix-xxii; Lehmann, *Aufbruch*, p. 15; Griep/Steinbrecher, *Herausbildung des FDGB*, p. 29; Klein, *Vereint . . . alles!*, p. 234.

77. Bednareck/Behrendt/Lange, *Gew. Neubeginn*, p. xxii; Lehmann, *Aufbruch*, pp. 15-16; Klein, *Vereint . . . alles!*, p. 42.

78. Bednareck/Behrendt/Lange, *Gew. Neubeginn*, p. xxiv; "Aufruf des Vorbereitenden Gewerkschaftsausschusses für Gross-Berlin" (15 June 1945), in ibid., pp. 8-11; Lehmann, *Aufbruch*, p. 16.

79. Bednareck/Behrendt/Lange, *Gew. Neubeginn*, pp. xxiv-xxv; "Der Vorbereitende Gewerkschaftsausschuss für Gross-Berlin, Sitzungsbericht Nr. 1" (14 June 1945), in ibid., pp. 12-13; "Sitzungsbericht No. 2" (16 June 1945), in ibid., p. 17.

80. Exceptions to this "one shop, one union" rule were granted grudgingly to the powerful clerical employees' and technical employees' associations, whose cause was championed in the Preparatory Committee by Bernhard Göring. In the Weimar era, these autonomous white-collar workers' associations had remained rather aloof from and to the right of their respective trade union leagues, and had succumbed more readily to Nazism. The KPD—and some Social Democrats as well—thus regarded these nonproletarians as unreliable allies and would have liked to see them neutralized by absorption into the proletarian-dominated industrial unions. Rather than risk having them reject the FDGB altogether, however, the Communists finally made the tactical concession of allowing them to organize separately and to elect their own representatives to the single trade union

council in each shop. "This occurred in the realization that winning over the salaried employees for the Organization was prerequisite for their ideological education to solidarity of action in the trade union movement." (Dietrich Hurrelmann, "Bewusste Mitgestalter der neuen Ordnung," in Lehmann, *Aufbruch*, p. 165.)

As the above quote implies, the issue was by no means resolved in KPD eyes. There followed three years of skirmishing over the rights and jurisdiction of the employees' associations, during which the Communists worked to undercut their position. Final resolution came in 1948, when a formal conference of the FDGB leadership ended the compromise and achieved the KPD's original goal. See Klein, *Vereint . . . alles!*, pp. 40-41, 280-81; Germer, *Grotewohl-Brandt*, pp. 55-56; "Vorläufige Satzung des Freien Deutschen Gewerkschaftsbundes," in FDGB, *Protokoll der ersten . . . Delegiertenkonferenz*, p. 235; Hans Eckart, "Zum Anteil des FDGB im Land Sachsen an der Herausbildung und Entwicklung des neuen Inhalts der Arbeiterbewegung in den Jahren 1945 bis 1950" (Ph.D. dissertation, Univ. of Leipzig, 1975), p. 33.

81. "Anweisungen des vorbereitenden Gewerkschaftsausschusses für Gross-Berlin über den Neuaufbau der freien Gewerkschaften," *DVZ*, 19, June 1945, p. 3.

82. Griep/Steinbrecher, *Herausbildung des FDGB*, pp. 35, 41; Thomas, *Entscheidung*, p. 146; Fritz Rettmann, "Die Metallarbeiter gingen voran," in Lehmann, *Aufbruch*, pp. 27-30.

83. Ulbricht, *Gesch. d. n. Zeit*, p. 151.

84. "Richtlinien über den Aufbau der neuen Gewerkschaften, Beschluss des ZK der KPD zur Mitteilung an die Parteibezirksleitungen" (June 1945), in Bednareck/Behrendt/Lange, *Gew. Neubeginn*, p. 4.

85. "Die Berliner Gewerkschaften beraten über Festigung der Organisation und Klare Aufgabenstellung," *DVZ*, 18 July 1945, p. 1; "Sitzungsbericht No. 6" (of the Berlin Preparatory Committee, 25-26 July 1945), in Bednareck/Behrendt/Lange, *Gew. Neubeginn*, pp. 57-59.

86. Cf. Griep/Steinbrecher, *Herausbildung des FDGB*, pp. 16, 76-77.

87. Krisch, *German Politics*, p. 71; Letter from Lt. Gen. Lucius Clay to the U.S. Secretary of War (13 October 1945), in Smith,

ed., *Clay*, p. 102; Volker Wahl, "Der Beginn der antifaschistisch-demokratischen Umwälzung in Thüringen—Die Organisierung der gesellschaftlichen Kräfte und der Neuaufbau der Landesverwaltung 1945" (Ph.D. dissertation, Univ. of Jena, 1976), pp. 132-35.

88. Doernberg, *Geburt*, p. 44; Diepenthal, *Drei Volksdem.*, pp. 99-100; Eisermann, "Mittelschichten," pp. 25-27. The LDP, the weakest of the parties, was not even established in Mecklenburg until the end of 1945, and only extended its authority over the Thuringian "Democratic Party" in 1946. See: *Vereint sind wir Alles. Erinnerungen an die Gründung der SED* (Berlin: Dietz Verlag, 1966), p. 639; Wahl, "Beginn . . . in Thüringen," p. 132.

89. Moraw, *Parole*, pp. 87-88, 97-98, 103; Staritz, *Sozialismus*, pp. 36, 70-72; Thomas, *Entscheidung*, pp. 44, 151-52.

90. See below, p. 75. Moraw, *Parole*, pp. 96-97, 107-12.

91. Ibid., pp. 106, 118-20 (citation taken from p. 106); Hans Warnke, "In der grössten Not erkennt man seinen wahren Freund," in *Vereint sind wir alles*, pp. 656-57.

92. Edinger, *German Exile Politics*, p. 70.

93. Letter by Lt. Gen. Lucius Clay to Maj. Gen. John H. Hilldring, dated 5 July 1945, in Smith, ed., *Clay*, p. 47.

94. Walter Ulbricht, "Das Aktionsprogramm der KPD in der Durchführung," *DVZ*, 14 October 1945, p. 7; Krisch, *German Politics*, pp. 31-32; Leonhard, *Rev. entlässt*, p. 412.

95. Otto Buchwitz, "Nur die Arbeiterklasse besass die Kraft," in *Beginn eines neuen Lebens. Eine Auswahl von Erinnerungen an den Beginn des Neuaufbaus in Dresden im Mai 1945*, "Beiträge zur Geschichte der Dresdener Arbeiterbewegung," Vol. 7 (Dresden: Museum für Geschichte der Dresdener Arbeiterbewegung, 1960), p. 30.

96. Ibid.; Moraw, *Parole*, pp. 103-4; Krisch, *German Politics*, pp. 84-100 passim; Vosske, "Zur Tätigkeit," p. 195.

97. Thomas, *Entscheidung*, p. 25; Tjulpanov, "Rolle der SMAD," pp. 243-44; Stefan Doernberg, "Die Hilfe der sowjetischen Besatzungsmacht beim Aufbau eines neuen Deutschland 1945/49," *Deutsche Aussenpolitik*, Vol. 10, special issue 1 (1965), p. 101.

98. Thomas, *Entscheidung*, pp. 62-63, 81; Paul Gerhard Esche, "Die Überwindung der kapitalistischen Verhältnisse im Zeiss-Werk Jena und die Neuformierung des Zeiss-Konzerns in Westdeutschland (1945-1949/50). Ein Beitrag zur Geschichte des VEB

Carl Zeiss Jena" (Ph.D. dissertation, Univ. of Jena, 1962), pp. 91, 94-95; Johannes Emmrich, "Die Entwicklung demokratischer Selbstverwaltungsorgane und ihr Kampf um die Schaffung der antifaschistisch-demokratischen Ordnung in Chemnitz vom 8. Mai 1945 bis Mitte 1948" (Ph.D. dissertation, Univ. of Leipzig, 1974), pp. 43-44; Franz Dahlem, "Mit Wilhelm Pieck im Flugzeug zurück nach Deutschland," in *Vereint sind wir alles*, p. 28.

99. Germer, *Grotewohl-Brandt*, pp. 44-45; Gottwald, "Entmachtung," p. 158; Interview with Walter Bartel, 26 May 1977.

100. Krieger, "Inter-Regnum," pp. 530-31; Roman Erdmann, "Die Enteignung der Kriegsverbrecher und aktiven Faschisten in Mecklenburg-Vorpommern 1945/46," *Wissenschaftliche Zeitschrift der Ernst-Moritz-Arndt-Universität Greifswald*, Gesellschafts- und sprachwissenschaftliche Reihe, 18, no. 3/4, pt. 2 (1969), p. 298; Doernberg, *Geburt*, p. 86.

101. Thomas, *Entscheidung*, pp. 144-45; Moraw, *Parole*, pp. 103-5.

102. Walter Weidauer, "Hermann Matern und Otto Buchwitz—zwei hervorragende Funktionäre der Arbeiterklasse," in Wehner, *Kampfgefährten*, p. 145.

103. Emmrich, "Entwicklung . . . in Chemnitz," pp. 66-67.

104. Schöneburg, *Von den Anfängen*, p. 49.

105. "Mitteilung über die Bestätigung der Provinzialverwaltung Brandenburg und der Landesverwaltungen Mecklenburg und Sachsen" (4 July 1945), in *Dokumente 1945-49*, pp. 82-83; "Mitteilung über die Bestätigung der Provinzialverwaltung Sachsen und der Landesverwaltung Thüringen" (16 July 1945), in ibid., pp. 94-95; Doernberg, *Geburt*, pp. 88-89; cf. Diepenthal, *Drei Volksdem.*, pp. 146-48. Administrations were directly appointed in Thuringia and Saxony-Anhalt because these areas had only recently been evacuated by U.S. troops, and the political system of the Soviet Zone was not yet firmly established there (cf. Krieger, "Inter-Regnum," p. 529).

106. Bednareck/Behrendt/Lange, *Gew. Neubeginn*, p. xxxii; "Richtlinien über den Aufbau der neuen Gewerkschaften," in ibid., pp. 1-7.

107. This reluctance was particularly evident in the areas of the Soviet Zone under temporary U.S. occupation. Trade union committees formed expressly on the basis of the Aachen pro-

gram were refused recognition in Jena, Halle, and Erfurt. See Klein, *Vereint . . . alles?*, p. 179.

108. Ibid., pp. 165-68.

109. Ibid., p. 224; Bednareck/Behrendt/Lange, *Gew. Neubeginn*, pp. xlii-xliii, lii, 201.

110. Klein, *Vereint . . . alles?*, pp. 175-79, 227-30; Bednareck/Behrendt/Lange, *Gew. Neubeginn*, pp. xxxii-xxxiv, 193-95; Fritz Apelt, "Zum Aufbau freier Gewerkschaften in Sachsen," in Institut für Marxismus-Leninismus beim ZK der SED, *Wir sind die Kraft: Der Weg zur Deutschen Demokratischen Republik. Erinnerungen* (Berlin: Dietz Verlag, 1959), p. 334; Fritz Apelt, "Gewerkschaftseinheit—Arbeitereinheit," in *Vereint sind wir alles*, pp. 370, 274. Apelt was sent to Dresden by Ulbricht (in an SMA vehicle) in June 1945 to help organize the Saxon FDGB.

111. Bednareck/Behrendt/Lange, *Gew. Neubeginn*, pp. xxxvii-xlii; Rudolf Jäger, "Heisse Spätsommertage in Halle," in Lehmann, *Aufbruch*, pp. 57-58, 60; Wahl, "Beginn . . . in Thüringen," pp. 150-55.

112. Wolfgang G. Friedmann, *The Allied Military Government of Germany*, "Library of World Affairs," No. 8 (London: Stevens and Sons, 1947), p. 124.

113. Wahl, "Beginn . . . in Thüringen," pp. 46-47, 89-95, 104-8, 148-50; Letter, Clay to Hilldring (5 July 1945), in Smith, ed., *Clay*, p. 46; Klein, *Vereint . . . alles?*, p. 175; Esche, "Überwindung . . . im Zeiss-Werk," pp. 66, 98, 272-75.

114. Wahl, "Beginn . . . in Thüringen," pp. 159-66, 171-77, 183-84, 207, 213.

115. Ibid., p. 117.

116. The "Manifesto of the Democratic Socialists of the Former Concentration Camp Buchenwald," an important document of anti-fascist political thought within Nazi Germany, asserted that with the destruction of the fascist regime the capitalist system itself would be destroyed, and with it the social basis for parliamentary democracy. The manifesto called for a new "People's Republic" without separation of powers, to be based on a system of local and regional soviets dominated by a united proletarian party. A socialist planned economy would be established, and foreign policy would be conducted "in closest

harmony" with the USSR. See Moraw, *Parole*, pp. 113-15; Sywottek, *Dt. Volksdem.*, pp. 195-96.

117. Wahl, "Beginn . . . in Thüringen," pp. 110-11, 121-27;
Esche, "Überwindung . . . im Zeiss-Werk," p. 86; Gottwald,
"Entmachtung," p. 162; Moraw, *Parole*, p. 115.

118. Wahl, "Beginn . . . in Thüringen," p. 258.

119. Ibid., pp. 272-73; Doernberg, *Geburt*, pp. 92-95; Esche,
"Überwindung . . . im Zeiss-Werk," pp. 102-3; "Teilniederschrift
über eine Beratung mit kommunistischen und sozialdemokratischen Funktionären im Hotel 'Ölmühle' in Jena" (5 July 1945),
in Ulbricht, *Gesch. . . . Arbeiterbew.*, 2:1st supp., p. 245.

120. Wahl, "Beginn . . . in Thüringen," pp. 110, 257, 260-66.
Ironically, Dr. Paul also proved unsatisfactory to the KPD and
was removed some months later.

121. Ibid., pp. 156-57, 267-68; Bednareck/Behrendt/Lange, *Gew.
Neubeginn*, pp. xli-xlii; Krisch, *German Politics*, pp. 152-61.

122. Deckers, *Transf. des Bankensystems*, pp. 27-29; Interview with Walter Bartel, 26 May 1977.

123. A memo-for-record by LDP chairman Waldemar Koch of
an interview with Marshal Zhukov on 5 September 1945 documents Zhukov's keen interest in the bourgeois parties' expansion into the U.S. and British zones. Zhukov also remarked
during the audience that, in creating governmental organs where
all parties were represented, the Soviets had seized the political
initiative. "The Americans and English would have to follow
them." See Waldemar Koch, "Aktennotiz 5.9.1945. Betrifft: Besprechung bei Marschall Schukow," in Ekkehart Krippendorf,
"Die Gründung der Liberal-Demokratischen Partei in der
sowjetischen Besatzungszone 1945," *Vierteljahresheft für
Zeitgeschichte* 8 (1960):303-5.

124. U.S. Department of State, *Foreign Relations of the United
States. Diplomatic Papers. The Conference of Berlin (The Potsdam Conference), 1945*, 2 vols. (Washington: U.S. Govt. Printing
Office, 1960), 2:493, 824; U.S. Headquarters Berlin District,
G-2 Division, "Special Report on Formation of a Central Administration in the Russian Zone," dated 7 August 1945 (NARS
RG 260). This report is based on information supplied to U.S.
intelligence services on 27 July by Ernst Lemmer and later cor-
roborated by Jakob Kaiser and Friedrich Ernst, a banker. All three
were offered positions in the new organs as CDU representatives,

but refused "on the grounds that they were unwilling to participate in any government not sanctioned by all three major oc-
cupational powers."

125. W. Averell Harriman, "Report to the Secretary of State"
(10 January 1945), in U.S. Dept. of State, *Conferences at Malta
and Yalta*, p. 450.

126. Sywottek, *Dt. Volksdem.*, pp. 168-72; U.S. Dept. of State,
Conference of Berlin 1:440-41; Letter by Col. Azel F. Hatch,
Chief of Local Government Branch OMGUS, dated 15 August
1945, appended to U.S. Hq. Berlin, "Report on Central Admins."

127. The U.S. had meanwhile concluded that its ban on political activities was impractical and was working to the Communists' advantage. See Sywottek, *Dt. Volksdem.*, pp. 168-72;
U.S. Dept. of State, *Conference of Berlin*, 1:438, 472-73.

128. U.S. Dept. of State, *Conference of Berlin*, 2:493, 824,
1502-3.

129. Ibid., pp. 1504-5.

130. Cf. Waltraud Falk, "Die politische, organisatorische und
ökonomische Konstituierung des volkseigenen Sektors der Wirtschaft und seine Entwicklung in der ersten Etappe der volksdemokratischen Revolution in der DDR 1945 bis 1950," *Wissenschaftliche Zeitschrift der Humboldt-Universität zu Berlin*,
Gesellschafts- und Sprachwissenschaftliche Reihe 16 (1967):21;
Sywottek, *Dt. Volksdem.*, pp. 165-68.

CHAPTER THREE: THE LAND REFORM

1. Leonhard, *Rev. entlässt*, pp. 390-91.

2. Hermann Dölling, *Wende der deutschen Agrarpolitik* (Berlin: Deutscher Bauernverlag, 1950), p. 88; Raup, "Land Reform,"
pp. 136-47 passim, 250. The parallel between American planning
and subsequent Soviet policies on land reform, as evidenced in
a series of documents cited by Raup, is astonishing. As Raup
himself comments (p. 411), "Each major step taken in executing
the Soviet land reform in 1945 was anticipated and recommended for the guidance of United States Military Government
in Germany . . . before the end of the war."

3. V. I. Lenin, "Preliminary Draft Theses on the Agrarian
Question," in V. I. Lenin, *Collected Works*, Vol. 31 (Moscow:
Progress Publishers, 1966), pp. 152-64 passim. Gottwald, "Ent-

machtung," pp. 83-86. The KPD took seriously the danger that landowners deprived of political power would sabotage the new regime by withholding food. See Ulbricht, *Gesch. d. n. Zeit*, p. 216; Grigori G. Kotov, *Agrarverhältnisse und Bodenreform in Deutschland*, 2 vols. (Berlin: Deutscher Bauernverlag, 1959), 2:195-96.

4. Joseph Stalin, *Foundations of Leninism* (New York: International Publishers, 1932), p. 60.

5. Doernberg, *Geburt*, pp. 152-53.

6. Raup, "Land Reform," p. 325; Gottwald, "Entmachtung," p. 160; Walter Ulbricht, *Die Bauernbefreiung in der Deutschen Demokratischen Republik*, 2 vols. (Berlin: Dietz Verlag, 1961), 1:20-21, 43-45; Doernberg, *Geburt*, p. 158.

7. Siegfried Stein, *Die demokratische Bodenreform in Mecklenburg—ein Schlag gegen den Imperialismus und Militarismus* (Schwerin: Bezirksleitung Schwerin der SED-Kommission zur Erforschung der Geschichte der örtlichen Arbeiterbewegung, n.d.), pp. 27-28; Rudolf Woderich, "Zu den Anfängen der Demokratisierung des Dorfes in Ostmecklenburg von 1945 bis Ende 1947, dargestellt vornehmlich am Beispiel des Kreises Neubrandenburg" (Ph.D. dissertation, Univ. of Rostock, 1965), p. 19; Doernberg, *Geburt*, p. 158; Rolf Stöckigt, *Der Kampf der KPD um die demokratische Bodenreform, Mai 1945 bis April 1946* (Berlin: Dietz Verlag, 1964), pp. 68-70; Leonhard, *Rev. entlässt*, pp. 409-10.

8. Cf. Andrzej Korbonski, *Politics of Socialist Agriculture in Poland: 1945-60*, "East Central European Studies of Columbia University" (New York and London: Columbia University Press, 1965), pp. 68-69.

9. Siegfried Kuntsche, "Die Hilfe der Sowjetischen Militäradministration bei der demokratischen Bodenreform in Mecklenburg-Vorpommern," in Schildhauer, *Befreiung*, p. 227. Cf. Ulbricht, *Bauernbefreiung*, 1:45.

10. Hermes, *CDU und Bodenreform*, pp. 20-22; Wolfgang Hoffmann, "Die demokratische Bodenreform und die LDPD," *ZfG* 13 (1965):992-97; Walter Ulbricht, *Die demokratische Bodenreform—ein ruhmreiches Blatt in der deutschen Geschichte* (Berlin: ZK der SED, [1955]), p. 32.

11. See Edwin Hoernle, "Das Bündnis zwischen Arbeitern und Bauern," in Hoernle, *Zum Bündnis*, pp. 379-81.

12. Stöckigt, *Kampf der KPD*, p. 67; Doernberg, *Geburt*, p. 165; Ulbricht, *Bauernbefreiung*, 1:50. West German authors have generally contended that the KPD land reform decree was actually written by the Soviets. Wolfgang Leonhard in fact claims to have done the translation from Russian into German himself (see *Rev. entlässt*, pp. 410-11). GDR historians, on the other hand, insist that the KPD's draft was of German origin, and point to the obvious similarities between it and earlier KPD documents dealing with land reform. Asked by the author about this discrepancy, Prof. Walter Bartel suggested that the first draft may have been drawn up by KPD emigrés in Moscow and submitted to the Central Committee of the Communist Party of the Soviet Union. There it would have been discussed and rewritten into a suitable legal format, then sent on as a Russian text to the SMA in Germany, who had it retranslated by Leonhard. (Interview with Walter Bartel, 26 May 1977.)

13. "Verordnung der Provinzialverwaltung Sachsen über die demokratische Bodenreform" (3 September 1945), in *Dokumente 1945-49*, pp. 132-38; Leo Herwegen, "Stellungnahme des CDU-Landesverbandes zur Bodenreform in der Provinz Sachsen/Anhalt" (letter dated 4 September 1945, from a member of the CDU provincial leadership to party headquarters in Berlin, explaining the actions of the CDU in Halle in accepting the KPD land reform program), in Hermes, *CDU und Bodenreform*, p. 115.

14. Stöckigt, *Kampf der KPD*, pp. 56-61, 78-87. Herwegen, "Stellungnahme," pp. 116-22; Ulbricht, Bauernbefreiung, 1:50-51; Robert Siewert, "Ein neuer Weg wird beschritten," in IML, *Wir sind die Kraft*, p. 375.

15. Herwegen, "Stellungnahme," p. 117.

16. Hermes, *CDU and Bodenreform*, p. 27; "Sitzungsbericht No. 9" (29 August 1945), in Bednareck/Behrendt/Lange, *Gew. Neubeginn*, p. 80; Siewert, "Ein neuer Weg," p. 375.

17. Gottwald, "Entmachtung," pp. 106, 109, 111-15; Stein, *dem. Bodenreform*, pp. 31-35; "Ausführungsverordnung zum Gesetz über die Bodenreform im Lande Thüringen" (15 September 1945), *Regierungsblatt für das Land Thüringen*, Pt. 1, vol. 1, no. 5 (22 September 1945), p. 17. On 26 September, with the land reform well under way, the KPD's *Thüringer Volkszeitung* insisted that "All large estates over 100 hectares are to be ex-

propriated. . . ." In all cases where landowners had applied for exemptions as anti-fascists, "a closer investigation revealed that none of these applicants could present concrete proof of his anti-fascist, democratic convictions *during the entire time* of the Nazi regime. And that is the decisive point: *that the anti-fascist, democratic activity extend throughout the entire time of the Nazi regime.*" (*TVZ*, 26 September 1945, p. 1. Original italics.)

18. Hermes, *CDU und Bodenreform*, pp. 27, 31-33. KPD doctrine on this point followed to the letter Lenin's "Preliminary Draft Theses on the Agrarian Question," which stated (p. 159): "Under no circumstances is it permissible for Communist parties to advocate or practise compensating the big landowners for the confiscated lands, for under present-day conditions in Europe and America this would be tantamount to a betrayal of socialism and the imposition of new tribute upon the masses of working and exploited people, to whom the war has meant the greatest hardships, while it has increased the number of millionaires and enriched them."

19. Koch, "Aktennotiz," pp. 303-5.

20. Hermes, *CDU und Bodenreform*, pp. 33-34; Doernberg, *Geburt*, pp. 167-68.

21. Siegfried Schulze, "Der Prozess der Herausbildung der Provinzialverwaltung Mark Brandenburg und ihre Politik zur Einleitung der antifaschistisch-demokratischen Revolution (Sommer 1945 bis Frühjahr 1946)" (Ph.D. dissertation, Pädagogische Hochschule Potsdam, 1971), pp. 193-94; Kotov, *Agrarverhältnisse* 1:203; Hermes, *CDU und Bodenreform*, pp. 42-44, 46-47.

22. See Koch, "Aktennotiz," pp. 303-5.

23. Cf. V. I. Lenin, " 'Left-Wing' Communism—An Infantile Disorder," in Lenin, *Collected Works*, 31:75.

24. Stöckigt, *Kampf der KPD*, p. 95; Office of . . . Intelligence, OMGUS, "Russian Interference," p. A-3; Ekkehart Krippendorf, *Die Liberal-Demokratische Partei Deutschlands in der Sowjetischen Besatzungszone 1945/48*, "Beiträge zur Geschichte des Parlamentarismus und der politischen Parteien," Vol. 21 (Düsseldorf: Droste Verlag, n.d.), p. 40.

25. Hermes, *CDU und Bodenreform*, pp. 60-63; "Gemeinsamer Aufruf der KPD, der SPD, und der LDP zur Sicherung der

Ernährung und zur Hilfe für die Neubauern" (8 December 1945), in *Dokumente 1945-49*, pp. 215-18.

26. Hermes, *CDU und Bodenreform*, pp. 66-70, 86-96; Office of . . . Intelligence, OMGUS, "Russian Interference," p. A-3; "Den Neubauern Haus, Stall und Vieh: Aufruf der vier antifaschistisch-demokratischen Parteien der Mark Brandenburg," *DVZ*, 16 December 1945, p. 1; "CDU Provinz Sachsen für Neubauernhilfe," *DVZ*, 19 December 1945, p. 1; "Erklärung aktiver Mitglieder der CDU Leipzig," *DVZ*, 20 December 1945, p. 1; "Führungswechsel in der CDU: Die Verabschiedung von Dr. Hermes und Dr. Schreiber," *DVZ*, 22 December 1945, p. 2.

27. Herwegen, "Stellungnahme," p. 120; Doernberg, *Geburt*, pp. 173, 191-92.

28. Rudolf Reutter, *Grossgrundbesitz wird wieder Bauernland* (Berlin: Verlag neuer Weg, 1945) p. 7; Wilhelm Pieck, *Junkerland in Bauernhand: Rede zur demokratischen Bodenreform, Kyritz, 2. September 1945* (Berlin: Dietz Verlag, 1955), pp. 21-24.

29. Edwin Hoernle, "Deutschland wird ein neues Gesicht bekommen," in Hoernle, *Zum Bündnis*, pp. 348-52; Reutter, *Grossgrundbesitz*, pp. 8, 13; Pieck, *Junkerland*, pp. 9-10.

30. Reutter, *Grossgrundbesitz*, p. 22. Reporting on the "free peaks" system to U.S. authorities, the OSS noted that it had been used throughout the war in the USSR as a means of stimulating production and getting extra food to the cities. To give an idea of the kind of profits being made, the report cited the current prices for one pound of meat as 2½ marks on the official exchange in Berlin, but 300 marks on the open market. This disparity struck many well-meaning socialists as capitalist opportunism at its worst, and the KPD had to battle constantly against attempts by local officials to fix maximum prices or otherwise control the "free peaks." See: OSS, "Russian Econ. Policies," pp. 12, 20; Schulze, "Prozess der Herausbildung," pp. 164-66; Ulbricht, *Bauernbefreiung*, pp. 63-65.

31. Reutter, *Grossgrundbesitz*, pp. 15, 21; Pieck, *Junkerland*, pp. 14-15; Doernberg, *Geburt*, p. 155.

32. "Anweisungen des ZK der KPD an die Bezirks- und Kreisleitungen über die Durchführung der Bodenreform im sowjetisch besetzten Gebiet," in "KPD und demokratische Bodenreform," *BzG* 17, no. 5 (1975):853; Hoernle, "neues Gesicht," p. 349; Ernst

Altenkirch, "Vorurteile wurden in der gemeinsamen Aktion überwunden," in *Vereint sind wir alles*, p. 592.

33. Griep/Steinbrecher, *Herausbildung des FDGB*, pp. 66-67; "Sitzungsbericht No. 5" (11 July 1945), in Bednareck/ Behrendt/Lange, *Gew. Neubeginn*, pp. 44-45; Siewert, "Ein neuer Weg," pp. 370-71; Dölling, *Wende*, pp. 115-16.

34. Rackow/Heyne/Kleinpeter, *Rostock*, p. 62; Kotov, *Agrarverhältnisse*, 1:219; Esche, "Überwindung . . . im Zeiss-Werk," p. 102; [Siegfried] Graffunder et al., "Die Landwirtschaftspolitik in der antifaschistisch-demokratischen Ordnung und die Heranführung der Bauern an die sozialistische Umgestaltung" (undated typewritten manuscript in archive of Zentralvorstand der Vereinigung der gegenseitigen Bauernhilfe, Berlin), pp. 34-35; Griep/Steinbrecher, *Herausbildung des FDGB*, pp. 68-69; Gottwald, "Entmachtung," pp. 148-49; "Die Stadt hilft dem Dorf, der Arbeiter dem Bauer," *TVZ*, 4 February 1946, p. 1.

35. Cf. Korbonski, *Politics of Soc. Agriculture*, p. 73ff.; Gustav Beuer, *New Czechoslovakia and her Historical Background* (London: Lawrence and Wishart, 1947), p. 149.

36. "Verordnung der Provinzialverwaltung Sachsen über die demokratische Bodenreform," pp. 135-36.

37. Ulbricht, *Gesch. d. n. Zeit*, p. 221; Raup, "Land Reform," p. 270; "Bauern, Landarbeiter, handelt," *DVZ*, 12 September 1945, p. 2; Edwin Hoernle, "Bauchschmerzen," in Hoernle, *Zum Bündnis*, p. 360.

38. Kotov, *Agrarverhältnisse*, 1:211; "Verordnung der Provinzialverwaltung Sachsen über die demokratische Bodenreform," pp. 137-38; Nettl, *Eastern Zone*, p. 174; Horst Duhnke, *Stalinismus in Deutschland* (n.p.; Verlag für Politik und Wirtschaft, [1955?]), p. 120.

39. Dölling, *Wende*, p. 103. These figures no doubt reflect as well the refusal of many CDU and LDP members to associate themselves with the KPD's land reform.

40. "Verordnung der Provinzialverwaltung Sachsen über die demokratische Bodenreform," p. 135; "Decree on Land Reform in Land Saxony (10 September 1945)," in Ruhm von Oppen, *Documents on Germany*, p. 62.

41. Gottwald, "Entmachtung," pp. 127-31; Schulze, "Prozess der Herausbildung," p. 202; Edwin Hoernle, "Grosse Entscheidungen—kleine Bedenken," *TVZ*, 26 September 1945, p. 4.

42. "Über die Enteignung von Nazibesitz," *DVZ*, 16 December 1945, p. 1; Interview with Walter Bartel, 27 April 1977; Provinzausschuss der Gegenseitigen Bauernhilfe Mark Brandenburg, *Parlament der Bauern. Erster Provinz-Kongress der Gegenseitigen Bauernhilfe der Mark Brandenburg am 16. und 17. März 1946 in Potsdam* (Potsdam: Verlag "Märkische Volksstimme," [1946?]) p. 26; Schulze, "Prozess der Herausbildung," pp. 191-95. Schulze relates (pp. 194-95) that fully 3 percent of expropriations at the village and county levels in Brandenburg had to be revoked as "not according to law." Cf. Korbonski, *Politics of Soc. Agriculture*, pp. 84-85 for parallel Polish experience.

43. Raup, "Land Reform," p. 271; Doernberg, *Geburt*, p. 177; "Vermessung und Bodenzuteilung" (24 September 1945), *Verordnungsblatt der Provinz Mark Brandenburg*, No. 3 (30 November, 1945), p. 54; Arbeitsgemeinschaft deutscher Landwirte und Bauern, *Weissbuch über die "Demokratische Bodenreform"* (Hanover: Arbeitsgemeinschaft deutscher Landwirte und Bauern E.V., 1955), p. 5; "Auflösung und Enteignung der Konzerne," *DVZ*, 9 October 1945, p. 1.

44. "Bauern fragen, wir antworten," *DVZ*, 9 October 1945, p. 2; "Gemeinschaftseinsatz in der Landwirtschaft," *DVZ*, 19 August 1945, p. 1.

45. Kuntsche, "Hilfe der Sow. Militäradm.," pp. 225-26; Siegfried Kuntsche, "Die Unterstützung der Landesverwaltung bzw. Landesregierung Mecklenburg durch die Sowjetische Militäradministration bei der Leitung der demokratischen Bodenreform," *Jahrbuch für Geschichte* 12 (1974):152-56, 162; Dölling, *Wende*, pp. 127-28; Nettl, *Eastern Zone*, p. 115; Matthias Kramer, *Die Bolschewierung der Landwirtschaft: in Sowjetrussland, in den Satellitenstaaten, in der Sowjetzone* (Cologne: Rote Weissbücher, 1951) p. 95; Viacheslav Nevsky, "Soviet Agricultural Policy in Eastern Germany 1945-1949," in Robert Slusser, ed., *Soviet Economic Policy in Postwar Germany* (New York: Research Program on the USSR, 1953), pp. 87-89.

46. Kuntsche, "Hilfe der Sow. Militäradm.," pp. 224, 277; Kuntsche, "Unterstützung der Landesverw.," pp. 157, 162-66, 170; Kommunistische Partei Deutschlands, Zentralkomitee, "An die BL Mecklenburg-Schwerin" (20 October 1945), in "KPD und dem. Bodenreform," p. 856.

47. Kotov, *Agrarverhältnisse*, 1:221; Gottwald, "Entmachtung," pp. 165, 181-84; "Grundbesitz der Nazis" (10 October 1945), *Verordnungsblatt... Brandenburg*, No. 3, p. 55; Stöckigt, *Kampf der KPD*, pp. 137, 194-95; "Sabotage bei der Ernte," *TVZ*, 10 September 1945, p. 1.

48. Kuntsche, "Unterstützung der Landesverw.," p. 157; Kuntsche, "Hilfe der Sow. Militäradm.," pp. 229-30; Gottwald, "Entmachtung," pp. 139-40, 186-90, 192-93; Kotov, *Agrarverhältnisse*, 1:202, 237; Interview with Walter Bartel, 27 April 1977.

49. Erdmann, "Enteignung... in Mecklenburg," p. 298; Gottwald, "Entmachtung," pp. 17-18, 170-76.

50. Rumors of an impending Anglo-American advance against the Soviets, fomented by Nazi propaganda toward the end of the war, were still current in the first months of occupation. Some Mecklenburg peasants were so fearful of eventual retribution that they fastened plaques to equipment they received from liquidated estates, bearing the inscription "Property of the Landowner." See Tjulpanov, "Rolle der Sow. Militäradm.," pp. 38-39.

51. Raup, "Land Reform," pp. 277-78; Stöckigt, *Kampf der KPD*, pp. 138, 180-81; Woderich, "Anfängen der Demokratisierung," p. 54; Interview with Walter Bartel, 27 April 1977, and other conversations in the GDR.

52. Rudolf Reutter, "KPD und Bodenreform," *DVZ*, 14 September 1945, p. 1.

53. Gottwald, "Entmachtung," pp. 138-39, 141-42, Appendix p. 12; "Bauern, seid wachsam!" *TVZ*, 5 November 1945, p. 3; Werner Eggerath, "Unser Kampf für ein neues Deutschland," *ZfG*, 17, no. 7 (1969):866.

54. Stöckigt, *Kampf der KPD*, pp. 180-81; Doernberg, *Geburt*, pp. 170, 184; Gottwald, "Entmachtung," pp. 138-39, 199; Kuntsche, "Unterstützung der Landesverw.," pp. 160-61, 170-71.

55. Kotov, *Agrarverhältnisse*, 1:217, 219; Korbonski, *Politics of Soc. Agriculture*, pp. 80-81.

56. Dölling, *Wende*, pp. 119, 121-22, 130-31; Raup, "Land Reform," p. 282; "Die ersten Güter aufgeteilt," *DVZ*, 28 September 1945, p. 1.

57. Raup, "Land Reform," pp. 280-83, 299; Doernberg, *Geburt*,

pp. 185-86; Gottwald, "Entmachtung," pp. 130-31, 180-81; Warnke, "In der gr. Not," p. 658.

58. Dölling, *Wende*, pp. 112, 114; Raup, "Land Reform," p. 310; Eberhard, *Magdeburg*, pp. 26-27; Kotov, *Agrarverhältnisse*, 1:205-6.

59. "Bauern heraus! Sichert die Bodenreform," *Der Freie Bauer* (official weekly of the Central Administration for Agriculture and Forestry, hereafter *DFB*) 1, no. 7 (December 1945):1.

60. Dölling, *Wende*, pp. 107-8; Raup, "Land Reform," p. 267; "Zur Bodenreform in der Provinz Brandenburg," *DVZ*, 13 September 1945, p. 1.

61. Rudolf Reutter, "Antifaschisten, Neubauern, seid wachsam!" *DVZ*, 26 January 1946, p. 2; Georg Wehner, "Im Kampf um das Bündnis der Arbeiterklasse mit den werktätigen Bauern," in Wehner, *Kampfgefährten*, pp. 226-27; "Bauern heraus! Sichert die Bodenreform," *DFB* 1, no. 7 (December 1945):1; "Ein Naziverbrecher erhält 5 ha.," *DFB* 1, no. 16 (February 1946):4; Gottwald, "Entmachtung," p. 164.

62. Dölling, *Wende*, pp. 95-96, 114-15; Duhnke, *Stalinismus*, p. 121; Reutter, *Grossgrundbesitz*, pp. 25, 31; Edwin Hoernle, "Bodenreform sichert unsere Ernährung," *DVZ*, 7 April 1946, p. 1; Edwin Hoernle, "Das Errungene sichern," *DFB* 1, no. 3 (November 1945):1; Interview with Claus Montag, historian and representative of the Institute for International Relations of the GDR, 12 March 1975.

63. Dölling, *Wende*, pp. 110, 113; Edwin Hoernle, "Mehr Sorgen für unsere Neubauern in den kriegsverwüsteten Gebieten," *DVZ*, 18 April 1946, p. 3.

64. Raup, "Land Reform," pp. 327-29, 385-86; Dölling, *Wende*, p. 110; Matthias Kramer, *Die Landwirtschaft in der sowjetischen Besatzungszone*, "Bonner Berichte aus Mittel- und Ostdeutschland" (Bonn: Bundesministerium für gesamtdeutsche Fragen, 1953), p. 16.

65. Hans Liebe, "Die Organisation der Landwirtschaft in der sowjetischen Besatzungzone," in Deutsches Institut für Wirtschaftsforschung (hereafter DIW), *Wirtschaftsprobleme der Besatzungszonen* (Berlin: Duncker & Humbolt, 1948), pp. 195-98; Ulbricht, *Gesch. d. n. Zeit*, p. 237; Ulbricht, *Bauernbefreiung*, p. 85.

66. Communist writers insist that this phenomenon has been

grossly exaggerated by Western accounts, and that only 2 percent of new land recipients had actually abandoned their plots by 1947. Philip Raup notes, however ("Land Reform," pp. 377-78), that this figure is based on the total number of land recipients, including many industrial workers and city dwellers who received small garden plots which they could easily maintain. If the 2 percent figure, equaling about 13,500 abandonments, were applied to the number of actual new *farms* created, about 210,000, it would give a rate of farm abandonment in the range of 5 or 6 percent—high enough to account for the regime's alarmed reaction. (The same problem also occurred in Poland; cf. Korbonski, *Politics of Soc. Agriculture*, pp. 85-86.)

67. Liebe, "Org. der Landw.," pp. 193, 198; "Befehl No. 62 des Obersten Chefs der Sowjetischen Militäradministration in Deutschland über die Kredithilfe für Neubauern," in *Dokumente 1945-49*, pp. 248-49; Kuntsche, "Unterstützung der Landesverw.," pp. 172-73; Gottwald, "Entmachtung," pp. 152-55; Dölling, *Wende*, pp. 136-37, 148, 150; Raup, "Land Reform," pp. 378, 387; Kramer, *Bolschewierung*, p. 103; FDGB, *Protokoll der ersten . . . Delegiertenkonferenz*, p. 94.

68. Dölling, *Wende*, pp. 105, 109-10, 112, 143; Gottwald, "Entmachtung," p. 195.

69. Raup, "Land Reform," pp. 270, 321-26, 329-32, 336-37; Kramer, *Bolschewierung*, pp. 103, 109; Hoernle, "Bündnis zw. Arbeitern u. Bauern," pp. 379-81.

70. Raup, "Land Reform," pp. 106, 326-27.

71. Ibid., pp. 306-8, 310, 316; Horst Bartel and Heinz Heitzer, "Die Anwendung grundlegender Erfahrungen der Sowjetunion in der DDR," *ZfG* 22, no. 9 (1974):924; Woderich, "Anfängen der Demokratisierung," p. 52; Karl Mewis, *Die Lage auf dem Lande und die Aufgaben der Partei* (Schwerin, 1951), p. 54, as quoted in Doernberg, *Geburt*, p. 214. Cf. Doreen Warriner, *Revolution in Eastern Europe* (London: Turnstile Press, 1950), pp. 138-39.

72. Walter Ulbricht, *Die nationale Mission der DDR und das geistige Schaffen in unserem Staat* (Berlin: Dietz Verlag, 1965), p. 17; Hans Immler, *Agrarpolitik in der DDR* (Cologne: Verlag Wissenschaft und Politik, 1971), p. 32; Raup, "Land Reform," pp. 318-19. Raup notes pointedly: "Save for the absence of mystical references to race, blood, and soil, there is very little dif-

ference between the tenure under . . . the Soviet Zone land reform laws and the tenure that was involved in the Nazi *Erbhof* laws."
73. Hoernle, "Agrarprogramm," p. 333.
74. Kotov, *Agrarverhältnisse*, 2:11; Raup, "Land Reform," pp. 41-43. Cf. Laschitza, *Kämpf Dem.*, p. 154; Warriner, *Rev. in E. Europe*, p. 141.
75. Kommunistische Partei Deutschlands, Zentralkomitee, "An die BL Mecklenburg" (letter signed by Wilhelm Pieck, dated 17 October 1945), in "KPD und dem. Bodenreform," p. 854; KPD, *Bericht . . . des 15. Parteitages*, p. 67; "Kleinbauern treten der KPD bei," *TVZ*, 1 November 1945, p. 2; Thomas, *Entscheidung*, p. 158; Woderich, "Anfängen der Demokratisierung," p. 18; Sywottek, *Dt. Volksdem.*, p. 208.
76. Lenin, "Prel. Draft Theses," pp. 156-58; Gottwald, "Entmachtung," pp. 51-52; Kuntsche, "Hilfe der Sow. Militäradm.," pp. 227-28; Doernberg, *Geburt*, pp. 221-22, 172-73; Liebe, "Org. der Landw.," p. 192; Raup, "Land Reform," pp. 416ff.; [Franz Rupp], "Die wirtschaftliche und soziale Entwicklung in der sowjetischen Besatzungszone Deutschlands" (unpublished manuscript in archives of the Hoover Institution for War, Revolution and Peace, Stanford, California), pp. 135-36. Cf. Warriner, *Rev. in E. Europe*, p. 141.
77. Stöckigt, *Kampf der KPD*, pp. 52, 109; Hoernle, "Agrarprogramm," p. 334. Cf. Rupp, "wirtsch. und soc. Entwicklung," p. 134.

CHAPTER FOUR: NEW INSTITUTIONS FOR A NEW ORDER

1. Karl Marx, *The Civil War in France*, in Saul K. Padover, ed. and trans., *Karl Marx on Revolution* (New York: McGraw-Hill Book Co., 1971), pp. 347ff.
2. Tjulpanov, "Rolle der SMAD," p. 244.
3. Paul Schwenk and Paul Wandel, "Richtlinien für die Tätigkeit der lokalen Volksausschüsse auf dem Gebiet der Wirtschaft," in Laschitza, *Kämpf, Dem.*, p. 230. Cf. Diepenthal, *Drei Volksdem.*, pp. 121-22.
4. "Zentrale Steuerung der Ernährungswirtschaft" (8 September 1945), *Verordnungsblatt der Provinz Sachsen*, Vol. 1, no. 2 (20 October 1945), p. 14; "Verordnung über den Übergang der Landwirtschaftskammer auf die Provinzialverwaltung," ibid., p.

17; Fritz Wessel, "Der Kampf ums tägliche Brot. Ein Jahr Aufbau der Landwirtschaft in Sachsen," in Sozialistische Einheitspartei Deutschlands, Landesvorstand Sachsen, *Ein Jahr demokratischer Aufbau im Land Sachsen* (Dresden: Sachsenverlag Drückkerei-und Verlags-Gesellschaft m.b.H., [1946]), p. 27; Combined Resources and Allocations Board (CRAB), Combined Food and Agriculture Committee, "Recommendations Regarding Overall German Administrative Machinery for Food, Agriculture and Forestry" (NARS RG 260), p. 3; "Aktionsprogramm," p. 196.

    5. OSS, "Russian Econ. Policies," pp. 20-21; Raup, "Land Reform," p. 406.

    6. Lenin, "Prel. Draft Theses," pp. 157-58, 164; Leonard Schapiro, *The Communist Party of the Soviet Union* (New York: Random House, 1960), p. 455; Sywottek, *Dt. Volksdem.*, p. 177; Hugh Seton-Watson, *The East European Revolution*, 3d ed. (London: Methuen & Co., 1956), p. 363; Korbonski, *Politics of Soc. Agriculture*, pp. 103-4; Eugen Varga, "Demokratie neuer Art," *Neue Welt* 2, no. 11 (1947):39. This article by a leading Soviet economist is probably the most important Communist theoretical treatment of the postwar "People's Democracies."

    7. "Ausführungsverordnung der Provinzialverwaltung der Mark Brandenburg über die Bildung der Ausschüsse der gegenseitigen Bauernhilfe" (20 October 1945), in *Dokumente 1945-49*, p. 181.

    8. Ibid., p. 180; Raup, "Land Reform," p. 396; Rudolf Reutter, *Was will die Vereinigung der gegenseitigen Bauernhilfe?* (Berlin: Verlag Neuer Weg, 1946), p. 20; Edwin Hoernle, "Unsere Vereinigungen," in: Hoernle, *Zum Bündnis*, pp. 371-72; Dölling, *Wende*, p. 158.

    9. KPD, "An die BL Mecklenburg," p. 855; Rudolf Reutter, "Es geht um die Verwirklichung des grossen Planes," *DVZ*, 10 March 1946, p. 1; Kommunistische Partei Deutschlands, Zentralkomitee, "Betr. Kreis-, Provinz-, bzw. Landesdelegiertenkonferenzen der Vereinigung der gegenseitigen Bauernhilfe" (letter addressed to KPD District Secretaries, signed by Walter Ulbricht), in "KPD und dem. Bodenreform," p. 856; Edwin Hoernle, "VdgB— die bäuerliche Interessengemeinschaft: was soll und kann die VdgB?" in Hoernle, *Zum Bündnis*, pp. 391-92; Doernberg, *Geburt*, p. 216; Wolfgang Heyl, *Zwanzig Jahre demokratische Bodenreform*, "Hefte aus Burgscheidungen," No. 140 (n.p.: Sekretariat des Hauptvorstandes der Christlich-Demokrat-

ischen Union, 1965), pp. 33-34; "Wirtschaftliche Entwicklungen in der sowjetischen Zone seit Potsdam," *Europa-Archiv*, 1 (1946-47):295.

VdgB membership was also weighted in the KPD's favor by a decision to admit workers, artisans, etc., employed in any industry related to agriculture, as well as their family members over the age of eighteen (see Kotov, *Agrarverhältnisse*, 2:47-48).

10. Walter Ulbricht, "Der grosse Plan des demokratischen Neuaufbaus," *DVZ*, 3 March 1946, p. 6.

11. "Ausführungsverordnung . . . über die Bildung der AdgB," pp. 181-82; Reutter, *Was will die VdgB?*, pp. 19, 27-31, 40-41; Kramer, *Bolschewierung*, pp. 100-101; Liebe, "Organis. der Landw.," p. 202; Edgar Tümmler, Konrad Merkel, and Georg Blohm, *Die Agrarpolitik in Mitteldeutschland*, Bundesministerium für gesamtdeutsche Fragen, "Wirtschaft und Gesellschaft in Mitteldeutschland," Vol. 3 (Berlin: Duncker & Humbolt, 1969), p. 34; Robert Siewert, "Ein neuer Weg wird beschritten," in IML, *Wir sind die Kraft*, pp. 377-78.

12. Liebe, "Organis. der Landw.," pp. 189-90, 201; Raup, "Land Reform," pp. 393-96; Reutter, *Was will die VdgB?*, pp. 25-27; Tümmler/Merkel/Blohm, *Agrarpolitik*, p. 34; "Verordnung über die Arbeit der Traktoren bei der Frühjahrsbestellung" (4 April 1946), *Verordnungsblatt . . . Brandenburg*, No. 8 (10 May 1946), pp. 131-32.

13. "Entschliessung der ersten Tagung der Landes-und Provinzialausschüsse der Vereinigungen der gegenseitigen Bauernhilfe" (9-10 May 1946), in *Dokumente 1945-49*, p. 266.

14. Reutter, *Was will die VdgB?*, pp. 21, 32-35; Hoernle, "VdgB," p. 393; "An die Bauern in Mitteldeutschland, Thüringen und Sachsen," *TVZ*, 25 January 1946, p. 3; "Bauprogramm und Viehverteilung" (12 December 1945), *Verordnungsblatt . . . Brandenburg*, No. 3 (5 February 1946), p. 39.

15. Hoernle, "VdgB," p. 393; Hoernle, "Unsere Vereinigungen," pp. 371-73; Reutter, *Was will die VdgB?*, p. 19; Interview with Claus Montag, 12 March 1975.

16. Fritz Selbmann et al., *Volksbetriebe im Wirtschaftsplan. Der Auftakt in Leipzig* (Berlin, n.p., 1948), p. 42; Hoernle, "VdgB," pp. 394-95; Raup, "Land Reform," pp. 291-94; Nettl, *Eastern Zone*, p. 176; Hoernle, "Die Agrarpolitik des Blocks der kämpferischen Demokratie," in Laschitza, *Kämpf. Dem.*, p. 214.

17. Ulbricht, *Dem. Bodenreform*, p. 46.

18. "Entschliessung der ersten Tagung . . . der VdgB," pp. 268-69; Hoernle, "VdgB," pp. 392-93; Liebe, "Organis. der Landw.," p. 202; Wehner, "Kampf um das Bündnis," pp. 212-13.

19. Hoernle, "Agrarpolitik des Blocks," p. 219; Hermes, *CDU und Bodenreform*, p. 20; *Neuaufbau . . . Referat*, pp. 99-100; "Genossenschaften—wichtige Bausteine beim Neuaufbau der Wirtschaft," *DVZ*, 2 December 1945, p. 1; Freier Deutscher Gewerkschaftsbund Berlin, *Gewerkschaften und Konsumgenossenschaften*, "Schulungs- und Referentenmaterial," No. 12 (Berlin, 1946), p. 14.

20. Paul Gärtner, *Die Genossenschaftsbewegung* (Berlin: Dietz Verlag, 1947), pp. 39, 55; "Auflösung von Wirtschaftsverbänden" (11 July 1945), *Verordnungsblatt . . . Pr. Sachsen*, Vol. 1, no. 2 (20 October 1945), p. 22; "Vollendet die Bodenreform!" *DVZ*, 30 October 1945, p. 1; "Befehl Nr. 146 des Obersten Chefs der Sowjetischen Militäradministration in Deutschland zur Wiederaufnahme der Tätigkeit der landwirtschaftlichen Genossenschaften" (20 November 1945), in *Dokumente 1945-49*, pp. 206-8.

21. Reutter, *Was will die VdgB?*, pp. 38, 41; "Freigabe unserer Genossenschaften," *DFB* 1 (November 1945):3; "Befehl 146 . . . der SMAD," p. 207; Gärtner, *Genossenschaftsbew.*, pp. 43-44, 66-68; Kotov, *Agrarverhältnisse*, 2:56.

22. See pp. 96-97, including n. 30.

23. Kotov, *Agrarverhältnisse*, 2:56; Robert Nieschlag, "Die Organisation des Handels in der sowjetischen Besatzungszone," in DIW, *Wirtschaftsprobleme*, pp. 272, 279-80; Dörrier, *Pankow*, p. 67; "Freier Markt nicht für Spekulanten," *DFB* 2 (November 1945):4; "Raiffeisen und freier Markt," *TVZ*, 20 October 1945, p. 2; "Um die freien Erntemengen," *TVZ*, 27 November 1945, p. 3; "Privathandel und freie Erntemengen," *TVZ*, 28 December 1945, p. 4; "Verbotene Lebensmitteleinkäufe," *DVZ*, 13 March 1946, p. 2; *Neuaufbau . . . Referat*, p. 100; Liebe, "Organis. der Landw.," pp. 194, 200-201. Liebe offers several reasons why peasants continued to prefer the black market: (1) despite official KPD insistence that "free market" prices not be artificially restricted (see Ulbricht, *Bauernbefreiung* 1:63-65), black market prices remained higher; (2) by selling in the open market, a peasant risked drawing attention to his favorable quota allot-

ment; (3) although premiums of sugar and tobacco were offered to sellers in the free markets, black-market traders could offer a much wider selection of coveted goods.

24. Gärtner, *Genossenschaftsbew.*, p. 39; David Schoenbaum, *Hitler's Social Revolution: Class and Status in Nazi Germany 1933-1939* (Garden City, N.Y.: Doubleday-Anchor Books, 1967), pp. 136-39; Heinz Bleich et al., *Weg und Erfolg. Zur Entwicklung der Konsumgenossenschaften in der Deutschen Demokratischen Republik* (Berlin: Verband Deutscher Konsumgenossenschaften, [1960]), pp. 9, 17-18.

25. Bleich, *Weg und Erfolg*, pp. 20-25; "Befehl no. 176 des Obersten Chefs der Sowjetischen Militäradministration in Deutschland über die Wiederherstellung der Konsumgenossenschaften" (18 December 1945), in *Dokumente 1945-49*, pp. 219-21.

26. Bleich, *Weg und Erfolg*, pp. 21-26; Nieschlag, "Org. des Handels," pp. 278-79; FDGB, *Gewerksch. und Konsumgenoss.*, pp. 4, 8-9; "Richtlinien der SPD und KPD für die Neugründung der Konsumgenossenschaften," in Gärtner, *Genossenschaftsbew.*, pp. 48-51; Freier Deutscher Gewerkschaftsbund, Landesvorstand Sachsen, "Rundschreiben No. 3," dated 29 March 1946 (Zentralarchiv des FDGB, Folder No. A868); "Wiederaufrichtung der Konsumgenossenschaften" (5 January 1946), *Verordnungsblatt . . . Brandenburg*, No. 5 (5 March 1946), p. 74; "Neugründung der Konsumgenossenschaften," *TVZ*, 21 February 1946, p. 2; Eisermann, "Mittelschichten," pp. 48-51.

27. Gärtner, *Genossenschaftsbew.*, pp. 81-82; Konsum-Hauptsekretariat, *Die Entwicklung der Konsumgenossenschaften von ihrem Neuaufbau seit 1945 bis zum 31. Dezember 1948* (Berlin: Das Neue Berlin, [1949?]), pp. 87-88.

28. "Befehl No. 146 . . . der SMAD," p. 207; "Befehl No. 176 . . . der SMAD," p. 220; Bleich, *Weg und Erfolg*, pp. 21-22, 26-27; Reutter, *Was will die VdgB?*, p. 38; Gärtner, *Genossenschaftsbew.*, p. 72; FDGB, *Gewerksch. und Konsumgenoss.*, pp. 10-11; "Neuaufbau der Genossenschaften," *TVZ*, 23 October 1945, p. 2; Konsum-Hauptsek., *Entwicklung der Konsumgenoss.*, p. 87.

29. "Genossenschaften—wichtige Bausteine beim Neuaufbau der Wirtschaft," *DVZ*, 2 December 1945, p. 1; "Richtlinien . . . für die Neugründung," pp. 48-49, 51; Kramer, *Bolschewierung*,

pp. 110-12; "Die Genossenschaften der freien Bauern," *DFB* 1, no. 5 (December 1945):3; Kotov, *Agrarverhältnisse*, 2:59; FDGB, *Gewerksch. und Konsumgenoss.*, p. 9; "Freigabe unserer Genossenschaften," *DFB* 1 (November 1945):3.

30. Doernberg shows a total of 813,300 farms operating in the Soviet Zone in 1949 (*Geburt*, p. 208); and by 9 January 1946, the *Thüringer Volkszeitung* claimed that half of Thuringia's conservative peasantry were already coop members ("Raiffeisen und Bodenreform," p. 3).

31. Dölling, *Wende der dt. Agrarpolitik*, p. 162; "Aus den Ländern und Provinzen," *DFB* 1 (January 1946):2; "Raiffeisen und Bodenreform," p. 3.

32. Raup, "Land Reform" pp. 394-96; Ernst Busse, *Die Bauerngenossenschaften. Der neue demokratische Aufbau der ländlichen Genossenschaften und ihre Aufgaben* (Berlin: Deutscher Bauernverlag, [1949?]), p. 14. Cf. Liebe, "Organis. der Landw.," p. 190.

33. FDGB, *Gewerksch. und Konsumgenoss.*, p. 14; "Genossenschaften—wichtige Bausteine beim Neuaufbau der Wirtschaft," *DVZ*, 2 December 1945, p. 1; Konsum-Hauptsek., *Entwicklung der Konsumgenoss.*, p. 87; FDGB, *Protokoll der ersten . . . Delegiertenkonferenz*, pp. 57, 233; FDGB Landesvorstand Sachsen, "Rundschreiben No. 3" (29 March 1946); Bleich, *Weg und Erfolg*, p. 21; "Neugründung der Konsumgenossenschaften," *TVZ*, 21 February 1946, p. 2.

34. Cf. Germer, *Grotewohl-Brandt*, p. 63; Griep/Steinbrecher, *Herausbildung des FDGB*, p. 160; Diepenthal, *Drei Volksdem.*, pp. 121-22.

35. Greip/Steinbrecher, *Herausbildung des FDGB*, pp. 60-61.

36. "Sitzungsbericht No. 10" (31 August 1945) and "Sitzungsbericht No. 16" (29 September 1945), in Bednareck/Behrendt/Lange, *Gew. Neubeginn*, pp. 82-84, 125. Walter's indiscretion was a particular provocation to Göring, the chief proponent of white-collar workers' unique status (see Chapter 2, n. 80).

37. See p. 90 above.

38. Walter Ulbricht, "Neue Aufgaben der freien Gewerkschaften. Rede auf der 1. Gewerkschaftskonferenz in Halle, 29. August 1945," in Ulbricht, *Gesch. . . . Arbeiterbew.*, 2:454-81 pas-

sim; Rudolf Jäger, "Heisse Spätsommertage in Halle," in Lehmann, *Aufbruch*, pp. 61-62.

39. Klein, *Vereint . . . alles!*, p. 288; "Sitzungsbericht No. 15" (24 September 1945) and "Sitzungsbericht No. 16" (29 September 1945), in: Bednareck/Behrendt/Lange, *Gew. Neubeginn*, pp. 118-19, 121. The minutes of session no. 15 were changed at the following session to state merely that the Editorial Commission had authorized reprinting Ulbricht's speech "in order to make publication possible." There is no indication as to who requested the change.

40. "Sitzungsbericht No. 9" (29 August 1945), "Sitzungsbericht No. 15" (24 September 1945), "Sitzungsbericht No. 18" (31 October, 1945), and "Sitzungsbericht No. 19" (12 and 14 November 1945), in Bednareck/Behrendt/Lange, *Gew. Neubeginn*, pp. 77, 119, 136-37, 147; Freier Deutscher Gewerkschaftsbund, Berlin, *Betriebsräte und Wiederaufbau*, "Schulungs- und Referentenmaterial," No. 5 (Berlin, 1945), passim.

41. Jäger, "Heisse Spätsommertage," pp. 59-64; Arthur Baumann, "Ein gutes Wort, ein kluger Rat," in Lehmann, *Aufbruch*, pp. 180-81. Even while U.S. troops were still in occupation, Communist agitators had already begun trying to win rank-and-file factory workers away from ADGB influence. See Gerhard Hering, *Der Neuaufbau einheitlicher freier Gewerkschaften 1945 in Leipzig*, "Schriftenreihe des Museums für Geschichte der Stadt Leipzig," No. 8 (Leipzig: Museum für Geschichte der Stadt Leipzig, 1965), pp. 9-10, 13-15.

42. Germer, *Grotewohl-Brandt*, pp. 60-61; Thomas, *Entscheidung*, pp. 137-39; "Greulmärchen des 'Tagesspiegel,' " *DVZ*, 13 March 1946; Berlin-Lichtenberg, *Grosse Kraft*, p. 23; Esche, "Überwindung . . . im Zeiss-Werk," pp. 90-91.

43. Ulbricht, *Gesch. d. n. Zeit*, pp. 152-54; Ulbricht, "Neue Aufgaben der freien Gewerkschaften," p. 477; Ulbricht, "Das Aktionsprogramm der KPD in Durchführung," *DVZ*, 14 September 1945, p. 6.

44. Bednareck/Behrendt/Lange, *Gew. Neubeginn*, pp. xxx-xxxi; "Sitzungsbericht No. 9" (29 August 1945) and "Sitzungsbericht No. 11" (6 September 1945), ibid., pp. 80-81, 94. It is worthy of note that on 27 August, SMA General Bokov politely rejected the Preparatory Committee's request that its area of responsibility be extended beyond Berlin, with a remark that such a step

was still "premature," but that it might be reconsidered at a later time. In the meantime, he said, the Berlin FDGB should make every effort to build up an "exemplary and precedent-setting" organization (ibid., pp. 79-80).

45. Germer was alerted, according to his memoirs, by the following remark in an official FDGB circular: "The election of delegates must be accompanied by a mobilization of all workers in the factories. Their interest, too, is to be awakened in trade union work, and they should be induced to join the trade union." See Germer, *Grotewohl-Brandt*, p. 60; Freier Deutscher Gewerkschaftsbund, Berlin, "Rundschreiben No. 10," dated 1 September 1945 (Zentralarchiv des FDGB, Folder No. A2631).

46. Germer, *Grotewohl-Brandt*, pp. 57-62; Interview with Karl Germer, 21 April 1977; "Sitzungsbericht No. 10" (31 August, 1945) and "Situngsbericht No. 11" (6 September 1945), in Bednareck/Behrendt/Lange, *Gew. Neubeginn*, pp. 82-84, 92, 94.

47. "Sitzungsbericht No. 11" (6 September 1946), in Bednareck/Behrendt/Lange, *Gew. Neubeginn*, pp. 92-94; Griep/Steinbrecher, Herausbildung des FDGB, p. 57; Ulbricht, *Gesch. . . . Arbeiterbew.*, Vol. 2, 1st supp., p. 216; FDGB Berlin, "Rundschreiben No. 16" (21 September 1945), and "Rundschreiben No. 18" (25 September 1945); Interview with Karl Germer, 21 April 1977. Cf. Thomas, *Entscheidung*, p. 116.

48. Staritz, *Sozialismus*, pp. 70-72; Moraw, *Parole*, pp. 129-31; Germer, *Grotewohl-Brandt*, p. 63.

49. Krisch, *German Politics*, pp. 102, 148; Thomas, *Entscheidung*, pp. 164-65; Duhnke, *Stalinismus*, p. 57; Klein, *Vereint . . . . alles?*, pp. 297-98; Moraw, *Parole*, pp. 130-32.

50. Moraw, *Parole*, pp. 132-34; Klein, *Vereint . . . alles?*, pp. 297-98; Office of . . . Intelligence, OMGUS, "Russian Interference," p. A-2.

51. Bednareck/Behrendt/Lange, *Gew-Neubeginn*, p. 1; "Sitzungsbericht No. 19" (12 and 14 November 1945), ibid., p. 148; Albert Behrendt, "Der FDGB und die Vereinigung von KPD und SPD zur SED," *ZfG* 24 (1976):1136-37.

52. Walter Ulbricht, "Die Gewerkschaftswahlen und die Aufgaben der Gewerkschaftsmitglieder beim demokratischen Wirtschaftsaufbau," in Ulbricht, *Gesch. . . . Arbeiterbew.*, Vol. 2, 1st supp., pp. 287-91.

53. Bednareck/Behrendt/Lange, *Gew. Neubeginn*, p. li; "Mit-

teilung des Organisationsausschusses zur Vorbereitung der Delegiertenkonferenz des Freien Deutschen Gewerkschaftsbundes für die sowjetische Besatzungszone" (5 December 1945), ibid., pp. 255-57.

54. "Sitzungsbericht No. 23" (11 December 1945) and "Protokoll der 25. Sitzung des Bundesvorstandes" (18 December 1945), in Bednareck/Behrendt/Lange, *Gew. Neubeginn*, pp. 160, 166; "Sichert die Einheit in den Betrieben. Entwurf einer Plattform uber die Grundsätze und Aufgaben des Freien Deutschen Gewerkschaftsbundes" (5 December 1945), ibid., pp. 249, 253.

55. In this connection it is also noteworthy that the Organization Committee set up by the Brandenburg meeting had tried to hammer out statutes for the FDGB, but had been unable to reach agreement on some questions. The matter was thereupon referred to the provincial FDGB organizations, who were invited to submit their own drafts for statutes to the coming General Delegates' Conference. The statutes finally accepted by the KPD-dominated conference were drawn up on the basis of the provincial recommendations, "as well as other drafts submitted." See Bednareck/Behrendt/Lange, *Gew. Neubeginn*, p. 271, n. 1.

56. Ibid., pp. lii-liii; Behrendt, "FDGB und Vereinigung," p. 1138; FDGB Landesvorstand Sachsen, "Rundschreiben No. 1" (14 March 1946), p. 6; FDGB, *Protokoll der ersten . . . Delegiertenkonferenz*, pp. 150-54; Office of . . . Intelligence, OMGUS, "Russian Interference," p. A-1.

The Thuringian FDGB recorded the following figures for convocations there during the period December 1945 to June 1946:

	No. held	Participants
Public trade union rallies	258	130,986
Trade union meetings	850	103,858
Shop meetings	10,044	431,287
Shop council plenary meetings	828	42,393
Industrial union meetings	1,506	103,190
Shop stewards' conferences	1,526	22,511

SOURCE: Freier Deutscher Gewerkschaftsbund, Landesvorstand Thüringen, *Ein Jahr FDGB* (Erfurt [?], 1946 [?]), p. 14.

57. Griep/Steinbrecher, *Herausbildung des FDGB*, pp. 119-20.

58. Fred Oelssner, "Die Anfänge unserer Parteischulung," in *Vereint sind wir Alles*, p. 162.

59. Griep/Steinbrecher, *Herausbildung des FDGB*, pp. 119-20; Moraw, *Parole*, pp. 136-37; Krisch, *German Politics*, pp. 121-22; Office of . . . Intelligence, OMGUS, "Russian Interference," p. A-1.

60. FDGB, *Protokoll der ersten . . . Delegiertenkonferenz*, p. 179.

61. Ibid., p. 120; *Neuaufbau . . . Richtlinien*, p. 11; *Neuaufbau . . . Referat*, p. 117; Walter Ulbricht, "Die Aufgaben der KPD im Kampf um die Herstellung der Einheit der Arbeiterklasse," in Ulbricht, *Gesch. . . . Arbeiterbew.*, Vol. 2, 1st supp., pp. 336-38; Griep/Steinbrecher, *Herausbildung des FDGB*, p. 122.

62. "Erklärung des Zentralkomitees der KPD und des Zentralausschusses der SPD zur Vorbereitung einer Delegiertenkonferenz des Freien Deutschen Gewerkschaftsbundes für die sowjetische Besatzungszone" (10 December 1945), in Bednareck/Behrendt/Lange, *Gew. Neubeginn*, pp. 261-62; Fritz Rettmann, "Verteidigt die Einheit in den Betrieben," *DVZ*, 16 January 1946, p. 1; "Wählt nur Anhänger der Einheit," *DVZ* 18 January 1946, p. 1; "Wie die Gewerkschaftsdelegiertenwahl nicht durchgeführt werden soll," *DVZ*, 18 January 1946, p. 2; Germer, *Grotewohl-Brandt*, pp. 79-82.

63. Leonhard, *Rev. entlässt*, pp. 428-30.

64. These figures do not include the delegates from Berlin. Western authorities refused to permit FDGB elections in their sectors of the city and later forbade, through the Kommandatura, the newly-elected representatives of the Berlin FDGB from participating in the zonal conference except as observers.

65. FDGB, *Protokoll der ersten . . . Delegiertenkonferenz*, pp. 129, 163; "Demokratie der Millionen. Die Zonenkonferenz der Freien Gewerkschaften Deutschlands," *DVZ*, 9 February 1946, p. 1; "Im Geiste der Einheit. Wahlergebnisse der Allgemeinen Gewerkschaftskonferenz," *DVZ*, 13 February 1946, p. 3. Karl Germer has made further allegations of KPD chicanery at the General Delegates' Conference itself (*Grotewohl-Brandt*, p. 82).

66. FDGB, *Protokoll der ersten . . . Delegiertenkonferenz*, pp. 34-35, 48-49, 78-81, 210-11; Germer, *Grotewohl-Brandt*, p. 83.

67. FDGB, *Protokoll der ersten . . . Delegiertenkonferenz*, pp. 170-71, 230-31; Thomas, *Entscheidung*, pp. 200-201, 238. The leverage gained by the KPD through control of the unions is indicated by the following statistics: the 1946 census of the

Soviet Zone classified 56 percent of all gainfully employed people, with their families, as "workers," and 18 percent as white-collar employees (Doernberg, *Geburt*, p. 37). According to FDGB membership statistics as of June 1946, 53 percent of all workers, white-collar employees, and "members of the intelligentsia" were organized in trade unions (Behrendt, "FDGB und Vereinigung," p. 1133).

68. Freier Deutscher Gewerkschaftsbund, Bundesvorstand, "Bericht über die organisatorische Entwicklung des FDGB," dated 9 February, 1947 (Zentralarchiv des FDGB, Folder No. A0005); Wilhelm Koenen, "Unser jahrelanges Ringen im Sinne des Marxismus-Leninismus trug seine Früchte," in IML, *Wir sind die Kraft*, p. 235; Bundesministerium für gesamtdeutsche Fragen, *Der FDGB* ("Bonner Fachberichte aus der Sowjetzone"; Berlin, 1959), p. 14.

69. Selbmann, "Anfänge der Wirtschaftsplanung," p. 82.

70. The SPD tended to become a catchall for opportunists of all political persuasions (or none) who wanted the presumed shelter of belonging to a socialist party, but shunned the rigid discipline of the KPD. The SPD's democratic organizational style enabled such people, as well as bona fide Social Democrats with dissident views, to affect the party's local political coloration to a degree that would have been unthinkable in the KPD.

71. Thomas, *Entscheidung*, p. 140; Lenin, " 'Left-Wing' Comm.," p. 75; Germer, *Grotewohl-Brandt*, pp. 88-89; Interview with Hein Peglow, chairman of the KPD organization in Berlin-Lichtenberg after October 1945, 20 May 1977.

72. Eckart, "Zum Anteil des FDGB," p. 55; Freier Deutscher Gewerkschaftsbund, Landesausschuss Sachsen, "Programm für Volkssolidarität," dated 22 November 1945 (Zentralarchiv des FDGB, FDGB Bundesvorstand: Folder No. A867); Interview with Walter Bartel, 27 April 1977.

73. V. I. Lenin, "Über die Rolle und die Aufgaben der Gewerkschaften unter den Verhältnissen der Neuen Ökonomischen Politik," in *Lenin und Stalin über die Gewerkschaften*, 2 vols. (Berlin: Tribüne Verlag, 1955), 1:160, 164-65.

74. Esche, "Überwindung . . . im Zeiss-Werk," pp. 115-16.

75. Ibid., pp. 81, 92-93; Wally Vollmer, "Die Fallstricke der AEG und das Votum der Arbeiter," in Lehmann, *Aufbruch*, pp. 85-89; Fritz Rettmann, "Verteidigt die Einheit in den Betrieben,"

DVZ, 16 January 1946, p. 1; Karl Fugger, "Worüber diskutieren gewerkschaftliche Funktionäre?" undated typewritten report (Zentralarchiv des FDGB, Folder No. A0697).

76. Fugger, "Worüber diskutieren gew. Funktionäre?"; Griep/Steinbrecher, *Herausbildung des FDGB*, pp. 14, 16; *Neuaufbau . . . Referat*, p. 63; FDGB, *Protokoll der ersten . . . Delegiertenkonferenz*, p. 110; *Aus der Praxis*, p. 9. Cf. Staritz, *Sozialismus*, p. 95; Lenin, "Über die Rolle . . . der Gewerksch.," pp. 165-66.

77. "Richtlinien für die Tätigkeit der lokalen Volksausschüsse auf dem Gebiete der Wirtschaft," in Laschitza, *Kämpf. Dem.*, p. 231; "Richtlinien für die Arbeit der deutschen Antifaschisten in dem von der Roten Armee besetzten deutschen Gebiet," ibid., pp. 251-52.

78. Stefan Doernberg, "Aus der Geschichte des Kampfes um die ökonomische Entmachtung des Monopolkapitals im Osten Deutschlands (1945-46)," *ZfG* 7 (1959):502; Thomas, *Entscheidung*, pp. 92-94; FDGB, *Protokoll der ersten . . . Delegiertenkonferenz*, p. 70.

79. "Welche Vertretung gibt es im Betrieb?" *DVZ*, 5 July 1945, p. 2.

80. "Richtlinien über den Aufbau der Gewerkschaften. Beschluss des ZK der KPD zur Mitteilung an die Parteibezirksleitungen" (June 1945), in Bednareck/Behrendt/Lange, *Gew. Neubeginn*, p. 4.

81. Walter Ulbricht, "Die Bewältigung der Aufgaben des Aufbaus," in Ulbricht, *Gesch. . . . Arbeiterbew.*, 2:484; Freier Deutscher Gewerkschaftsbund, Berlin, *Betriebsräte und Wiederaufbau*, "Schulungs- und Referentenmaterial," No. 5 (Berlin, October 1945), pp. 2, 7, 10; Freier Deutscher Gewerkschaftsbund, Berlin, *Die Gewerkschaftseinheit und unsere Zukunft*, "Schulungs- und Referentenmaterial," No. 2 (Berlin, 1945), p. 4; Freier Deutscher Gewerkschaftsbund, *Geschäftsbericht des Freien Deutschen Gewerkschaftsbundes 1946* (Berlin: "Die Freie Gewerkschaft" Verlagsgesellschaft m.b.H., 1947), p. 153; Bednareck/Behrendt/Lange, *Gew. Neubeginn*, pp. xlvi-xlvii; "Betrieb und Gewerkschaft," *DVZ*, 31 August 1945, p. 1.

82. FDGB, *Betriebsräte*, pp. 5-6.

83. FDGB Berlin, "Rundschreiben No. 7" (15 August 1945); FDGB, *Geschäftsber. 1946*, pp. 153-54.

84. This list can be summarized as follows: (1) cooperation in efforts for reconstruction, reparations, and denazification; (2) cooperation in expanding production and introducing new work methods; (3) representation of workers' interests vis-à-vis management; (4) participation in negotiations regarding wages and hours; (5) supervision of health and safety arrangements in the factory; (6) coadministration of company kitchens, housing, day-care centers, pension funds, etc.; (7) "securing harmony among the workforce and guarding freedom of combination"; (8) "close cooperation" with the factory trade union committee and protection of its activities from management interference. Source: "Gesetz des Landes Thüringen über die Bildung vorläufiger Betriebsräte, ihre Rechte und Aufgaben" (10 October 1945), in *Dokumente 1945-49*, pp. 169-74.

85. *Aus der Praxis*, p. 15; Thomas, *Entscheidung*, p. 95; FDGB, *Betriebsräte*, p. 7; Roman Chwalek, "Organe der Werktätigen, die sich ergänzen," *DVZ*, 27 December 1945, p. 3; Fritz Rettmann, "Verteidigt die Einheit in den Betrieben," *DVZ*, 16 January 1946, p. 1; "Betriebsräte jetzt und später," ibid., p. 4; Bednareck/Behrendt/Lange, *Gew. Neubeginn*, p. xlvii.

86. *Neuaufbau . . . Richtlinien*, pp. 15-18, 26; *Aus der Praxis*, p. 17; Ulbricht, "Gewerkschaftswahlen," pp. 294-95; FDGB, *Geschäftsber. 1946*, pp. 91, 409-10; Fritz Apelt, "Zum Aufbau freier Gewerkschaften in Sachsen," in IML, *Wir sind die Kraft*, pp. 333-34; FDGB Bundesvorstand, "Informationsmaterial; Hauptabteilung 7—Betriebsräte. Betrifft: Vierteljahresberichte der Betriebsräte," unpublished reports assembled during 1946 (Zentralarchiv des FDGB, Folder No. A0697); Griep/Steinbrecher, *Herausbildung des FDGB*, p. 82; FDGB Berlin, "Rundschreiben No. 72" (9 March 1946); Selbmann, "Anfänge der Wirtschaftsplanung," p. 80.

87. *Neuaufbau . . . Referat*, p. 50. From a speech by Fritz Rettmann.

88. FDGB, *Geschäftsber. 1946*, p. 168.

89. Ibid., pp. 154-56, 159-61, 303; Freier Deutscher Gewerkschaftsbund Berlin, *Das Betriebsrätegesetz*, "Schulungs- und Referentenmaterial," No. 16 (Berlin, 1946), pp. 4-6; "Betriebsrätegesetz," *DVZ*, 18 April 1946, p. 2; Roman Chwalek, "Zum Betriebsrätegesetz," *DVZ*, 19 April 1946, p. 2; Doernberg, *Geburt*, p. 289.

90. FDGB, *Geschäftsber. 1946*, p. 17.

91. Selbmann, *Dem. Wirtschaft*, p. 58; FDGB, *Protokoll der ersten . . . Delegiertenkonferenz*, pp. 55-56; "Mitbestimmung der Werktätigen in der Wirtschaft," *TVZ*, 17 November 1945, p. 3. Mecklenburg was something of an anomaly in this regard: workers' production cooperatives were tolerated and even encouraged for a time by provincial FDGB and party leaders, including Communists, despite warnings from the KPD in Berlin. Only in 1947-48 were these cooperatives finally converted to state enterprises. See FDGB, *Protokoll der ersten . . . Delegiertenkonferenz*, pp. 98-99; Erdmann, "Enteignung . . . in Mecklenburg," p. 305.

92. For a discussion of parallel experiences in Russia in 1917 and their influence on Communist policy regarding worker control in postwar Germany, see Hildegard Dech, "Die Rolle der Gewerkschaften in der Übergangsperiode in der Gewerkschaftsdiskussion der Sowjet-Union bis 1921 und die politische Praxis des FDGB in der SBZ bzw. DDR bis 1955" (Diploma-thesis, Free University of Berlin, 1971), pp. 2-7.

93. By the end of 1946, shop councils existed in 20 percent of Soviet Zone enterprises, mostly larger ones, and included about 50 percent of the workforce. Source: Freier Deutscher Gewerkschaftsbund, Bundesvorstand, "Aus der Betriebsräte-Arbeit des FDGB in der SBZ," report dating from about early 1947 (Zentralarchiv des FDGB, Folder No. A0005).

94. Freier Deutscher Gewerkschaftsbund, Bundesvorstand, "Protokoll: Sitzung der Hauptabteilung II mit Vizepräsidenten der Industrie- und Handelskammern Brandenburg und Mecklenburg," dated 14 February 1947 (Zentralarchiv des FDGB, Folder No. A1708); FDGB, "Betriebsräte-Arbeit"; FDGB, Bundesvorstand, "Rundschreiben No. 23" (10 September 1946); FDGB, Landesvorstand Sachsen, "Rundschreiben No. 9" (undated); FDGB, *Geschäftsber. 1946*, pp. 156-59, 167, 171.

95. Staritz, *Sozialismus*, pp. 105-6; Sarel, *Classe ouvrière*, p. 29.

96. "Aktionsprogramm des Blockes der kämpferischen Demokratie," in Laschitza, *Kämpf. Dem.*, p. 195; Doernberg, *Geburt*, pp. 89-90; Emmrich, "Entwicklung . . . in Chemnitz," pp. 43-44, 94-98; Eberhard, *Magdeburg*, p. 15; Rackow/Heyne/Kleinpeter, *Rostock*, p. 51; FDGB, Landesvorstand Sach-

sen, "Rundschreiben No. 1" (14 March 1946), pp. 3-4; Griep/Steinbrecher, *Herausbildung des FDGB*, pp. 63-64; FDGB, *Protokoll der ersten . . . Delegiertenkonferenz*, p. 62; Bednareck/Behrendt/Lange, *Gew. Neubeginn*, p. xxix.

97. Walter Ulbricht, "Wo ist der Ausweg aus der Katastrophe?" *DVZ*, 19 December 1945, p. 3; Walter Ulbricht, "Der grosse Plan des demokratischen Neuaufbaus," *DVZ*, 6 March 1946, pp. 6-7; Willi Thiele and Horst Bednareck, "Die Gründung des FDGB im Kampf um die Vernichtung der Grundlagen des deutschen Imperialismus und Militarismus, für den Aufbau einer antifaschistisch-demokratischen Ordnung (1945-1946)," *ZfG* 8 (1960):638; FDGB, Landesausschuss Sachsen, "Rundschreiben No. 5" (21 September 1945); Eberhard, *Magdeburg*, pp. 17-18.

98. Griep/Steinbrecher, *Herausbildung des FDGB*, pp. 60-61; Ulbricht, "Neue Aufgaben der Freien Gewerkschaften," p. 456; *Neuaufbau . . . Referat*, p. 30; FDGB, *Geschäftsber. 1946*, p. 90; FDGB, Landesausschuss Sachsen, "Rundschreiben No. 18" (18 December 1945); FDGB Thüringen, *Ein Jahr FDGB*, p. 7.

99. Doernberg, *Geburt*, pp. 282-83; "Selbstverwaltung der Wirtschaft," *TVZ*, 28 July 1945, p. 2; Wahl, "Beginn . . . in Thüringen," pp. 326-27; Emmrich, "Entwicklung . . . in Chemnitz," p. 175; FDGB, *Protokoll der ersten . . . Delegiertenkonferenz*, p. 61; FDGB, Landesausschuss Sachsen, "Rundschreiben No. 14" (14 November 1945); Anton Ackermann, "Nie wieder Reichsverbände!" *DVZ*, 4 October 1945, p. 3; FDGB, Bundesvorstand, "Bericht über die Entnazifizierung der Wirtschaft in der sowjetischen Besatzungszone und Berlin," typewritten report prepared for an interzonal trade union conference in Hanover, 18-20 December 1946 (Zentralarchiv des FDGB, Folder No. 4182).

100. "Wirtschafts-Runderlass No. 8, Betr: Wiederaufnahme der Produktion in demontierten Betrieben" (8 September 1945), *Verordnungsblatt . . . Pr. Sachsen*, Vol. 1, no. 2 (20 October 1945), p. 26; Barthel, "Probleme der . . . Entwicklung," pp. 130-31; Kommunistische Partei Deutschlands, Bezirksleitung der Provinz Sachsen, *Sofortprogramm der KPD für die Wirtschaft der Provinz Sachsen* (n.p., [1946?]), p. 14; "Selbstverwaltung der Wirtschaft," *TVZ*, 28 July 1945, p. 2.

101. Erdmann, "Enteignung . . . in Mecklenburg," pp. 299-301.

102. Ibid., p. 301; Willi Diecker, "Wirtschaft und Staat gingen in die Hände des Volkes über," *ZfG* 17 (1969):874-75; "Richtlinien über den Aufbau der neuen Gewerkschaften. Beschluss des ZK der KPD zur Mitteilung an die Parteibezirksleitungen" (June 1945), in Bednareck/Behrendt/Lange, *Gew. Neubeginn*, p. 5; FDGB, "Entnazifizierung," pp. 9, 16.

103. B. Leuschner, "Die Demokratisierung der Industrie- und Handelskammern," *DVZ*, 28 December 1945, p. 1; FDGB, Landesausschuss Sachsen, "Rundschreiben No. 22" (17 January 1946); Kotov, *Agrarverhältnisse* 1:184; "Verordnung zur Ergänzung der Verordnung über die Bildung der Industrie- und Handelskammer in der Provinz Mark Brandenburg" (8 April 1946), *Verordnungsblatt... Brandenburg*, No. 8 (10 May 1946), p. 132; "Verordnung der Provinzialverwaltung Sachsen über die politische Säuberung der Wirtschaft" (13 September 1945), in *Dokumente 1945-1949*, pp. 150-53.

104. Freier Deutscher Gewerkschaftsbund, Bundesvorstand, "Aufbau und Aufgaben der Fachausschüsse in den IHK," letter dated 11 November 1947 (Zentralarchiv des FDGB, Folder No. A1708); FDGB, "Sitzung der Hauptabt. II mit... IHK"; *Neuaufbau... Referat*, pp. 66-67.

105. Walter Ulbricht, "Der Aufbau der demokratischen Selbstverwaltung," in Ulbricht, *Gesch.... Arbeiterbew.*, Vol. 2, 1st supp., p. 318; FDGB, *Protokoll des ersten... Delegiertenkonferenz*, p. 116; FDGB, "Sitzung der Hauptabt. II mit... IHK"; Eberhard, *Magdeburg*, p. 28; Freier Deutscher Gewerkschaftsbund Berlin, *Gewerkschaften und Selbstverwaltungsorgane. Aufruf des FDGB Gross-Berlin zu den Stadtverordnetenwahlen* (Berlin, [1946]), p. 11; Eisermann, "Mittelschichten," pp. 35-36.

106. "Einige dringende Fragen der Landwirtschaft," *DVZ*, 7 July 1945, p. 2; *Neuaufbau... Richtlinien*, p. 14; *Neuaufbau... Referat*, p. 93; "Sofortprogramm der Gewerkschaften," *TVZ*, 23 August 1945, p. 1; Freier Deutscher Gewerkschaftsbund, IG Metall, Berlin, *Tätigkeitsbericht, 1945-47* (Berlin, [1948?]), p. 37.

107. Doernberg, *Geburt*, pp. 41-44; Laschitza, *Kämpf. Dem.*, p. 196; Eisermann, "Mittelschichten," pp. 56-57; *Neuaufbau... Referat*, p. 18.

108. Eisermann, "Mittelschichten," pp. 9, 30-31, 36-39; "Sitzungsbericht No. 7" (1 August 1945), in Bednareck/Behrendt/Lange, *Gew. Neubeginn*, p. 62; Freier Deutscher Ge-

werkschaftsbund, Bundesvorstand, "Der Einfluss der Gewerk-schaften in Wirtschaft und Verwaltung," report dating from late 1946 or early 1947 (Zentralarchiv des FDGB, Folder No. A0005); FDGB, "Entnazifizierung," p. 10; "Die Demokratisierung des Handwerks," *DVZ*, 16 April 1946, p. 2.

109. Gärtner, *Genossenschaftsbew.*, pp. 57, 60, 68-69; Eisermann, "Mittelschichten," pp. 39-40; Hans Haarfeld, "Die neuen Handwerksorganisationen," *DVZ*, 10 January 1946; Interview with Hein Peglow, 20 May 1977.

110. FDGB, *Geschäftsber. 1946*, p. 92.

111. FDGB, "Einfluss der Gewerksch."; Eisermann, "Mittelschichten," pp. 37-39, 42.

112. "Beste Kräfte als Nachwuchs," *DVZ*, 16 April 1946, p. 2; Eisermann, "Mittelschichten," pp. 43-45; Eckart, "Zum Anteil des FDGB," pp. 101-3; Freier Deutscher Gewerkschaftsbund Berlin, *Gewerkschaften und Wirtschaft. Zur Vorbereitung des Wirtschaftsplanes für 1946*, "Schulungs- und Referentenmaterial," No. 8 (Berlin, 1946), p. 14.

113. Skrypscinski, "Neue Wirtschaftsmoral," *TVZ*, 1 October 1945, p. 1.

114. Walter Ulbricht, *Demokratischer Wirtschaftsaufbau* (Berlin: JHW Dietz Nachf., [1946?]), pp. 36, 44; Friedrich Sarow, *Von der Kriegsproduktion zur Friedenswirtschaft* (Weimar: Thüringer Volksverlag GmbH, [1946?]), p. 11; Laschitza, *Kämpf. Dem.*, pp. 102, 195, 231; *Neuaufbau . . . Referat*, p. 87.

115. Jörg Roesler, "Allgemeines und Besonderes bei der Herausbildung der sozialistischen Planwirtschaft in der DDR (1945-1950)," *Jahrbuch für Geschichte* 12 (1974):287, 290-92; Erna Trübenbach, "Unsere Ernährung," in SED Sachsen, *Ein Jahr . . . Aufbau*, pp. 41-42; FDGB, *Protokoll der ersten . . . Delegiertenkonferenz*, pp. 97-98; "Aus der Diskussionsrede auf der Wirtschaftstagung des Magistrats von Gross-Berlin mit Gewerbetreibenden, Unternehmern, und Gewerkschaftsvertretern," in Ulbricht, *Gesch. . . . Arbeiterbew.*, Vol. 2, 1st supp., p. 252; Willi Stoph, "Streiflichter vom Neuaufbau der Industrie," in IML, *Wir sind die Kraft*, p. 60; "Sitzungsbericht No. 7" (1 August 1945) and "Sitzungsbericht No. 9" (29 August 1945), in Bednareck/Behrendt/Lange, *Gew. Neubeginn*, pp. 63, 77-79; Dieter Sell, "Die Herausbildung und Entwicklung der staatlichen Leitung und Planung in der volkseigenen Industrie beim Aufbau

der antifaschistisch-demokratischen Ordnung und Grundlagen des Sozialismus in der DDR (1945 bis 1955)," (Ph.D. dissertation, Humboldt Univ. Berlin, 1976), p. 24.

The Central Administrations were apparently intended to serve both as a potential nucleus for a future government of all Germany (see pp. 78-79), and in the shorter run as a central economic authority for the Soviet Zone, to remove the SMA as much as possible from visible, day-to-day direction of German economic affairs. In effect they were also a training school for those who would administer the new planned economy.

116. Sell, "Herausb. . . . Planung," pp. 24-27; *Neuaufbau . . . Richtlinien*, p. 11; Stoph, "Streiflichter," p. 69; Selbmann, "Anfänge der Wirtschaftsplanung," pp. 78-80; "Sitzungsbericht No. 20" (26 November 1945), in Bednareck/Behrendt/Lange, *Gew. Neubeginn*, pp. 149-50. Although the East German sources cited here make no mention of any allowance being made in the plan for reparations payments, it is safe to assume that a significant portion of production was earmarked for this purpose as well.

117. Horst Barthel, *Die wirtschaftlichen Ausgangsbedingungen der DDR*, "Forschungen zur Wirtschaftsgeschichte," Vol. 14 (Berlin: Akademie Verlag, 1979), pp. 108, 121-22; *Neuaufbau . . . Referat*, pp. 16-17, 46-47, 93-96; Sell, "Herausb. . . . Planung," p. 27.

118. FDGB, *Geschäftsber. 1946*, pp. 14-15.

119. Ulbricht, *Bauernbefreiung*, p. 87.

120. Griep/Steinbrecher, *Herausbildung des FDGB*, p. 85; *Neuaufbau . . . Referat*, pp. 45-46; Ulbricht, "Gewerkschaftswahlen," pp. 297-98.

121. *Neuaufbau . . . Referat*, pp. 12-13, 45-46; Sarow, *Von der Kriegsprod.*, p. 11; Fugger, *Akt. Fragen*, pp. 16-17. Cf. Rolf Badstübner et al., *DDR: Werden und Wachsen* (Berlin: Dietz Verlag, 1975), p. 96.

CHAPTER FIVE: THE EXPROPRIATION OF MAJOR INDUSTRIES

1. Doernberg, *Geburt*, pp. 272-76; Thomas, *Entscheidung*, pp. 100-101.

2. Badstübner et al., *DDR: Werden und Wachsen*, pp. 53-54; "Directive of the United States Joint Chiefs of Staff to the Commander-in-Chief of the United States Forces of Occupation Re-

garding the Military Government of Germany" (April 1945), in Ruhm von Oppen, *Documents on Germany*, p. 13; "Military Government—Germany, United States Zone, Law No. 52," in OMGUS, "Property Control in the U.S.-Occupied Area of Germany 1945-1949: Special Report of the Military Governor," typewritten report dated July 1949 (Univ. of Wisconsin Memorial Library, Madison, Wis.), p. 65; "Betr.: Erfassung von Beschlagnahmten und herrenlosen Vermögen" (21 August 1945), *Verordnungsblatt . . . Pr. Sachsen*, Vol. 1, no. 2 (20 October 1945), pp. 12-13; Wahl, "Beginn . . . in Thüringen," pp. 331-39. Cf. Sywottek, *Dt. Volksdem.*, pp. 202-3.

3. Erdmann, "Enteignung . . . in Mecklenburg," p. 298; Emmrich, "Entwicklung . . . in Chemnitz," pp. 151-52; Wahl, "Beginn . . . in Thüringen," pp. 331-39; Dörrier, *Pankow*, p. 76; "Berliner Magistrat beschliesst: Nazivermögen wird beschlagnahmt," *DVZ*, 12 July 1945, p. 1; "Zentrale Regelung der Beschlagnahme der Nazivermögen" (16 August 1945), *Verordnungsblatt . . . Brandenburg*, No. 1 (20 October 1945), p. 3; "Beschlagnahme von Industriebetrieben" (25 August 1945), ibid., pp. 3-4; "Mitbestimmung der Werktätigen in der Wirtschaft," *TVZ*, 17 November 1945, p. 3; Interview with Walter Bartel, 26 May 1977. For a comparison of developments in Russia 1917-18 see Dech, "Rolle der Gewerkschaften," pp. 2-3, 9-10.

4. *Neuaufbau . . . Referat*, pp. 110-11; "Betr.: Erfassung von . . . Vermögen," pp. 12-13; "Wirtschaftsrundschreiben No. 12, Betr.: Politische Säuberung der Wirtschaft" (26 September 1945), *Verordnungsblatt . . . Pr. Sachsen*, Vol. 1, no. 1 (6 October 1945), p. 42; "Verordnung No. 12c Betr.: Politische Bereinigung der Wirtschaft" (29 October 1945), *Amtsblatt der Landesverwaltung Mecklenburg-Vorpommern mit amtlicher Beilage*, Vol. 1 [?], no. 1 (25 June 1946), p. 5; Erdmann, "Enteignung . . . in Mecklenburg," pp. 298-99; Doernberg, *Geburt*, p. 312.

5. *Neuaufbau . . . Referat*, pp. 63, 65-66; Thomas, *Entscheidung*, pp. 87-88; Dietrich Staritz, Die National-Demokratische Partei Deutschlands 1948-1953: Ein Beitrag zur Untersuchung des Parteiensystems der DDR" (Ph.D. dissertation, Free Univ. of Berlin, 1968), p. 34; Emmrich, "Entwicklung . . . in Chemnitz," p. 157.

6. "Verordnung . . . Betr.: Politische Bereinigung"; Erdmann, "Enteignung . . . in Mecklenburg," pp. 298-99; Wahl, "Beginn

. . . in Thüringen," pp. 342-43; "Thüringer Verwaltungsgesell-schaft m.b.H.," *TVZ*, 29 October 1945, p. 3; Esche, "Überwin-dung . . . im Zeiss-Werk," pp. 93, 114; Doernberg, *Geburt*, pp. 278-80, 312; Thomas, *Entscheidung*, pp. 95-97; *Neuaufbau . . . Referat*, pp. 82-83; Günther Krüger, "Der Kampf um die Ent-eignung der Kriegsverbrecher und Naziaktivisten in Leipzig" (Ph.D. dissertation, Univ. of Leipzig, 1958), pp. 100-101; Griep/Steinbrecher, *Herausbildung des FDGB*, pp. 92-93.

7. Doernberg, "Aus der Geschichte," p. 502; Doernberg, *Ge-burt*, pp. 300-301; Thomas, *Entscheidung*, pp. 100-101; Inter-view with Walter Bartel, 26 May 1977.

8. V. I. Lenin, *Imperialism: The Highest Stage of Capitalism*, "Little Lenin Library," Vol. 15 (New York: International Pub-lishers, 1939), passim; Fritz Rettmann, "Die Metallarbeiter gin-gen voran," in Lehmann, *Aufbruch*, p. 31; Ulbricht, *Gesch. d. n. Zeit*, pp. 256-60; Thomas, *Entscheidung*, pp. 114-15; Doern-berg, *Geburt*, pp. 247-48; FDGB, *Protokoll der ersten . . . De-legiertenkonferenz*, p. 184.

9. Thomas, *Entscheidung*, pp. 97, 100; Vollmer, "Fallstricke der AEG," pp. 85-86; Esche, "Überwindung . . . im Zeiss-Werk," pp. 100-101; Ulbricht, *Gesch. d. n. Zeit*, pp. 260-61, 270-71; *Neuaufbau . . . Referat*, pp. 58, 62-63.

10. Thomas, *Entscheidung*, p. 97; FDGB Landesausschuss Sachsen "Rundschreiben No. 4" (21 September 1945); Griep/Steinbrecher, *Herausbildung des FDGB*, p. 91; Vollmer, "Fallstricke der AEG," pp. 86-89; "Entschliessung der Gross-kundgebung der KPD," *DVZ*, 20 September 1945, p. 1; "Dele-giertenkonferenz des FDGB fordert: Auflösung und Enteignung der Konzerne," *DVZ*, 9 October 1945, p. 1; "Wer hat das Recht, die Berliner Konferenz zu missachten?" *DVZ*, 28 October 1945, p. 1; Fritz Rettmann, "Die Liquidierung der Konzerne," *DVZ*, 14 November 1945, p. 1; Fritz Rettmann, "Verteidigt die Einheit in den Betrieben," *DVZ*, 16 January 1946, p. 1.

11. *Neuaufbau . . . Referat*, pp. 17-18.

12. Doernberg, *Geburt*, 300-302; Ulbricht, "Gewerkschafts-wahlen," p. 304; "Liquidierung der Konzerne—Voraussetzung der Produktion," *DVZ*, 29 November 1945, p. 1; *Neuaufbau . . . Referat*, pp. 24-25.

13. "Beschluss des Präsidiums der Landesverwaltung Sachsen

über die Enteignung des Kriegsverbrechers Flick" (29 October 1945), in *Dokumente 1945-49*, pp. 184-85.

14. *Neuaufbau . . . Referat*, p. 112; "Verstaatlichung der Bodenvorkommen," *TVZ*, 15 September 1945, p. 1; Pieck, "An die BL Mecklenburg," p. 854; Selbmann, *Anfänge der Wirtschaftsplanung*, pp. 80-81; Diepenthal, *Drei Volksdem.*, pp. 153-54; Doernberg, *Geburt*, pp. 304-7.

15. "Entschliessung einer Kundgebung der SPD in Halle am 31. August 1945," in IML, *Dokumente und Materialien*, Series 3, Vol. 1, p. 123; Sozialdemokratische Partei Deutschlands, Zentralausschuss, "Richtlinien für die Bekämpfung der Monopole und Konzerne," dated 27 November 1945 (Zentralarchiv des FDGB, Folder No. A0123); Doernberg, *Geburt*, pp. 277, 303; Pieck, "An die BL Mecklenburg," p. 854; Wahl, "Beginn . . . in Thüringen," pp. 344-46, 352-53; Wehner, "Dresden," p. 79. Cf. Sywottek, *Dt. Volksdem.*, pp. 208-9.

16. Doernberg, *Geburt*, pp. 307-8, 311, 320; Ulbricht, *Gesch. d. n. Zeit*, p. 264; Falk, "Politische . . . Konstituierung des volkseigenen Sektors," p. 21. It bears mentioning that a committee had been established in the Allied Control Council in September 1945 to study the decartelization issue, but that its activities were "severely inhibited," in the Communist view, by Anglo-American foot-dragging. On 20 December 1945, Control Council Law No. 10 on the "Punishment of Persons Guilty of War Crimes, Crimes Against Peace and Against Humanity" was published, which specified forfeiture of property among other penalties for those falling under its provisions. While Communists claimed this Control Council law to be a ratification of SMA Order No. 124, they remained dissatisfied with Western implementation of this and other radical-sounding legislation. See Doernberg, *Geburt*, pp. 307-8, 316-17; Ruhm von Oppen, *Documents on Germany*, pp. 97-101.

17. "Befehl No. 124 des Obersten Chefs der Sowjetischen Militäradministration in Deutschland über die Beschlagnahme und Übernahme einiger Eigentumskategorien" (30 October 1945), in *Dokumente 1945-49*, pp. 189-92; "Befehl No. 126 des Obersten Chefs der Sowjetischen Militäradministration in Deutschland zur Konfiskation des Eigentums der nationalsozialistischen Partei, ihrer Organe und der ihr angeschlossenen organisationen"

(31 October 1945), ibid., pp. 194-96; Doernberg, *Geburt*, pp. 313-15.

18. Ulbricht, "Gewerkschaftswahlen," pp. 305-6. In his 29 August 1945 speech in Halle, Ulbricht hinted at a further reason for the Communists' rejection of formal nationalization: it would raise questions of compensation that need not arise in a purely punitive expropriation of "war criminals" such as the Communists had in mind. See Ulbricht, *Gesch. . . . Arbeiterbew.*, 2:467.

19. "Befehl No. 124 . . . der SMAD"; Emmrich, "Entwicklung . . . in Chemnitz," pp. 154-56; Wahl, "Beginn . . . in Thüringen," pp. 353-55; Erdmann, "Enteignung . . . in Mecklenburg," p. 300.

20. Werner Krause, *Die Entstehung des Volkseigentums in der Industrie der DDR* (Berlin: Verlag Die Wirtschaft, 1958), p. 47; Günther Krüger, "Der Volksentscheid in Sachsen—ein Beweis für die geschichtsbildende Kraft der Volksmassen," *ZfG* 7 (1959):1610; Federal Republic of Germany, Bundesministerium für gesamtdeutsche Fragen, *Die Enteignungen in der Sowjetischen Besatzungszone* (Bonn: Deutscher Bundes-Verlag, 1958), pp. 23-24; Doernberg, *Geburt*, pp. 318-19; Erdmann, "Enteignung . . . in Mecklenburg," pp. 300-303.

21. Erdmann, "Enteignung . . . in Mecklenburg," pp. 300-303; Emmrich, "Entwicklung . . . in Chemnitz," pp. 155-56; Eckart, "Zum Anteil des FDGB," p. 86, n. 83c; Bundesmin. für g. Fragen, *Enteignungen*, p. 23; Krause, *Entstehung des Volkseigentums*, pp. 42, 46.

22. Erich Mückenberger, "Alle Kannten wir nur ein Ziel: die Einheit der Arbeiterklasse," in *Vereint sind wir Alles*, pp. 330-31.

23. Original italics. FDGB Landesvorstand Sachsen, "Rundschreiben No. 8" (31 May 1946), p. 5; Doernberg, *Geburt*, pp. 318-19; Otto Schröder, *Der Kampf der SED in der Vorbereitung und Durchführung des Volksentscheids in Sachsen Februar bis 30. Juni 1946* (Berlin: Dietz Verlag, 1961), p. 127; Emmrich, "Entwicklung . . . in Chemnitz," p. 157; Esche, "Überwindung . . . im Zeiss-Werk," pp. 112-13; Sozialistische Einheitspartei Deutschlands, Abteilung Werbung und Schulung, "Die politische Bedeutung des Volksentscheids zur Enteignung der Naziverbrecher und Kriegsinteressenten und unsere Agitation und Propaganda" (16 May 1946), in "Rundschreiben der SED zum

Volksentscheid in Sachsen," *BzG* 18, no. 3 (1976):466; Griep/Steinbrecher, *Herausbildung des FDGB*, pp. 92-93; Eckkart, "Zum Anteil des FDGB," p. 51; Interview with Walter Bartel, 26 May 1977.

24. Doernberg, *Geburt*, pp. 335-37; Krause, *Entstehung des Volkseigentums*, pp. 61, 66-68; Krüger, "Volksentscheid," pp. 1609-10; "Befehl No. 97 des Obersten Chefs der Sowjetischen Militäradministration in Deutschland über die Schaffung einer Deutschen Zentralkommission für Beschlagahme und Sequestrierung mit Ausführungsbestimmungen" (29 March 1946), in *Dokumente 1945-49*, pp. 252-53.

25. Krüger, "Volksentscheid," pp. 1605-6; Doernberg, *Geburt*, p. 304; Schröder, *Kampf der SED*, p. 47; Walter Ulbricht, "Der grosse Plan des demokratischen Neuaufbaus," *DVZ*, 6 March 1946, p. 6; "Befehl No. 154/181 des Obersten Chefs der Sowjetischen Militäradministration in Deutschland zur Übergabe des beschlagnahmten und sequestrierten Vermögens in den Besitz und die Nutzniessung der deutschen Selbstverwaltungsorgane" (21 May 1946), in *Dokumente 1945-49*, pp. 272-74.

26. Ulbricht, *Volksentscheid*, pp. 7-8; Doernberg, *Geburt*, pp. 333-34; Leonhard, *Rev. entlässt*, p. 445.

27. Schröder, *Kampf der SED*, pp. 93-95; Ulbricht, *Volksentscheid*, pp. 5-6, 11-12.

28. "Aufruf des Parteivorstandes der SED zum Volksentscheid in Sachsen" (14 June 1946), in Institut für Marxismus-Leninismus beim ZK der SED, *30 Jahre Volkseigene Betriebe: Dokumente und Materialien zum 30. Jahrestag des Volksentscheids in Sachsen* (Berlin: Dietz Verlag, 1976), p. 114; "Interview der 'Sächsischen Zeitung' mit Generalmajor Dubrowski, Chef der SMA des Landes Sachsen, zum Volksentscheid und zur Ernährungslage" (22 June 1946), ibid., pp. 118-19; Ulbricht, *Volksentscheid*, p. 7; Ulbricht, "Der grosse Plan," pp. 6-7; "Der Volksentscheid in Sachsen" (anonymous, undated manuscript, William Sander Collection, archive of the Hoover Institution for War, Revolution and Peace, Stanford, California), pp. 4-6, 9, 11. Political Advisor to the [British] Commander-in-Chief, Germany, "Weekly Political Summary," No. 2, Part 3, dated 28 January 1946 (Public Record Office, Foreign Office file No. 371/55579; hereafter PRO FO 371/55579). According to this report "a number of independent and reliable sources" were quoting senior

Soviet officers as having told SPD leaders as early as January 1946 that Soviet troops would be withdrawn after the KPD-SPD merger, land reform, and industrial expropriations were complete.

29. Schröder, *Kampf der SED*, pp. 66-68, 102-6; Krüger, "Volksentscheid," pp. 1606-8; Doernberg, *Geburt*, pp. 338; Ulbricht, *Volksentscheid*, p. 6; FDGB Landesvorstand Sachsen, "Rundschreiben No. 8" (31 May 1946), pp. 1-2.

30. FDGB Landesvorstand Sachsen, "Rundschreiben No. 8," pp. 1-2; Schröder, *Kampf des SED*, pp. 93-98; Krüger, "Volksentscheid," pp. 1606-8.

31. As an added demonstration of its humane intent, the proposed expropriation law provided that proceeds from any properties resold by the administrations would be used to aid widows, orphans, refugees, etc.

32. FDGB Landesvorstand Sachsen, "Rundschreiben No. 8," pp. 2-3; SED Sachsen, "Die pol. Bedeutung," pp. 465-67; Emmrich, "Entwicklung . . . in Chemnitz," pp. 164, 168-69; "Aufruf des Landesfrauenausschusses von Sachsen zum Volksentscheid" (1 June 1945), in IML, *30 Jahre VEB*, pp. 96-97; Doernberg, *Geburt*, p. 337.

33. FDGB Landesvorstand Sachsen, "Rundschreiben No. 8," pp. 1, 5; Freier Deutscher Gewerkschaftsbund Berlin, "Rundschreiben No. 72" (9 March 1946); Eckart, "Zum Anteil des FDGB," p. 98.

34. SED Sachsen, "Die pol. Bedeutung," p. 466; Freier Deutscher Gewerkschaftsbund, Landesvorstand Sachsen, *Informationsblatt für den Gewerkschaftsfunktionär*, Vol. 1, no. 1 (1946), p. 3; Freier Deutscher Gewerkschaftsbund, Bundesvorstand, "Rundschreiben No. 9" (7 May 1946); FDGB Landesvorstand Sachsen, "Rundschreiben No. 8," p. 4, and "Rundschreiben No. 9" (undated), pp. 1-2; Eckart, "Zum Anteil des FDGB," p. 94; Emmrich, "Entwicklung . . . in Chemnitz," pp. 171-72; "Hinweise des Landesvorstandes der SED Sachsen für die Arbeit der Betriebsgruppen zum Volksentscheid" (June 1946), in IML, *30 Jahre VEB*, pp. 130-31.

35. Dana Adams Schmidt, "Saxon Plebiscite Reveals Dissent," *New York Times*, 5 July 1946, p. 9; Schröder, *Kampf der SED*, p. 230; "Der Volksentscheid in Sachsen," pp. 9-11; Anatoli Waks, "Proletarischer Internationalismus in Aktion," in Wehner,

Kampfgefährten, p. 249; "Kanzelverkündung des Bischofs von Meissen zum Volksentscheid" (Whitsun, 1946), in IML, *30 Jahre VEB,* p. 104; Doernberg, *Geburt,* pp. 340-41.

36. Ulbricht, *Volksentscheid,* p. 10.

37. Schröder, *Kampf der SED,* pp. 82-83, 87; "Der Volksentscheid in Sachsen," pp. 6-9; SED Sachsen, "Die pol. Bedeutung," p. 469; FDGB Landesvorstand Sachsen, "Rundschreiben No. 8," p. 3; Doernberg, *Geburt,* p. 341.

38. Doernberg, *Geburt,* pp. 342-44; Schröder, *Kampf der SED,* pp. 82-83, 87, 89; Emmrich, "Entwicklung . . . in Chemnitz," p. 168.

39. "Aufruf . . . der SED zum Volksentscheid," p. 112; Ulbricht, *Volksentscheid,* pp. 8-9; "Der Volksentscheid in Sachsen," p. 13; Krüger, "Volksentscheid," p. 1608; Emmrich, "Entwicklung . . . in Chemnitz," p. 169. Emmrich notes that in the entire city of Chemnitz only 720 residents were disqualified from voting.

40. Secretary of State Byrnes remarked at the conference that the U.S. would "frankly always be suspicious of elections in countries where our representatives are not free to move about and where the press cannot report freely" (U.S. Dept. of State, *Conference of Berlin,* 2:231).

41. Percy Stulz and Siegfried Thomas, *Die Deutsche Demokratische Republik auf dem Wege zum Sozialismus,* Part 1 (Berlin: Volk und Wissen Volkseigener Verlag, 1959), p. 96; Krüger, "Volksentscheid," p. 1617; Schröder, *Kampf der SED,* p. 169; Schmidt, "Saxon Plebiscite."

42. Quoted in Krüger, "Volksentscheid," p. 1618; Doernberg, *Geburt,* pp. 337-40.

43. "Blendwerk Volksentscheid," *Der Sozialdemokrat,* 24 May, 1946, p. 1.

44. *Neuaufbau . . . Referat,* p. 62; Krüger, "Volksentscheid," p. 1617; Krüger, "Enteignung . . . in Leipzig," p. 127; Krause, *Entstehung des Volkseigentums,* pp. 77, 84-86; Erdmann, "Enteignung . . . in Mecklenburg," p. 305; Emmrich, "Entwicklung . . . in Chemnitz," p. 174; Gärtner, *Genossenschaftsbew.,* p. 75; Doernberg, *Geburt,* pp. 335, 337; Schröder, *Kampf der SED,* pp. 76-77; Rupp, "wirtsch. u. soz. Entwicklung," pp. 113, 120.

45. Krause, *Entstehung des Volkseigentums,* pp. 80-82; Doernberg, *Geburt,* pp. 356-58; Karl Thalheim, "Wirtschaft," in Berlin,

Büro für gesamtberliner Fragen, *Berlin, Sowjet Sektor. Die politische, rechtliche, wirtschaftliche, soziale und kulturelle Entwicklung in acht Berliner Verwaltungsbezirken* (Berlin: Colloquium Verlag, 1965), p. 89; Kathleen McLaughlin, "Berlin Properties Reported Seized," *New York Times*, 7 July 1946, Sect. 1, p. 20; Thomas, *Entscheidung*, pp. 242-43; FDGB Berlin, "Rundschreiben" (no number, 28 February 1947).

46. Krüger, "Enteignung . . . in Leipzig," p. 164; Rupp, "Wirtsch. u. soz. Entwicklung," pp. 114-15; Wehner, "Dresden," p. 80; Doernberg, *Geburt*, pp. 435-38; Deckers, *Transf. des Bankensystems*, pp. 30-32; Krause, *Entstehung des Volkseigentums*, p. 82; "Control Council Directive No. 38: The Arrest and Punishment of War Criminals, Nazis and Militarists and the Internment, Control and Surveillance of Potentially Dangerous Germans" (12 October 1946), in Ruhm von Oppen, *Documents on Germany*, pp. 168-79. The provincial administrations also passed a series of laws confiscating all mining industries and mineral resources in 1947; these amounted, however, to little more than a ratification of measures already taken under earlier legislation. See Doernberg, *Geburt*, pp. 377-78.

47. Doernberg, *Geburt*, pp. 370-75, 382-87; Emmrich, "Entwicklung . . . in Chemnitz," pp. 174-76.

48. Schröder, *Kampf der SED*, pp. 63-64, 86, 120-21, 126.

49. "Befehl No. 64 des Obersten Chefs der Sowjetischen Militäradministration in Deutschland zur Beendigung des Sequesterverfahrens" (17 April 1946), in *Dokumente 1945-49*, pp. 620-22; Krause, *Entstehung des Volkseigentums*, p. 108.

CHAPTER SIX: CONCLUSION

1. Kramer, *Bolschewierung*, pp. 102-3, 112; Rupp, "Wirtsch. und soz. Entwicklung," p. 196; Doernberg, "Aus der Geschichte," pp. 496-97.

2. See pp. 7-8, 12ff. above.

3. Varga, "Dem. neuer Art." p. 33.

4. Ibid., pp. 33-34; Anton Ackerman, "Gibt es einen besonderen deutschen Weg zum Sozialismus?" *Einheit* 1 (1946):22ff.; Wolfgang Leonhard, "Über den deutschen Weg zum Sozialismus," *DVZ*, 24 March 1946, p. 3.

5. Leonhard, *Rev. entlässt*, pp. 242-43.

6. Deutscher, *Stalin*, pp. 542-43. Ulbricht commented in 1958: "One can just imagine what would have happened if we had proclaimed the immediate construction of socialism in the year 1945! We did not do that; rather, we carefully applied Lenin's teaching about the two tactics in the democratic revolution, in order to lead people forward step by step. . . ." See Ulbricht, *Die Staatslehre des Marxismus-Leninismus und ihre Anwendung in Deutschland* (Berlin: Deutscher Zentralverlag, 1958), p. 59; Anton Ackermann, "Der ideologische Kampf der Partei," in KPD, *Bericht . . . des 15. Parteitages,* pp. 114-16.

7. Cf. Ulam, *Exp. and Coex.*, p. 370; Vojtech Mastny, *Russia's Road to the Cold War* (New York: Columbia University Press, 1979), pp. 223-24, 278.

8. Doernberg, *Geburt*, p. 67; Falk, "Politische . . . Konstituierung des Volkseigenen Sektors," p. 21; Mastny, *Russia's Road*, p. 128. See also Koch, "Aktennotiz," passim. The Communists evidently expected significant support from Germans in the West, either out of sympathy with Soviet Zone democratization measures or out of fear of a permanent division of the nation. Asked by the author whether he and his colleagues had ever seriously hoped to implement their program in the Western zones, KPD veteran Walter Bartel replied that "it was more than just a hope." Demonstrations by Rhineland workers calling for expropriation of major industries, an attempt to imitate the Saxon referendum in Hesse, efforts to establish the SED in Bavaria and elsewhere, and the generally "progressive" character of the bourgeois parties' original platforms all led Communists to overestimate their chances in the West and to underestimate opposing forces, especially the determined opposition of the U.S. Djilas also recalled that in his conversations with Soviet leaders in 1946 they seemed to be "caught up by the flush of military victories and by their hopes for the economic and other dissolution of Western Europe" (*Conv. with Stalin*, p. 154).

9. Economic Information Section, British Delegation to the Control Commission for Germany, "Current Status of Industry and General Economy in the USSR Zone of Germany," dated 11 June 1946 (PRO FO371/55581); Telegram from Frank Roberts, British Ambassador to Moscow, to the Foreign Office regarding Soviet policy towards Germany, dated 30 March 1946 (PRO FO371/55579).

10. Harriman, "Report to the Secretary of State"; Sywottek, *Dt. Volksdem.*, pp. 168-72; John Gimbel, *The American Occupation of Germany* (Stanford: Stanford University Press, 1968), pp. 117, 126-28, 229; Thomas, *Entscheidung*, pp. 121-22; Edinger, *German Exile Politics*, p. 237.

11. Griep/Steinbrecher, *Herausbildung des FDGB*, pp. 114-15; Constantine Fitzgibbon, *Denazification* (London: Michael Joseph Ltd., 1969), pp. 166-67; Friedmann, *Allied Military Govt.*, pp. 113, 124.

12. Fitzgibbon, *Denazification*, pp. 95-99, 178-80; Tjulpanov, "Zusammenarbeit," p. 96; Niethammer, *Entnazifizierung*, pp. 47, 653, 666; Friedmann, *Allied Military Govt.*, p. 122. The idea of collective guilt was not totally foreign to the Soviet occupiers, but to them it meant national responsibility for reparations, not an abstract moral issue. It is interesting to observe that in recent years East German intellectuals have been trying to force their society to confront questions of moral responsibility for fascism which official dogma has hitherto sloughed off with the facile equation, "socialist equals anti-fascist."

13. Nevertheless it is worth noting, that, with rare exceptions, former Nazis have remained permanently excluded from even low-level positions of power in the GDR, in contrast to later developments in the Federal Republic. Since the old elites were left in place in the West, members of these elites who temporarily fell from grace were able to recover their positions relatively easily when times changed and experienced managers were needed. In East Germany the elites themselves had been displaced by a new elite.

14. Sywottek, *Dt. Volksdem.*, p. 192. Walter Ulbricht commented revealingly at the time of local elections in the U.S. Zone in January 1946 on the difference between Eastern and Western concepts of democracy: "Some are of the opinion that elections should measure the relative strength of all parties. From the standpoint of democratic progress . . . we regard this concept as false. Elections should be a means of influencing the masses in an anti-fascist direction" (Walter Ulbricht, "Offene Antwort an sozial-demokratische Genossen," *DVZ*, 16 January 1946, p. 5).

15. Tjulpanov, "Rolle der SMA," p. 61. Italics added.

Bibliography

ARCHIVAL SOURCES

Freier Deutscher Gewerkschaftsbund (Bundesvorstand), Berlin, Zentralarchiv des FDGB:
Freier Deutscher Gewerkschaftsbund, Berlin. "Rundschreiben" (1945-1950). Folder No. A2631.
Freier Deutscher Gewerkschaftsbund, Bundesvorstand. "Aufbau und Aufgaben der Fachausschüsse in den IHK," letter dated 11 November 1947. Folder No. A1708.
———. "Aus der Betriebsräte-Arbeit des FDGB in der SBZ," report dating from about early 1947. Folder No. A0005.
———. "Bericht über die Entnazifizierung der Wirtschaft in der sowjetischen Besatzungszone und Berlin," report presented to an interzonal trade union conference in December 1946. Folder No. 4182.
———. "Bericht über die organisatorische Entwicklung des FDGB," report dated 9 February 1947. Folder No. A0005.
———. "Der Einfluss der Gewerkschaften in Wirtschaft und Verwaltung," report dating from late 1946 or early 1947. Folder No. A0005.
———. "Informationsmaterial; Hauptabteilung 7—Betriebsräte. Betrifft: Vierteljahresberichte der Betriebsräte," report dating from late summer or early autumn 1946. Folder No. A0697.
———. "Protokoll: Sitzung der Hauptabteilung II mit Vizepräsidenten der Industrie- und Handelskammern Brandenburg und Mecklenburg," dated 4 February 1947. Folder No. A1708.
———. "Rundschreiben," (1946). Folder No. A2632.
Freier Deutscher Gewerkschaftsbund, Landesausschuss Sachsen. "Programm für die Volksolidarität," dated 22 November 1945. Folder No. A867.
———. "Rundschreiben," (1945-46). Folder No. A687.
Freier Deutscher Gewerkschaftsbund, Landesvorstand Sachsen. "Rundschreiben," (March-June 1946). Folder No. A868.

Fugger, Karl. "Worüber diskutieren gewerkschaftliche Funktionäre?" typewritten MS dating from 1946. Folder No. A0697.
Sozialdemokratische Partei Deutschlands, Zentralausschuss. "Richtlinien für die Bekämpfung der Monopole und Konzerne," date 27 November 1945. Folder No. A0123.

Hoover Institution for War, Revolution and Peace, Stanford, California:
[Rupp, Franz]. "Die wirtschaftliche und soziale Entwicklung in der sowjetischen Besatzungszone Deutschlands." Undated typewritten manuscript.
"Der Volksentscheid in Sachsen." Anonymous, undated manuscript, William Sander Collection.

National Archives and Records Service, Washington, D.C.; Record Group 260 (OMGUS documents):
Combined Resources and Allocations Board (CRAB), Combined Food and Agriculture Committee. "Recommendations Regarding Overall German Administrative Machinery for Food, Agriculture and Forestry."
Office of the Director of Intelligence, OMGUS. "Recent Evidences of Russian Interference in German Political Activity," dated 5 February 1946.
Office of Strategic Services (OSS). "Field Intelligence Study 8: Russian Economic Policies in Germany," dated 13 July 1945.
U.S. Headquarters Berlin District, G-2 Division. "Special Report on Formation of a Central Administration in the Russian Zone," dated 7 August 1945.

Public Record Office, London:
Economic Information Section, British Delegation to Control Commission for Germany. "Current Status of Industry and General Economy in the USSR Zone of Germany," dated 11 June 1946. FO371/55581.
Political Advisor to [British] Commander-in-Chief, Germany. "Weekly Political Summary," No. 2, Part 3. FO 371/55579.
Roberts, Frank (Ambassador). Reports analyzing Soviet policy toward Germany, dated 30 March and 27 April 1946. FO 371/55579 and /55580.

Strang, William. Memorandum on Soviet Policy in Germany, dated 6 April 1946.

Vereinigung ger gegenseitigen Bauernhilfe (Zentralvorstand), Berlin:
Graffunder, [Siegfried], et al. "Die Landwirtschaftspolitik in der antifaschistisch-demokratischen Ordnung und die Heranführung der Bauern an die sozialistische Umgestaltung." Undated typewritten manuscript.

OTHER PRIMARY SOURCES

Ackermann, Anton. "Gibt es einen bosonderen deutschen Weg zum Sozialismus?" *Einheit*, Vol. 1, no. 1 (1946).
Aus der Praxis der Betriebsräte: Tatsachen, Erfahrungen, Aufgaben in der sowjetischen Besatzungszone. Berlin: Freier Deutscher Gewerkschaftsbund, 1946.
Beginn eines neuen Lebens. Eine Auswahl von Erinnerungen an den Beginn des Neuaufbaus in Dresden im Mai 1945. "Beiträge zur Geschichte der Dresdener Arbeiterbewegung," Vol. 7. Dresden: Museum für Geschichte der Dresdener Arbeiterbewegung, 1960.
Bednareck, Horst; Behrendt, Albert; and Lange, Dieter, ed. *Gewerkschaftlicher Neubeginn. Dokumente zur Gründung des FDGB und zu seiner Entwicklung von Juni 1945 bis Februar 1946.* Berlin: Verlag Tribüne, 1975.
Berlin-Lichtenberg, Örtliche Kommission zur Erforschung der Geschichte der deutschen Arbeiterbewegung. *Die Grosse Kraft: Erlebnisberichte vom Kampf um die Einheit der Arbeiterklasse Berlin-Lichtenberg, Juni 1945-April 1946.* Berlin: SED Kreisleitung Lichtenberg, 1966.
Busse, Ernst. *Die Bauerngenossenschaften. Der neue demokratische Aufbau der ländlichen Genossenschaften und ihre Aufgaben.* Berlin: Deutscher Bauernverlag, [1949?].
Djilas, Milovan. *Conversations with Stalin.* Translated by Michael B. Petrovich. New York: Harcourt, Brace, & World. 1962.
Döring, H. *Von der Bodenreform zu den landwirtschaftlichen Produktionsgenossenschaften.* Berlin: VEB Deutscher Zentralverlag, [1953?].
Eberhard, Rudolf. *Ein Jahr Aufbauarbeit in Magdeburg. Re-*

chenschaftsbericht der Stadtverwaltung über die im ersten Jahr nach dem Hitlerkrieg geleistete Arbeit, erstattet in der 1. Beratenden Versammelung am 27. Juli 1946 von Oberbürgermeister Eberhard. Magdeburg: n.p., [1946?].

Ehrenburg, Ilya. *Men, Years—Life*, Vol. 5: *The War 1941-45.* Translated by Tatiana Shebunina and Yvonne Kapp. London: MacGibbon & Kee, 1964.

Einsiedel, Heinrich von. *I Joined the Russians.* New Haven: Yale University Press, 1953.

Freier Deutscher Gewerkschaftsbund. *Geschäftsbericht des Freien Deutschen Gewerkschaftsbundes 1946.* Berlin: "Die Freie Gewerkschaft," Verlagsgesellschaft m.b.H., 1947.

————. *Protokoll der ersten allgemeinen Delegiertenkonferenz des Freien Deutschen Gewerkschaftsbundes für das sowjetisch besetzte deutsche Gebiet, 9.-11. Februar 1946, Berlin.* Berlin: n.p., [1946].

Freier Deutscher Gewerkschaftsbund, Berlin. *Betriebsräte und Wiederaufbau.* "Schulungs- und Referentenmaterial," No. 5. Berlin, 1945.

————. *Das Betriebsrätegesetz.* "Schulungs- und Referentenmaterial," No. 16. Berlin, 1946.

————. *Gewerkschaften und Konsumgenossenschaften.* "Schulungs- und Referentenmaterial," No. 12. Berlin, 1946.

————. *Gewerkschaften und Selbstverwaltungsorgane. Aufruf des FDGB Gross-Berlin zu den Stadtverordnetenwahlen.* Berlin, [1946].

————. *Gewerkschaften und Wirtschaft. Zur Vorbereitung des Wirtschaftsplanes für 1946.* "Schulungs- und Referentenmaterial," No. 8. Berlin, 1946.

————. *Die Gewerkschaftseinheit und unsere Zukunft.* "Schulungs- und Referentenmaterial," No. 2. Berlin, 1945.

Freier Deutscher Gewerkschaftsbund, IG Metall, Gross-Berlin. *Tätigkeitsbericht, 1945-47.* Berlin: Vorstand des IG Metall Gross-Berlin, [1948?].

Freier Deutscher Gewerkschaftsbund, Landesvorstand Thüringen. *Ein Jahr FDGB.* Erfurt [?]: FDGB Landesvorstand Thüringen, [1946?].

Fugger, Karl. *Aktuelle Fragen der Gewerkschaftsbewegung.* Berlin: Vorstand des Freien Deutschen Gewerkschaftsbundes, [1946?].

Bibliography

German Democratic Republic, Ministerium für auswärtige Angelegenheiten, and Union of Soviet Socialist Republics, Ministerium für auswärtige Angelegenheiten. *Um ein antifaschistisch-demokratisches Deutschland: Dokumente aus den Jahren 1945-1949.* Berlin: Staatsverlag der DDR, 1968.

Germer, Karl J. *Von Grotewohl bis Brandt: ein dokumentarischer Bericht über die SPD in den ersten Nachkriegsjahren.* Landshut: Verlag Politisches Archiv, 1974.

Hoernle, Edwin. *Zum Bündnis zwischen Arbeitern und Bauern.* Berlin: Dietz Verlag, 1972.

Institut für Marxismus-Leninismus beim Zentralkomitee der SED. *Dokumente und Materialien zur Geschichte der deutschen Arbeiterbewegung.* Series 3, Vol. 1: *Mai 1945-April 1946.* Berlin: Dietz Verlag, 1959.

————. *30 Jahre Volkseigene Betriebe: Dokumente und Materialien zum 30. Jahrestag des Volksentscheids in Sachsen.* Berlin: Dietz Verlag, 1976.

————. *Wir sind die Kraft: Der Weg zur Deutschen Demokratischen Republik. Erinnerungen.* Berlin: Dietz Verlag, 1959.

Koch, Waldemar. "Aktennotiz 5.9. 1945. Betrifft: Besprechung bei Marschall Schukow." In "Die Gründung der Liberal-Demokratischen Partei in der sowjetischen Besatzungszone 1945," by Ekkehart Krippendorff. *Vierteljahreshefte für Zeitgeschichte*, Vol. 8, no. 3 (1960).

Kommunistische Partei Deutschlands. *Bericht über die Verhandlungen des 15. Parteitages der Kommunistischen Partei Deutschlands.* Berlin: Verlag Neuer Weg, 1946.

————. *Der Sieg des Faschismus in Deutschland und seine Lehren für unseren gegenwärtigen Kampf.* "Vortragsdisposition," No. 1. Berlin: Kommunistische Partei Deutschlands, [1945].

Kommunistische Partei Deutschlands, Bezirksleitung der Provinz Sachsen. *Sofortprogramm der KPD für die Wirtschaft der Provinz Sachsen.* n.p.: KPD Provinz Sachsen, [1946?].

"KPD und demokratische Bodenreform." *Beiträge zur Geschichte der Arbeiterbewegung*, Vol. 17, no. 5 (1975).

Lehmann, Erwin, ed. *Aufbruch in unsere Zeit. Erinnerungen an die Tätigkeit der Gewerkschaften von 1945 bis zur Gründung der Deutschen Demokratischen Republik.* Berlin: Verlag Tribüne, 1976.

Lenin, V. I. *Imperialism: The Highest State of Capitalism.* Little

Lenin Library, Vol. 15. New York: International Publishers, 1939.

————. *Collected Works.* Vol. 31. Moscow: Progress Publishers, 1966.

————. *Selected Works.* Vol. 3: *The Revolution of 1905-07.* New York: International Publishers, n.d.

Lenin und Stalin über die Gewerkschaften. 2 vols. Berlin: Tribüne Verlag, 1955.

Leonhard, Wolfgang. *Die Revolution entlässt ihre Kinder.* Cologne and Berlin: Kiepenhauer & Witsch, 1955.

Neuaufbau der deutschen Wirtschaft. Referat und Diskussion über die Richtlinien der KPD zur Wirtschaftspolitik. Berlin: Verlag Neuer Weg, [1946].

Neuaufbau der deutschen Wirtschaft. Richtlinien der KPD zur Wirtschaftspolitik. Berlin: Verlag Neuer Weg, [1946].

Office of Military Government for Germany (U.S.). "Property Control in the U.S.-Occupied Area of Germany 1945-1949: Special Report of the Military Governor," dated July 1949.

Padover, Saul K., ed. and trans. *Karl Marx on Revolution.* New York: McGraw-Hill Book Co., 1971.

Pieck, Wilhelm. *Advancing to Socialism. Report, Reply to the Discussion, and Resolution on the First Point of the Agenda: The Activities of the Executive Committee of the Communist International.* "Seventh World Congress of the Communist International." Moscow-Leningrad: Co-operative Publishing Society of Foreign Workers in the U.S.S.R., 1935.

————. *Junkerland in Bauernhand: Rede zur demokratischen Bodenreform, Kyritz, 2. September 1945.* Berlin: Dietz Verlag, 1955.

————. *Der neue Weg zum gemeinsamen Kampf für den Sturz der Hitlerdiktatur.* Berlin: Dietz Verlag, 1954.

Provinzausschuss der Gegenseitigen Bauernhilfe Mark Brandenburg. *Parlament der Bauern. Erster Provinz-Kongress der Gegenseitigen Bauernhilfe der Mark Brandenburg am 16. und 17. März 1946 in Potsdam.* Potsdam: Verlag "Märkische Volksstimme," [1946?].

Reutter, Rudolf. *Grossgrundbesitz wird wieder Bauernland.* Berlin: Verlag neuer Weg, 1945.

————. *Was will die Vereinigung der gegenseitigen Bauernhilfe?* Berlin: Verlag Neuer Weg, 1946.

Ruhm von Oppen, Beate, ed. *Documents on Germany under Occupation 1945-1954.* London: Oxford University Press, 1955.

"Rundschreiben der SED zum Volksentscheid in Sachsen." *Beiträge zur Geschichte der Arbeiterbewegung,* Vol. 18, no. 3 (1976).

Selbmann, Fritz. *Demokratische Wirtschaft.* "Dokumente der neuen Zeit," Vol. 3. Dresden: Dresdener Verlagsgesellschaft K.G., [1948].

Selbmann, Fritz, et al. *Volksbetriebe im Wirtschaftsplan. Der Auftakt in Leipzig.* Berlin, m.p., 1948.

Smith, Jean Edward, ed. *The Papers of General Lucius D. Clay: Germany 1945-1949.* Vol. 1:1945-47. Bloomington: Indiana University Press, 1974.

Stalin, Joseph. *Foundations of Leninism.* New York: International Publishers, 1932.

Stulz, Percy; and Thomas, Siegfried. *Die Deutsche Demokratische Republik auf dem Wege zum Sozialismus.* Part 1 (1945-1949). Berlin: Volk und Wissen Volkseigener Verlag, 1959.

Ulbricht, Walter. *Die Bauernbefreiung in der Deutschen Demokratischen Republik.* 2 vols. Berlin: Dietz Verlag, 1961.

————. *Die demokratische Bodenreform—ein ruhmreiches Blatt in der deutschen Geschichte.* Berlin: ZK der SED, [1955].

————. *Demokratischer Wirtschaftsaufbau.* Berlin: JHW Dietz Nachf., [1946?].

————. *Die nationale Mission der DDR und das geistige Schaffen in unserem Staat.* Berlin: Dietz Verlag, 1965.

————. *Die Staatslehre des Marxismus-Leninismus und ihre Anwendung in Deutschland.* Berlin: VEB Deutscher Zentralverlag, 1958.

————. *Volksentscheid und Wirtschaftsaufbau.* Dresden: Sachsenverlag, Druckerei und Verlags-Gesellschaft m.b.H., [1946?].

————. *Zur Geschichte der deutschen Arbeiterbewegung.* Vol. 2: (1933-1946), incl. first supplementary vol. Berlin: Dietz Verlag, 1953 and 1966.

————. *Zur Geschichte der neuesten Zeit.* Vol. 1. Berlin: Dietz Verlag, 1955.

U.S. Department of State. *Foreign Relations of the United States. Diplomatic Papers. The Conferences at Malta and Yalta, 1945.* Washington: U.S. Government Printing Office, 1955.

————. *Foreign Relations of the United States. Diplomatic Pa-*

pers. *The Conference of Berlin (The Potsdam Conference), 1945.* 2 vols. Washington: U.S. Government Printing Office, 1960.

Vereint sind wir alles. Erinnerungen an die Gründung der SED. Berlin: Dietz Verlag, 1966.

Wehner, Helfried, ed. *Kampfgefährten, Weggenossen: Erinnerungen deutscher und sowjetischer Genossen an die ersten Jahre der antifaschistisch-demokratischen Umwälzung in Dresden.* Berlin: Dietz Verlag, 1975.

Zur Geschichte der Kommunistischen Partei Deutschlands. Kiel: Rotfrontverlag und Literaturvertrieb, n.d.

PERIODICALS

Amtsblatt der Landesverwaltung Mecklenburg-Vorpommern mit amtlicher Beilage
Deutsche Volkszeitung
Der Freie Bauer
Informationsblatt für den Gewerkschaftsfunktionär (publication of FDGB Landesvorstand Sachsen)
New York Times
Regierungsblatt für das Land Thüringen
Der Sozialdemokrat
Thüringer Volkszeitung
Verordnungsblatt der Provinz Sachsen
Verordnungsblatt der Provinzialverwaltung Mark Brandenburg

INTERVIEWS

Bartel, Walter. Professor Emeritus, Humboldt University of Berlin; former personal consultant to Wilhelm Pieck, president of the German Democratic Republic. Interviews on April 27 and May 26, 1977.

Germer, Karl J. Co-founder of the SPD Central Committee in 1945; Recording Secretary of the FDGB Berlin Preparatory Committee. Interviews on April 21 and May 16, 1977.

Montag, Claus. Historian; representative of the Institute for International Relations of the German Democratic Republic. Interview on March 12, 1975.

Peglow, Hein. Former KPD Chairman of Berlin-Lichtenberg (1945-46). Interview on May 20, 1977.

Smettan, Kurt. Former KPD Chairman of Berlin-Lichtenberg (May-October 1945). Interview on May 27, 1977.

SECONDARY REFERENCES

Arbeitsgemeinschaft deutscher Landwirte und Bauern. *Weissbuch über die "Demokratische Bodenreform."* Hanover: Arbeitsgemeinschaft deutscher Landwirte und Bauern E.V., 1955.

Badstübner, Rolf, et al. *DDR: Werden und Wachsen.* Berlin: Dietz Verlag, 1975.

Bartel, Horst; and Heitzer, Heinz. "Die Anwendung grundlegender Erfahrungen der Sowjetunion in der DDR." *ZfG*, Vol. 22, no. 9 (1974).

Barthel, Horst. "Probleme der wirtschaftlichen Entwicklung der Deutschen Demokratischen Republik in der Nachkriegsperiode (1945-1949/50)." Dissertation for habilitation, Humboldt University of Berlin, 1968.

———. *Die wirtschaftlichen Ausgangsbedingungen der DDR.* "Forschungen zur Wirtschaftsgeschichte," Vol. 14. Berlin: Akademie-Verlag, 1979.

Behrendt, Albert. "Der FDGB und die Vereinigung von KPD und SPD zur SED." Vol. 24, no. 10 (1976).

Benser, Günter. "Die Anfänge der demokratischen Blockpolitik." *ZfG*, Vol. 23, no. 7 (1975).

———. "Die Befreiung Europas vom Faschismus durch die Sowjetunion und der Beginn des Übergangs vom Kapitalismus zum Sozialismus auf dem Territorium der DDR." *ZfG*, Vol. 23, no. 4 (1975).

Berlin, Büro für gesamtberliner Fragen. *Berlin, Sowjet Sektor. Die politische, rechtliche, wirtschaftliche, soziale und kulturelle Entwicklung in acht Berliner Verwaltungsbezirken.* Berlin: Colloquium Verlag, 1965.

Beuer, Gustav. *New Czechoslovakia and her Historical Background.* London: Lawrence and Wishart, 1947.

Bleich, Heinz, et al. *Weg und Erfolg. Zur Entwicklung der Konsumgenossenschaften in der Deutschen Demokratischen Republik.* Berlin: Verband Deutscher Konsumgenossenschaften, [1960].

Böttcher, Edgar. *Der Kampf des Nationalkomitees "Freies Deutschland" rettet Leipzig am Ende des zweiten Weltkriegs von der Zerstörung*. Leipzig: Museum für Geschichte der Stadt Leipzig, 1965.

Dech, Hildegard. "Die Rolle der Gewerkschaften in der Übergangsperiode in der Gewerkschaftsdiskussion der Sowjet-Union bis 1921 und die politische Praxis des FDGB in der SBZ bzw. DDR bis 1955." Diploma-thesis, Free University of Berlin, 1971.

Deckers, Josef. *Die Transformation des Bankensystems in der sowjetischen Besatzungszone/DDR von 1945 bis 1952*. Osteuropa-Institut an der Freien Universität Berlin, "Wirtschaftswissenschaftliche Veröffentlichungen," Vol. 36. Berlin: Duncker & Humbolt, 1974.

Deutscher, Isaac. *Stalin: A Political Biography*. 2nd ed. New York: Oxford University Press, 1967.

Deutsches Institut für Wirtschaftsforschung. *Wirtschaftsprobleme der Besatzungszonen*. Berlin: Duncker & Humbolt, 1948.

Diecker, Willi. "Wirtschaft und Staat gingen in die Hände des Volkes über." *ZfG*, Vol. 17, no. 7 (1969).

Diepenthal, Wolfgang. *Drei Volksdemokratien*. "Abhandlungen des Bundesinstituts für ostwissenschaftliche und internationale Studien," Vol. 29. Cologne: Verlag Wissenschaft und Politik, 1974.

Dölling, Hermann. *Wende der deutschen Agrarpolitik*. Berlin: Deutscher Bauernverlag, 1950.

Doernberg, Stefan. "Aus der Geschichte des Kampfes um die ökonomische Entmachtung des Monopolkapitals im Osten Deutschlands (1945-46)." *ZfG*, Vol. 7, no. 3 (1959).

―――. *Die Geburt eines neuen Deutschland 1945-1949*. Berlin: Rütten & Loening, 1959.

―――. "Die Hilfe der sowjetischen Besatzungsmacht beim Aufbau eines neuen Deutschland 1945/49." *Deutsche Aussenpolitik*, Vol. 10, special issue 1 (1965).

Dörrier, Rudolf. *Pankow. Kleine Chronik eines Berliner Bezirks*. Berlin: Das Neue Berlin, [1949].

Duhnke, Horst. *Stalinismus in Deutschland*. n.p.: Verlag für Politik und Wirtschaft, [1955?].

Eckart, Hans. "Zum Anteil des FDGB im Land Sachsen an der Herausbildung und Entwicklung des neuen Inhalts der Arbeiterbewegung in den Jahren 1945 bis 1950." Ph.D. dissertation, University of Leipzig, 1975.

Edinger, Lewis. *German Exile Politics: The Social Democratic Executive Committee in the Nazi Era*. Berkeley and Los Angeles: University of California Press, 1956.

Eggerath, Werner. "Unser Kampf für ein neues Deutschland." *ZfG*, Vol. 17, no. 7 (1969).

Eisermann, Horst. "Die städtischen Mittelschichten in der revolutionären Umwälzung von 1945 bis 1949/50, die Entwicklung ihrer Struktur und ihrer Stellung in der Gesellschaft, insbesondere zur Arbeiterklasse, dargestellt am Beispiel des ehemaligen Landes Sachsen-Anhalt." Ph.D. dissertation, University of Leipzig, 1973.

Emmrich, Johannes. "Die Entwicklung demokratischer Selbstverwaltungsorgane und ihr Kampf um die Schaffung der antifaschistisch-demokratischen Ordnung in Chemnitz vom 8. Mai 1945 bis Mitte 1948." Ph.D. dissertation, University of Leipzig, 1974.

Erdmann, Roman. "Die Enteignung der Kriegsverbrecher und aktiven Faschisten in Mecklenburg-Vorpommern 1945/46." *Wissenschaftliche Zeitschrift der Ernst-Moritz-Arndt-Universität Greifswald*, Gesellschafts- und Sprachwissenschaftliche Reihe, Vol. 18, no. 3/4, pt. 2 (1969).

Esche, Paul Gerhard. "Die Überwindung der kapitalistischen Verhältnisse im Zeiss-Werk Jena und die Neuformierung des Zeiss-Konzerns in Westdeutschland (1945-1949/50). Ein Beitrag zur Geschichte des VEB Carl Zeiss Jena." Ph.D. dissertation, University of Jena, 1962.

Falk, Waltraud. "Die politische, organisatorische und ökonomische Konstituierung des volkseigenen Sektors der Wirtschaft und seine Entwicklung in der ersten Etappe der volksdemokratischen Revolution in der DDR 1945 bis 1950." *Wissenschaftliche Zeitschrift der Humboldt-Universität zur Berlin*, Gesellschafts- und Sprachwissenschaftliche Reihe, Vol. 16, no. 1 (1967).

Federal Republic of Germany, Bundesministerium für gesamtdeutsche Fragen. *Die Enteignungen in der Sowjetischen Besatzungszone*. Bonn: Deutscher Bundes-Verlag, 1958.

———. *Der FDGB*. "Bonner Fachberichte aus der Sowjetzone." Berlin: n.p., 1959.

Feis, Herbert. *Between War and Peace*. Princeton: Princeton University Press, 1960.

Fischer, Alexander. *Sowjetische Deutschlandpolitik im Zweiten Weltkrieg 1941-1945*. Stuttgart: Deutsche Verlags-Anstalt, 1975.

Fitzgibben, Constantine. *Denazification*. London: Michael Joseph Ltd., 1969.

Friedmann, Wolfgang G. *The Allied Military Government of Germany*. "Library of World Affairs," No. 8. London: Stevens & Sons, 1947.

Gärtner, Paul. *Die Genossenschaftsbewegung*. Berlin: Dietz Verlag, 1947.

Gimbel, John. *The American Occupation of Germany*. Stanford: Stanford University Press, 1968.

Gottwald, Hans. "Die Entmachtung der Grossgrundbesitzer und Naziaktivisten und die Herausbildung neuer Produktionsverhältnisse in der Landwirtschaft während der ersten Etappe der demokratischen Bodenreform im Herbst 1945 auf dem Territorium des heutigen Bezirks Erfurt." Ph.D. dissertation, University of Halle-Wittenberg, 1974.

Gräfe, Karl-Heinz; and Wehner, Helfried. "Zur Politik der Sowjetischen Militäradministration in Sachsen." *ZfG*, Vol. 23, no. 8 (1975).

Griep, Günter; and Steinbrecher, Charlotte. *Die Herausbildung des Freien Deutschen Gewerkschaftsbundes. Zur Geschichte der deutschen Gewerkschaftsbewegung von 1945 bis 1946*. "Beiträge zur Geschichte der deutschen Gewerkschaftsbewegung," Vol. 9. Berlin: Tribüne Verlag, [1967].

Hauk, Roland, et al. *Zur Ökonomik der Übergangsperiode in der Deutschen Demokratischen Republik*. "Schriftenreihe des Institutes für Politische Ökonomie der Hochschule für Ökonomie." Berlin: Dietz Verlag, 1962.

Hering, Gerhard. *Der Neuaufbau einheitlicher freier Gewerkschaften 1945 in Leipzig*. "Schriftenreihe des Museums für Geschichte der Stadt Leipzig," No. 8. Leipzig: Museum für Geschichte der Stadt Leipzig, 1965.

Hermes, Peter. *Die Christlich-Demokratische Union und die Bodenreform in der Sowjetischen Besatzungszone Deutschlands im Jahre 1945*. Saarbrücken: Verlag der Saarbrücker Zeitung, 1963.

Heyl, Wolfgang. *Zwanzig Jahre demokratische Bodenreform.* "Hefte aus Burgscheidungen," No. 140. n.p.: Sekretariat des Hauptvorstandes der Christlich-Demokratischen Union, 1965.

Hoffmann, Wolfgang. "Die demokratische Bodenreform und die LDPD." *ZfG,* Vol. 13, no. 6 (1965).

Immler, Hans. *Agrarpolitik in der DDR.* Cologne: Verlag Wissenschaft und Politik, 1971.

Kirste, Peter. "Wirtschaftspolitik und antiimperialistische Umwälzung. Zur Erarbeitung wesentlicher Grundsätze der wirtschaftspolitischen Konzeption der KPD für die antifaschistisch-demokratische Umwälzung (Februar 1944-April 1945)." *Jahrbuch für Geschichte,* Vol. 14 (1976).

Klein, Jürgen. *Vereint sind sie alles? Untersuchungen zur Entstehung von Einheitsgewerkschaften in Deutschland von der Weimarer Republik bis 1946/47.* "Schriften der Stiftung Europa-Kolleg Hamburg," Vol. 23. Hamburg: Fundament-Verlag Dr. Sasse & Co., 1972.

Kleist, Peter. *Zwischen Hitler und Stalin, 1939-1945.* Bonn: Athenäum-Verlag, 1950.

Kohlmey, Günther; and Dewey, Charles. *Bankensystem und Geldumlauf in der Deutschen Demokratischen Republik 1945-1955.* Berlin: Verlag Die Wirtschaft, 1956.

Kolko, Gabriel. *The Politics of War: The World and United States Foreign Policy, 1943-45.* New York: Random House, 1968.

Konsum-Hauptsekretariat. *Die Entwicklung der Konsumgenossenschaften von ihrem Neuaufbau seit 1945 bis zum 31. Dezember 1948.* Berlin: Das Neue Berlin, [1949?].

Korbonski, Andrzej. *Politics of Socialist Agriculture in Poland: 1945-60.* "East Central European Studies of Columbia University." New York and London: Columbia University Press, 1965.

Kotov, Grigori G. *Agrarverhältnisse und Bodenreform in Deutschland.* 2 vols. Berlin: Deutscher Bauernverlag, 1959.

Kramer, Matthias. *Die Bolschewisierung der Landwirtschaft: In Sowjetrussland, in den Satellitenstaaten, in der Sowjetzone.* "Rote Weissbücher," No. 3. Cologne: Rote Weissbücher, 1951.

————. *Die Landwirtschaft in der sowjetischen Besatzungzone.* "Bonner Berichte aus Mittel- und Ostdeutschland." Bonn: Bundesministerium für gesamtdeutsche Fragen, 1953.

Krause, Werner. *Die Entstehung des Volkseigentums in der In-dustrie der DDR.* Berlin: Verlag Die Wirtschaft, 1958.

Krieger, Leonard. "The Inter-Regnum in Germany: March-August 1945." *Political Science Quarterly*, Vol. 64, no. 4 (1949).

Krippendorff, Ekkehart. *Die Liberal-Demokratische Partei Deutschlands in der Sowjetischen Besatzungszone 1945/48.* "Beiträge zur Geschichte des Parlamentarismus und der politischen Parteien," Vol. 21. Düsseldorf: Droste Verlag, n.d.

Krisch, Henry. *German Politics under Soviet Occupation.* New York and London: Columbia University Press, 1974.

Krüger, Günther. "Der Kampf um die Enteignung der Kriegsverbrecher und Naziaktivisten in Leipzig." Ph.D. dissertation, University of Leipzig, 1958.

————. "Der Volksentscheid in Sachsen—ein Beweis für die geschichtsbildende Kraft der Volksmassen." *ZfG*, Vol. 7, no. 7 (1959).

Kuntsche, Siegfried. "Die Unterstützung der Landesverwaltung bzw. Landesregierung Mecklenburg durch die Sowjetische Militäradministration bei der Leitung der demokratischen Bodenreform." *Jahrbuch für Geschichte*, Vol. 12 (1974).

Laschitza, Horst. *Kämpferische Demokratie gegen Faschismus.* Berlin: Deutscher Militärverlag, 1969.

Leptin, Gert. *Die deutsche Wirtschaft nach 1945: Ein Ost-West Vergleich.* Opladen: Leske Verlag, 1970.

Lipski, Horst. *Der Kampf der deutschen Arbeiterklasse und aller demokratischen Kräfte unter der Führung der Partei um die Errichtung der antifaschistisch-demokratischen Ordnung in Deutschland (1945-1949).* Berlin: Parteihochschule "Karl Marx" beim ZK der SED, 1960.

Loewe, Andreas. *Andreas Loewe: Eine Familie und ihr Werk von 1872 bis heute.* Lüneburg: Nordland-Druck, 1968.

McCagg, William O., Jr. *Stalin Embattled 1943-1948.* Detroit: Wayne State University Press, 1978.

Mastny, Vojtech. *Russia's Road to the Cold War.* New York: Columbia University Press, 1979.

Moraw, Frank. *Die Parole der "Einheit" und die Sozialdemokratie.* "Schriftenreihe des Forschungsinstituts der Friedrich-Ebert-Stiftung," Vol. 94. Bonn-Bad Godesberg: Verlag Neue Gesellschaft, 1973.

Nettl, J. P. *The Eastern Zone and Soviet Policy in Germany 1945-50.* London: Oxford University Press, 1951.

Niethammer, Lutz. *Entnazifizierung in Bayern.* Frankfurt: S. Fischer Verlag, 1972.

Puttkamer, Jesco von. *Irrtum und Schuld.* Neuwied-Berlin: Michael Verlag, 1948.

Rackow, Gerd; Heyne, Martin; and Kleinpeter, Oswald. *Rostock 1945 bis zur Gegenwart.* Rostock: VEB Hinstorff Verlag, 1969.

Raup, Philip M. "Land Reform in Post-War Germany: The Soviet Zone Experiment." Ph.D. dissertation, University of Wisconsin, 1949.

Roesler, Jörg. "Allgemeines und Besonderes bei der Herausbildung der sozialistischen Planwirtschaft der DDR (1945-1950)." *Jahrbuch für Geschichte,* Vol. 12 (1974).

Sarel, Benno. *La Classe ouvrière d'Allemagne orientale.* Paris: Les Éditions Ouvrières, 1958.

Sarow, Friedrich. *Von der Kriegsproduktion zur Friedenswirtschaft.* Weimar: Thüringer Volksverlag, [1946?].

Schapiro, Leonard. *The Communist Party of the Soviet Union.* New York: Random House, 1960.

Scheurig, Bodo. *Free Germany.* Translated by Herbert Arnold. Middletown, Conn.: Wesleyan University Press, 1969.

Schildhauer, Johannes, et al, ed. *Befreiung und Neubeginn.* Berlin: Staatsverlag der DDR, 1966.

Schmidt, Ute; and Fichter, Tilman. *Der erzwungene Kapitalismus. Klassenkämpfe in den Westzonen 1945-48.* "Rotbuch," No. 27. Berlin: Verlag Klaus Wagenbach, 1971.

Schoenbaum, David. *Hitler's Social Revolution: Class and Status in Nazi Germany 1933-1939.* Garden City, N.Y.: Doubleday-Anchor Books, 1967.

Schöneburg, Karl-Heinz. *Von den Anfängen unseres Staates.* Berlin: Staatsverlag der DDR, 1975.

Schöneburg, Karl-Heinz, et al. *Revolutionärer Prozess und Staatsentstehung.* Berlin: Akademie-Verlag, 1976.

Schröder, Otto. *Der Kampf der SED in der Vorbereitung und Durchführung des Volksentscheids in Sachsen Februar bis 30. Juni 1946.* Berlin: Dietz Verlag, 1961.

Schützler, Horst. "Die Unterstützung der Sowjetunion für die demokratischen Kräfte Berlins in den ersten Nachkriegsmonaten." *ZfG,* Vol. 13, no. 3 (1965).

Schulze, Siegfried. "Der Prozess der Herausbildung der Provinzialverwaltung Mark Brandenburg und ihre Politik zur Einleitung der antifaschistisch-demokratischen Revolution (Sommer 1945 bis Frühjahr 1946)." Ph.D. dissertation, Pädagogische Hochschule Potsdam, 1971.

Schumann, Wolfgang, et al. *Carl Zeiss Jena: Einst and Jetzt.* Berlin: Rütten & Loening, 1962.

Seemann, Ulrich. "Der Beginn des antifaschistisch-demokratischen Neuaufbaus in Rostock im Mai 1945." *Rostocker Beiträge,* Vol. 1 (1966).

Selbmann, Fritz. "Anfänge der Wirtschaftsplanung in Sachsen." *Beiträge zur Geschichte der deutschen Arbeiterbewegung,* Vol. 14, no. 1 (1972).

———. "Die UdSSR unterstützte den Wiederaufbau des Wirtschaftslebens." *Deutsche Aussenpolitik,* Vol. 10, special issue 1 (1965).

Sell, Dieter. "Die Herausbildung und Entwicklung der staatlichen Leitung und Planung in der volkseigenen Industrie beim Aufbau der antifaschistisch-demokratischen Ordnung und Grundlagen des Sozialismus in der DDR (1945 bis 1955)." Ph.D. dissertation, Humboldt University of Berlin, 1976.

Seton-Watson, Hugh. *The East European Revolution.* 3d ed. London: Methuen & Co., 1956.

Seydewitz, Max. *Zerstörung und Wiederaufbau von Dresden.* Berlin: Kongress-Verlag, 1955.

Slusser, Robert, ed. *Soviet Economic Policy in Postwar Germany.* New York: Research Program on the USSR, 1953.

Sozialistische Einheitspartei Deutschlands, Betriebsparteiorganisation Bewag. *Unsere Kraft: Betriebsgeschichte der Bewag.* Part 1 (1884-1949). Berlin: n.p., [1974?].

Sozialistische Einheitspartei Deutschlands, Kreisleitung VEB Leuna-Werke "Walter Ulbricht." *Befreites Leuna (1945-1950).* Part 2 "Geschichte der Fabriken und Werke," Vol. 8; Berlin: Verlag Tribüne, 1959.

Sozialistische Einheitspartei Deutschlands, Landesvorstand Sachsen. *Ein Jahr demokratischer Aufbau im Lande Sachsen.* Dresden: Sachsenverlag Druckerei- und Verlags-Gesellschaft m.b.H., [1946].

Staritz, Dietrich. "Die National-Demokratische Partei Deutschlands 1948-1953: Ein Beitrag zur Untersuchung des Parteiensystems der DDR." Ph.D. dissertation, Free University of Berlin, 1968.

————. *Sozialismus in einem halben Land. Zur Programmatik und Politik der KPD/SED in der Phase der antifaschistisch-demokratischen Unwälzung in der DDR.* Berlin: Verlag Klaus Wagenbach, 1976.

Stein, Siegfried. *Die demokratische Bodenreform in Mecklenburg—ein Schlag gegen den Imperialismus und Militarismus.* Schwerin: Bezirksleitung Schwerin der SED-Kommission zur Erforschung der Geschichte der örtlichen Arbeiterbewegung, n.d.

Stern, Carola. *Ulbricht: A Political Biography.* New York, Washington, London: Frederick A. Praeger, 1965.

Stöckigt, Rolf. *Der Kampf der KPD um die demokratische Bodenreform, Mai 1945 bis April 1946.* Berlin: Dietz Verlag, 1964.

Sywottek, Arnold. *Deutsche Volksdemokratie. Studien zur politischen Konzeption der KPD, 1935-1946.* "Studien zur modernen Geschichte." Düsseldorf: Bartelsmann Universitätsverlag, 1971.

Thiele, Willi; and Bednareck, Horst. "Die Gründung des FDGB im Kampf um die Vernichtung der Grundlagen des deutschen Imperialismus und Militarismus, für den Aufbau einer antifaschistisch-demokratischen Ordnung (1945-1946)." *ZfG,* Vol. 8, no. 3 (1960).

Thomas, Siegfried. *Entscheidung in Berlin. Zur Entstehungsgeschichte der SED in der deutschen Hauptstadt, 1945/46.* Berlin: Akademie-Verlag, 1964.

Tjulpanov, Sergei I. "Die Rolle der SMAD bei der Demokratisierung Deutschlands." *ZfG,* Vol. 15, no. 2 (1967).

————. "Die Rolle der Sowjetischen Militäradministration im demokratischen Deutschland." In *50 Jahre Triumph des Marxismus-Leninismus,* edited by Gertraud Teuschner et al. Berlin: Dietz Verlag, 1967.

————. "Die Zusammenarbeit der SMAD und der SED im Kampf für Demokratie und Sozialismus." In *Einheit—im Kampfe geboren,* edited by E. Kalbe and S. I. Tjulpanov. Leipzig: Karl-Marx-Universität Leipzig, 1975.

Tümmler, Edgar; Merkel, Konrad; and Blohm, Georg. *Die Agrarpolitik in Mitteldeutschland.* Bundesministerium für gesamtdeutsche Fragen, "Wirtschaft und Gesellschaft in Mitteldeutschland," Vol. 3. Berlin: Duncker & Humbolt, 1969.

Ulam, Adam B. *Expansion and Coexistence: The History of Soviet Foreign Policy 1917-67.* New York and Washington: Praeger Publishers, 1973.

Urban, Karl. "Die Herausbildung der Aktionseinheit der Arbeiterklasse und der demokratischen Selbstverwaltungsorgane unter Führung der KPD in der Provinz Brandenburg (Ende April bis Anfang Juni 1945)." *Beiträge zur Geschichte der deutschen Arbeiterbewegung.* Vol. 5, no. 5/6 (1963).

Varga, Eugen. "Demokratie neuer Art." *Neue Welt,* Vol. 2, no. 11 (1947).

Wahl, Volker. "Der Beginn der antifaschistisch-demokratischen Unwälzung in Thüringen—Die Organisierung der gesellschaftlichen Kräfte und der Neuaufbau der Landesverwaltung 1945." Ph.D. dissertation, University of Jena, 1976.

Warriner, Doreen. *Revolution in Eastern Europe.* London: Turnstile Press, 1950.

Weissel, Bernhard, ed. *Befreiung und Neubeginn. Zur Stellung des 8. Mai 1945 in der deutschen Geschichte.* Berlin: Akademie-Verlag, 1968.

"Wirtschaftliche Entwicklungen in der sowjetischen Zone seit Potsdam." *Europa Archiv,* Vol. 1 (1946-47).

Woderich, Rudolf. "Zu den Anfängen der Demokratisierung des Dorfes in Ostmecklenburg von 1945 bis Ende 1947, dargestellt vornehmlich am Beispiel des Kreises Neubrandenburg." Ph.D. dissertation, University of Rostock, 1965.

Index

Library of Congress Cataloging in Publication Data

Sandford, Gregory W., 1947-
From Hitler to Ulbricht.
Bibliography: p.   Includes index.
1. Communism—Germany (East) 2. Germany (East)—
Economic policy. 3. Reconstruction (1939-1951)—Germany (East)
4. Germany (East)—Politics and government. 5. Ulbricht,
Walter, 1893-1973. I. Title.
HX280.5.A6S245 1983 943.1087'4 82-47611
ISBN 0-691-05367-7

Dr. Gregory W. Sandford is a Foreign Service Officer
in the United States State Department.